UNION NOW
WITH BRITAIN

Plan for Union
Guide of the Free
Language of Freedom
Acts of Union
Of Life and Death

UNION NOW
WITH
BRITAIN

By
Clarence K. Streit

*This is rather an embryo state, a preparation
for living.* - Benjamin Franklin

HARPER & BROTHERS PUBLISHERS
New York   London

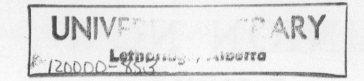

UNION NOW WITH BRITAIN

Copyright, 1941, by Clarence K. Streit
Printed in the United States of America

All rights in this book are reserved.
No part of the book may be reproduced in any
manner whatsoever without written permission
except in the case of quotations embodied in
critical articles and reviews. Applications will
be sympathetically considered. For information
address Harper & Brothers

"* * * * * * * dedicated to the great task remaining before us - that from these honored dead we take increased devotion to that cause for which they gave the last full measure of devotion - that we here highly resolve that these dead shall not have died in vain - that this nation, under God, shall have a new birth of freedom - and that government of the people, by the people, for the people, shall not perish from the earth."

The Federal Union Organization

To enroll with other Federal Unionists, write to:

U. S. A.: Federal Union, 10 East 40th Street, New York, N. Y.

Great Britain: Federal Union, 44 Gordon Square, P. O. Box 118, London, W. C. 1.

Canada: National Committee for Union Now, 2585 Cavendish Avenue, Victoria, B. C.;

Canadian Association for Federal Union, 73 Adelaide Street, West, Toronto.

Australia: Federal Union, 28 Bond Street, Sydney, New South Wales; Ronald L. Colman;

Federal Union, 34, The Crescent, Brighton, Adelaide, South Australia, E. Anthoney, Hon. Secretary;

Federal Union, 333, George Street, Brisbane, B. 12; J. M. Ahern, Secretary.

New Zealand: Federal Union, 104 Victoria Avenue, Remuera, Auckland; Telford MacLennan.

Union of South Africa: Federal Union, 101-102 A. B. C. Chambers, Simmonds Street, Johannesburg.

Eire: Federal Union, Killadreenan House, Newtown, Mount Kennedy, County Wicklow.

India: Federal Union Club, c/o Manickavelu, Palace Road, Bangalore; Mr. P. Strethill Wright.

Argentina: Federal Union, 285 Paseo Colon, Buenos Aires; Easton Garrett, Hon. Secretary.

If there isn't already a Federal Union Chapter in your community, help form one. Through *Federal Union World*, *The Student Federalist* (New York), *Federal Union News* (London), *Federal Union News Bulletin* (Auckland, New Zealand), *Federal Union Bulletin* (Edinburgh, Scotland), and other publications keep in touch with what other Unionists are doing, how the Union idea is rolling on around the world. Your Federal Union organization can tell you of many other things that you can do to help make The Union.

Contents

FOREWORD   xi

INTRODUCTION BY *Madison, Washington and Lincoln*   xv

Part I. Plan for Union

1. THE UNION PROPOSAL—BIRD'S-EYE VIEW   3
   First Glance   3
   Four Reasons for Union Now   6
   Background   10
   The War Makes Union with Britain Urgent   13
   The Union's Great, Imperiled Power   14
   If We Lose the Sea   17
   Union Needed to Win the War   19
   The European or the American Way?   21
   America Ueber Alles?   23
   A Limited Provisional Union First   24
   A Broader Permanent Union Later   27
   For Union in Peace   28
   Union How?—Action in Congress   29
   The Union Program in Outline   31
   The Alternative, an Alliance—Its Dangers   33
   Alliance Means Six Votes to Our One   34
   Alliance Means National Disunity   35
   Alliance Gives One Man All Our Power   36
   Alliance Means Partisan War   36
   Who Would Compose the Union Congress?   38
   Who Would Be the Union Executive?   42
   The Altars of Dabble and Dawdle   45
   Shall We Repeat the Errors of 1917-1920?   47
   Vision and Vigor Made America and Britain   50
   We Who Embody All Mankind   52

2. Union vs. Alliance (Diagramed)   54
     Fig. 1. Nationalism Leaves You Out on the Rim   56
     Fig. 2. Union Makes You the Hub of the World   57
     Fig. 3. What We Face in an Alliance   58
     Fig. 4. What We Get in a Federal Union   59

3. "First in Peace, First in War"   62
     Union as a Peace Policy   62
     The Flaw in "Pax Britannica"   63
     Pax Americana or *Pax Dei*?   64
     To Begin Peace Negotiations   66
     Union and the Japanese Alliance   70
     Could Hitler Accept the Union's Peace?   72
     If War Comes   74
     The Successful Wilsonian War Strategy   76
     No Great Expeditionary Force Needed   78
     The Moral Force of Union   81
     To Reassure Us and Everyone   85

Part II. Guide of the Free

4. Guide of the Free   91

Part III. Language of Freedom

5. Our Entangling World   103
     Wall Street's Crash Brought Us Hitler   103
     Ideas Can Invade Us, Too   106

6. What the French Did for Freedom   110
     Why France Fell   110
     Hitler's Great Blunder   112
     Why Did Hitler Turn on France?   115
     An Ocean of Responsibility   117

7. The Language of Freedom   119
     English Speech Is Free Speech   119
     We and the British Are Town-and-World-Minded   121

CONTENTS

8. How Federal Union Works: The American
   Example — 125
   - When the U. S. Was a League — 125
   - The Change from League to Union — 128
   - The Results of Union — 133

9. To an American Legion Official — 137

10. The Constitution Is Our Foreign Policy — 142

11. What We Are Bound to Defend — 144
    - Our Oath to Federal Union — 144
    - Losing Federal Union from Within — 147
    - Business in an Autocratic World — 149
    - Secret Budget vs. Public Budget — 152
    - Freedom for Spies or for the Press? — 153
    - The Prestige of Success — 154

12. The United States Must Keep on Uniting States — 156
    - Puny "Patriots" Who Would Halt America — 156
    - How Union Decentralizes Power — 158
    - Nationalism Brought Dictatorship — 160

13. Democracy and War — 162

14. The Constitutionality of Union Now — 167
    - The Forgotten Powers of the People — 167
    - Can the Constitution Be Unconstitutional? — 169
    - No Amendment Needed for Union Now — 172

15. Some Questions and Answers — 174
    - Would the British Accept? — 174
    - Party Lines in the Union — 177
    - Isn't the Economic Problem More Pressing? — 180
    - Is Union Just Another Imperialism? — 183
    - What About Latin America? — 186
    - What of China? Japan? — 188
    - India? Soviet Russia? — 191
    - Where Would the Capital Be? — 193
    - What of the Economic Problems? — 194
    - What Would I Gain or Lose? — 195
    - How Can I Help Get the Union Made? — 197

16. End, or Beginning? — 199

Annexes. Acts of Union

1. ILLUSTRATIVE DECLARATION OF INTER-DEPENDENCE
   AND UNION   205

2. ILLUSTRATIVE CONSTITUTION   212
   The Definitive Union   212
   The Provisional Union   223

Last Word

OF LIFE AND DEATH   231

INDEX   235

MAPS
   1. Control of the Sea Keeps the World Free.   16
   2. Where We Are Without the British Fleet.   18

Foreword

While surveying the public land in Alaska in 1916, I was once lost in the then primeval forest near Turnagain Arm. One of the axmen had slashed his leg; the rest of us were carrying him to camp, five or six miles away through the trackless woods. It was raining. When we found that we were circling we began to argue over the direction to take. Then it dawned on me that the quickest practical way out was not to continue moving through the wilderness, but to move up toward the sky: To climb that tall spruce tree and look for a sure landmark—a neighboring chain of mountains. It would quickly tell us where we were and where to go. And it did.

That tall spruce tree tells me today that, in this world emergency, too, we need to see not only where we really are but far ahead, all the way to our destination, if we are to move toward it as swiftly as we need to move. That tree tells me that, however "practical" it may seem to "stick always to the ground" and concentrate on getting past the nearest difficulties, our only practical course now is to stop long enough to climb up to where we can see beyond the immediate, blinding obstacles, and regain our true direction. And so I have tried in this book, as in *Union Now*, to help go on with freedom by going up to see how to go ahead, all the way home.

This book is not a revision of *Union Now*. It is a sequel to it, written in the light of subsequent, present and looming events. It has been necessary, of course, to cover some of the same ground, but that represents only a small part of this book.

The reader whose questions are unanswered here may find them answered by consulting *Union Now*. For example, he will find in it the philosophy of "Freedom and Union," details of the power of the democracies, analysis of the breakdown of the League of Nations and collective security, the reasons why Federal Unions work and leagues fail, and discussion of the economic, transitional and other technical problems involved in the establishment of The Union.

And if you do not find the answer to your objection in either book, I would ask you to try yourself to solve the problem that you raise. Since it was you who found the fault, may you not be the one to correct it or overcome it better than I, or anyone?

Indulgence is asked only for the faults in this book that rise from the speed with which it has been written and published. The writing of this book was done in only two months, though there are many years of study and observation behind it. I much prefer to put a manuscript aside for months, and then go over it again. But that was clearly impossible with this book; the events with which it deals are moving much too fast. And so it has been written as I have written many a news dispatch while a foreign correspondent—under such high pressure that I have not even reread it through from start to finish before sending it to the printer in New York or mailing it overseas. (I have, of course, read the book through in the proofs.)

I take this occasion to pay tribute to the work done by all the other authors who have cultivated this field, not only those in the distant past but such recent ones as Lionel Curtis (*World Order,* Oxford University Press), and W. B. Curry (*The Case for Federal Union,* Penguin)—to mention but two of the British champions of Federal Union of the democracies. I have been greatly encouraged to believe that this program is ripe by all the evidence I have found, since the publication of *Union Now,* of other contemporary, quite independent work in various parts of the world in the same general direction. Two outstanding American examples are Sinclair Kennedy's prophetic book, *The Pan-Angles* (Longmans, Green and Co., 1915), and John Francis Goldsmith's *President Randolph as I Knew Him* (Dorrance, 1935).

I have been deeply encouraged, too, by the reception given *Union Now* by people, prominent and obscure, in many countries. I have never received such eloquent, moving letters as it brought me from unknown men and women in many lands. I have been profoundly touched by the devotion this old idea of Federal Union inspires among so many people separated so widely and in so many ways—by land, sea, language, race, sex, age, education, wealth.

I remember the young married man who gave up his health insurance to help bring on The Union of the Free, the high school students who raised nearly $100 for it among themselves just before Christmas when money means so much to a boy or girl, the unemployed men and women who have volunteered their dimes, the overemployed who have yet given it their time, the old lady of eighty in Brooklyn who sent her Federal Union organization a dollar, explaining she had received a Thanksgiving Day basket for the poor and so could afford to help. I remember the lad whose letter is in the "Last Word" of this book, and I remember the young English soldier who wrote me from "Hell's Corner" in England, explaining he "might not be present" when The Union was made but trusted we would carry on with it.

I think of these and countless others (particularly the many to whom I am personally indebted and without whose help I could not have written either book), and I turn to Lincoln to express "thanks to all—for the Great Republic, for the principle it lives by and keeps alive, for Man's vast future—thanks to all."

C. K. S.

Washington, D. C.
Jan. 21, 1941.

Introduction by
Madison, Washington and Lincoln

Was, then, the American Revolution effected, was the American Confederacy formed, was the precious blood of thousands spilt, and the hard-earned substance of millions lavished, not that the people of America should enjoy peace, liberty, and safety, but that the government of the individual States . . . might enjoy a certain extent of power, and be arrayed with certain dignities and attributes of sovereignty? We have heard of the impious doctrine in the Old World, that the people were made for kings, not kings for the people. Is the same doctrine to be revived in the New, in another shape—that the solid happiness of the people is to be sacrificed to . . . political institutions of a different sort?—Madison, The Federalist, *No. 45.*

These considerations speak a persuasive language to every reflecting and virtuous mind, and exhibit the continuance of the Union as a primary object of patriotic desire. Is there a doubt whether a common government can embrace so large a sphere? Let experience solve it. To listen to mere speculation in such a case were criminal. We are authorized to hope that a proper organization of the respective subdivisions will afford a happy issue to the experiment. It is well worth a fair and full experiment.—Washington, Farewell Address.

Fellow-citizens, we cannot escape history. . . . The fiery trial through which we pass will light us down, in honor or dishonor, to the latest generation. We say we are for the Union. The world will not forget that we say this. We know how to save the Union. The world knows we do know how to save it.

We, even we here, hold the power and bear the responsibility. In giving freedom to the slave, we assure freedom to the free— honorable alike in what we give and what we preserve. We shall nobly save or meanly lose the last, best hope of earth. Other means may succeed; this could not fail. The way is plain, peaceful, generous, just—a way which, if followed, the world will for ever applaud, and God must for ever bless.—Lincoln, Message to Congress, *Dec. 1, 1862.*

Part I

PLAN FOR UNION

The subject speaks its own importance; compre-hending in its consequences nothing less than the existence of the Union . . . . the fate of an empire in many respects the most interesting in the world.
—Alexander Hamilton, opening The Federalist.

> *Sail on, O Ship of State!*
> *Sail on, O Union, strong and great!*
> *Humanity with all its fears,*
> *With all the hopes of future years,*
> *Is hanging breathless on thy fate!*
> *—Longfellow,* The Building of the Ship,

cited by President Roosevelt in the message Wendell Willkie carried from him to Prime Minister Churchill, who made it public in a world broadcast Feb. 9, 1941.

Chapter 1

The Union Proposal—Bird's-eye View

A new government must be made. Our all is depending on it.—*James Madison in the U. S. Constitutional Convention.*

When bad men combine, the good must associate; else they will fall one by one, an unpitied sacrifice in a contemptible struggle.—*Edmund Burke,* On the Conciliation of America.

As the barbarism of the present old Governments expires, . . . the moral condition of Nations with respect to each other will be changed. Man will not be brought up with the savage idea of considering his species as his enemy, because the accident of birth gave the individuals existence in countries distinguished by different names.—*Thomas Paine,* Rights of Man.

FIRST GLANCE

Long before this war began, I wrote *Union Now* to keep us all out of it. The book did not propose that we or any people should do this by blacking out our homes and burrowing for shelter down among the worms. It proposed nothing that required us or any people to work longer hours, pay heavier taxes, go without good food, centralize power more dangerously in the hands of any one man, or suspect our fellow citizens of being fifth columnists. It did not assign to us the parts of Pharisee and Pilate.

This proposal did not require us to conscript anyone. It handed no one a blank check. It obliged no one to produce like mad so as to lend, lease, or give the goods away, unconditionally. It gave no one dictatorial power over farmers, workers or businessmen. It did not call on us to appropriate thirteen billion dollars in a few months to keep us out of war, and then call for ten billion more. It cost nothing. And yet it proposed no method or procedure that had not been tested for generations.

3

Union Now pointed out that, to have freedom, peace and plenty, we must have good government in the world, and not merely in the town, county, state and nation. It held that, so long as we did not fill this rudimentary need, we were bound to suffer depression, dictatorship and war, no matter what else we did to avoid them. It proposed that we form this government before world lawlessness burst into world war. . . . Now it is proposed we act before this world war brings our world down to doom.

It is proposed here that we create now the nucleus of that free world republic that must be formed some day by men like you and me and the neighbors. It is proposed that we seize the present opportunity to start this Union of the Free as a United States of Man constituted to secure eventually, and in an ever-growing degree, the freedom, peace and prosperity of every man and woman.

To begin, it is proposed that we limit the first step to one that is well within our power, yet big enough to begin effectively this far-reaching enterprise. The proposal is that we Americans invite the men and women of the other democracies that speak our language—the United Kingdom, Eire, Canada, Australia, New Zealand and the Union of South Africa—to unite with us to form this nucleus on the following basis:

    1. *The End:* The Constitution of the government—called here *The Union*—that we thus establish shall have the same fundamental aims as the U. S. Constitution and uphold the universal principles of the Declaration of Independence.

    2. *The Means:* The new government shall be a Federal Union—that is, its machinery for governing the relations between the people of the member democracies shall be modeled on the U. S. A. system of Federal Union, in·the sense that the Canadian, Australian, South African and Swiss governments are already modeled on this American invention.

    3. *Citizenship and Representation:* The citizens of each member democracy, like those of each state in the U. S. A., shall be equal citizens of The Union with a

voice in its government in proportion to their numbers. They shall exercise this voice through the British system of representative government, in the sense in which the citizens of the U. S. A. and other democratic Federal Unions have already adopted this English invention, with the usual Federal safeguards for the less populous democracies.

4. *Union Rights:* The Union government shall have the same limited but effective powers as the U. S. government, notably: To make war and peace for all its members, to govern their foreign relations and their non-self-governing territory, to provide them with a common defense force, a common free trade market, a common currency, a common postal and communications system, and a common citizenship; and to operate directly on, through and *for* the citizens individually and equally, just as the governments of both the U. S. A. and the United Kingdom now do.

5. *Individual and National Rights:* The Constitution of The Union shall guarantee all persons living in it a Bill of Rights that shall include at least freedom of speech, press, religion and peaceful association. It shall also guarantee that all rights not specifically granted to The Union shall be retained exclusively by the member democracies respectively, or by the people. These rights shall include the right of Americans to retain their present Federal Republic, the right of the British to retain among themselves their monarchy, the right of organized, non-English-speaking member democracies to be as safeguarded in their language and customs as are the French in Canada, the Dutch Afrikaners in South Africa and the Spanish in New Mexico, and similar rights for every member people to maintain its national identity.

6. *Admission of New Members:* The Union shall provide that colonies and Latin American and other outside nations shall be admitted to it as states are admitted to the U. S. A., on a basis of equality with the founders and without being required to give more ef-

fective guarantees of democracy and disarmament than the founders themselves give, until The Union shall gradually become the government of all mankind and armament be reduced to a world police force.

7. *Peace Terms:* The Union shall offer at once to establish normal peaceful relations with all outside nations. As regards those now at war with any of its members it shall offer to do this on a basis of no annexations or occupation of foreign territory, no indemnities or reparations except the return of returnable property, and the settlement by arbitration, conciliation or judicial action of all disputes that led to this war, as well as all subsequent questions that cannot be settled by direct negotiation. To help hasten the establishment of real peace, The Union shall pledge itself to admit to it, once normal conditions are restored, those European peoples who have long governed themselves democratically, or who prove their readiness for membership by the way in which they restore at home their own free rights as men.

Four Reasons for Union Now

There are any number of sound and urgent reasons for this Union program. Many of them will be developed in this book, in addition to those already given in *Union Now*—for the aim here is to cover new ground. Four reasons for Union now with the British democracies may be noted here, for they will be developed most:

One. Union is the safest, surest, best policy for us no matter what course this unpredictable war takes—whether or not Britain can win with only our material aid, whether or not we declare war, whether or not Japan does, and so on.

Two. The Union policy is our safest, surest, best way to secure *real* peace—not appeasement, but the enduring, creative peace that all normal men desire.

Three. The Union policy is the safest, surest, best defense of our free principles from not only the foreign but the *domestic* dangers to them—from prolonged concentration of power in one man's hands, from national disunity, from the partisanship that makes us pay the highest price for victory and then costs us the peace, from the puny patriotism that perverts our principles, and from all that awaits those who refuse to admit their worst mistakes and right them.

Four. No alternative policy brings less difficulty and risk in the end; instead, they all bring far worse difficulties, insuperable difficulties, and they almost certainly lead only to both war and frustration.

The Union program is based on the conviction that we must first preserve the remaining democracies and prevent the victory of dictatorship in the Old World in order to have peace, prosperity and freedom anywhere, and that nothing short of Union now will enable us to do this.

To meet practically the existing and approaching dangers it is proposed that we form this Union:

A. In two steps
    first, immediately but provisionally,
    second, definitely but after long consideration
B. For two purposes
    first, to save freedom from defeat,
    second, to win the peace.

These four factors form a living, organic whole, each of vital importance to the others. To win the peace, the first essential is to keep autocracy from winning the war. To do that we must have Federal Union with Britain now—for we face a foe so powerful and cunning that any form of joint action short of Union will, like the Franco-British alliance, be unable to get its peace terms accepted, and liable to collapse when most needed. We can not safely take the time now that we need to work out a permanent Federal Union, but, by making our initial Federal Union strictly a provisional, emergency measure, we can organize it as safely and quickly as we can organize an inter-allied council, or any other alternative machinery.

Once we have the provisional Union government which we need to prevent defeat and to bring autocracy to reason, we can safely call a separate Federal Convention to begin the slower process of working out a definitive Constitution. Its text would then be submitted to each member democracy for ratification, and The Union would be permanent only for those that then freely decided to enter it. The details of its Constitution are secondary now, since they would depend on the discussion in the Convention, and would not bind any of us until we had studied the whole text and accepted it.

By this procedure none of us signs a check hastily or in blank, and we all avoid the pitfalls of prolonged inaction, or of activity too weak for the emergency's needs, or of overhasty definitive action. Moreover, this program allows us to profit from our practical experience in the provisional Union to draft a sounder permanent Constitution.

This permanent Constitution is a vital part of the program. Without it we win or stop the war in vain—for we then split apart and lose the peace. This is no question to put off till the peace conference. We need to begin this Constitution beforehand in order to win the war at the least cost and in the shortest time. To do this we must lean backwards—while still building soundly—to prove that we are not aiming at English-speaking hegemony or giving windy promises, but are actually establishing a nucleus World Federal Union open even to our enemies at the same price that we pay ourselves. The sooner we prove this concretely, the sooner we shall overthrow dictatorship from within, no matter where it is, or how strongly armed.

This is, then, a strategy for winning both the war and the peace by *first* halting autocracy's war machine in its traces— thus proving that democracy *is* better than autocracy, able to beat it even with its own choice of weapons—and, *then,* if it refuses to come to terms, overthrowing it in the way that costs the fewest lives and gives the best security for peace and freedom—by inducing the people on whom dictatorship has fastened itself to throw it off themselves.

The problem is to defeat dictatorship without thereby humiliating the people with whom it is now identified, or causing such bitterness as to make it extremely difficult for us and them to work together in a Union government. The answer is to make the victory over dictatorship a common one and divide the credit for it equally—we having the risk and credit of halting the dictator and they having the risk and credit of unhorsing him, we contributing the nucleus of the world republic and they contributing the proof that it is a living, growing nucleus.

Thus we and they shall keep our self-respect. Our peace can then breed no further war, for then all the children of The Union, no matter what their origin, can remember, with the equal pride that peace requires, the part their parents played in the great days when The Union of the Free began.

There, at a glance, is the Union plan for peace, prosperity and freedom—where it starts in Union now with Britain, where it goes on its long road, and how it gets there.

This plan is not frustration's wormy fruit; it is the sound fruit of success—the product of the practical experience of men of all varieties who, in four continents and under conditions as different as those of America and Switzerland, have put Federal Union to the test since it began a hundred and fifty years ago.

This is no attempt to achieve harmony among men by preaching either hatred of each other, or nonresistance of those who turn from ballots to bullets. Union would take men, as they are, where they want to go. It recognizes that society still rests on force, but that men are already capable of using force effectively without hate against men who are victims of ignorance or passion, or of diseases only less dangerous than virulent, warlike nationalism. Union puts the accent on what men die for, not on what they kill each other for.

This is no Utopia, and it is no mystic mirage. It involves great difficulties, but not the insuperable difficulties that will, in the end, defeat alternatives. Union is a program born of the needs and limitations of the normal human body, born of the reasoning of the normal mind, the sure instincts of the normal heart and the infinite longings of the normal soul—born of that healthy fusion of all these that men the world around call common sense.

Is not Union the program you yourself have long been seeking? Then let us go on with it together, now.

Have you ever wanted to do the very best you could with your life? To live supremely? Have you ever known this satisfaction? Ever had a chance to know how much you yourself can really do, how good you really are? Here is your chance.

Here is a proposal that we now do something really worthy of us, while we can. Something that will lift us out of our humdrum lives, and leave us each greater. Something that none of us will ever forget, that our whole species will always remember. Something worth our while on earth. Something deathless that we can do . . . but only if we do our best.

The Freedom that lets us honestly discuss these common problems was bound to reach some day the time when it must give mankind the world republic, or perish by the sword. It has reached that time today, when freedom depends on you and me.

None of us alone can decide this momentous issue. But enough of us, decided and united, can together shape the world nearer to the heart's desire—now while the metal's molten.

Men can hope to beat the sword into the plow only when the sword is white, and the sword is flaming now.

They cannot beat the sword who flee the showering sparks, shrink horror-stricken from the blast, fear for their fingers and their Sunday clothes. Nor can they shape the plow who are blinded by the glare or shaken by the clamor. This is work for men, coolheaded, sinewy men, born and wed to firm, stouthearted women. . . .

May the Almighty sustain the men who form the hammer and the anvil, guide the hands that guide the blows, and console the women whose tears, at long last, freeze in the plow the temper of the sword.

*   *   *   *   *   *   *

BACKGROUND

Our first basic question is how to organize world government without abolishing existing governments and states. At bottom, as *Union Now* made clear,* peoples can organize such government in two ways only. Either they must keep all power in the hands of their existing governments and try to get these governments to work together as equal units. Or they must take the individual in all the states concerned as the new state's equal unit and citizen, and form its government by giving each citizen a vote in electing representatives to it. In this case they transfer

* See *Union Now*, Chapters I, VI, VII.

from his existing to his new representatives the power to govern
him individually in certain limited fields of common interests.

The former, *government-to-government method* is the old
way of Europe. Examples of it are diplomacy, international
law, international conferences, alliances and leagues, including
our Joint Defense Board with Canada and our Pan-American
organization. To understand this system one need only imagine
the U. S. Government organized as an Alliance or League of
the 48 State Governments, each backed by an independent army,
currency, tariff and immigration act, trying to secure co-opera-
tion in these fields by acting through their governors, giving
each an equal vote and veto in the Alliance, and attempting to
enforce agreements by punishing, not an individual, but a whole
state. The other, *man-to-man system* is the Federal Union or
Union method. Since the United States Constitution is the first
example of it, it can be called the American way, though Canada, Australia, the Union of South Africa and Switzerland are
now organized on this basis.

Having explained this fundamental choice, *Union Now* made,
in sum, this proposal:

Let us organize government between nations the American way,
because our Federal Union way is the only system of inter-state
government that has proved it can do this task. Let us model world
government on our own Constitution which has stood the test of
time the longest, governing most successfully the largest and most
mixed population scattered among the most states in the widest area.

And let us learn, too, from the way in which our American Union
evolved and grew. Instead of trying to start the United States of
the World with all mankind at once, let us begin it, too, with a
nucleus, with a few of the greatest, oldest, most homogeneous and
closely linked democracies, the peoples most experienced and successful in solving the problem at hand—the peaceful, reasonable
establishment of effective inter-state democratic world government.

Let us hasten agreement by starting with as few of these as we
need to equip this Union from the start with overwhelming superiority in power. Let us begin The Union of the Free with these 15
founder democracies: The U. S. A., the United Kingdom, Canada,
Eire, Australia, New Zealand, the Union of South Africa, France,
Switzerland, Belgium, Holland, Denmark, Norway, Sweden and
Finland.

Let us so constitute their Union as to encourage the nations outside it and the colonies inside it to seek to unite with it instead of against it. Let us arrange for The Union to admit to it—just as the American Union does—new states that guarantee its basic rights of man.

Let us organize the Great Republic deliberately to spread peacefully round the earth as people grow ripe for it. Let its Constitution aim clearly at achieving eventually by this peaceful, ripening, natural method the goal millions have dreamed of individually, but not tried to get by carefully planning and patiently working together to achieve it. That goal would be achieved by The Union when every individual of our species was a citizen of it, a citizen of a disarmed world enjoying world free trade, a common money and a world communications system. Then Man's vast future would begin.

But, first and foremost, let us begin by forming the nucleus of this world government before it is too late. Let us make haste and begin The Union *now*.

Union Now sought to boil its whole proposal down to the two words in its title and to center attention on them as equally essential.

Few or none denied its main contentions. Few or none denied the need of government, or the failure of the League of Nations, diplomacy and the balance of power. Nearly everyone agreed that Federal Union had succeeded not only in the United States for one hundred and fifty years, but in Canada between the British and French, in the Union of South Africa between the Boers and British, in Switzerland among German, French and Italian cantons in the heart of Europe.

Few held that World Federal Union could be started on a universal scale. And none could challenge the facts that the fifteen proposed founders together governed nearly half of the human species, owned almost half the earth, ruled all its oceans, had more than 50 per cent control of practically every raw essential in peace or war, did 65 per cent of the world's trade, possessed virtually all the world's gold. None could deny that these fifteen democracies had the power to make half the world safe for democracy without a war, simply by changing their own minds and agreeing to seek their common ends—freedom, peace and plenty—in union rather than disunion. *None proposed a more promising, proven and practical answer to the world problem.*

A growing number, here and in all the democracies, began banding themselves together and working untiringly to make the Union. But the great majority remained indifferent. They could not see the need of action. They were too busy with other, now forgotten things. Many said the Union proposal appealed to their common sense but could not appeal to the common man. They assumed their common sense was quite uncommon.

THE WAR MAKES UNION WITH BRITAIN URGENT

Union, people said, was a dream. They acted as if a nightmare were more practical than a dream. They got the nightmare. Down the disunited democracies have gone, one after another, surprised, betrayed, invaded, ravaged, conquered, imprisoned, put to shame. Of those fifteen democracies only seven now remain free—the six democracies of the British Commonwealth of Nations and the United States of America.

In less than a year the question has changed from one of preventing the onslaught on democracy to one of preventing democracy's total defeat, from one of preventing war in Europe to one of preventing the invasion of America. We Americans, instead of uniting the fifteen while they faced a single foe, have let that Nazi foe unite in an alliance against us the three most heavily armed aggressor powers on earth. That is the first military alliance ever made to intimidate and coerce the United States. It is something which the opponents of Union have truly brought to America first. And this alliance has been made to force you and me to keep on following the disastrous policy of disunion when we showed signs of abandoning it.

What must our answer be? More urgently than ever, "Union Now"—Federal Union with the remaining democracies for nucleus, *Union now with Britain.*

The war has not destroyed or altered the basic principles of *Union Now.* Instead, it has proved their soundness, rendered their adoption much more necessary, and made the nuclear Union much less difficult to start. The advance of autocracy has changed the *Union Now* program mainly in matters of degree, and in these three respects:

1. The Union must start with a smaller nucleus than was first proposed.
2. The people of this nucleus, to save themselves from autocracy, must unite more hastily, in a provisional emergency Federal Union to hold the fort till they can agree upon a permanent Constitution.
3. To succeed in overthrowing autocracy they must stress all the more that their Union is not exclusive or imperialistic, but the genuine nucleus of the United States of Man.

The more democracies we lose, the truer these three principles will be. The longer we practice disunion and the weaker the possible nucleus becomes, the greater the danger will grow to its members and the more they will need to start The Union quickly, and promise to make it universal. So long as any democracies remain, the advance of autocracy cannot destroy or alter the basic principles of *Union Now.* It can only sharpen the ideas summed up in *Union* and in *Now,* and tie them more tightly together.

Though the nucleus must now be smaller than the original of fifteen, it is still possible, at this writing, to unite the great bulk of the original Union's population, land and power. No material power has been lost except the minor fractions of population and territory which were situated on the European continent. The vast non-European possessions of France, Holland, Belgium and Denmark are not in the hands of Germany. They can still count for democracy.

The Union's Great, Imperiled Power

Moreover, the seven democracies that remain free to found The Union now—the United States of America, Canada, the United Kingdom, Eire, the Union of South Africa, Australia and New Zealand—formed the great core and body of the original nucleus of fifteen.

Of the 280,000,000 self-governing citizens of the fifteen,

more than 200,000,000 are citizens of the seven. They supplied it the most practical experience in self-government and federal union. They gave it most of its power, for together they own one-third of the earth and govern one-third of humanity. And they already have the strongest natural bonds to draw and hold them together. Language, which helps divide the others, helps unite these seven. History and religion do not separate them so deeply. Politically, one can say that these seven are divided at bottom only into the United States of America and the British Commonwealth of Nations.

The one thing that divides them most is the thing they can together most easily control—the sea. While these seven states control the Seven Seas they can even suffer invasion of the British and Irish Isles and yet carry through the Union program. For they can then hold in trust for the European democracies their territory overseas, draw on the resources of half the earth and half the human race, blockade dictators from rubber, tin, nickel, copper, lead, gold, cotton, wool and oil, gain the time to control the air also . . . and so win the earth, too, for freedom.

But though the democracies still retain most of their tremendous actual and potential strength, their continued retention of it has become exceedingly precarious. They are in grave danger of losing most of it in one sudden catastrophe. Their hold on it depends on sea power. That power depends about equally on the British and the American navies. The control of the British navy resides solely in the London government. That government remains fearfully exposed.

The democracies of western Europe, particularly France, formed a protective covering for this great nerve center of democracy. Their defeat left autocracy installed within cannon range of England, and only too well placed, from Norway to Spain, to sap away with planes and submarines the sea power and supplies of the British. While it bombs, night after night, the island's docks, shipyards, factories, and people, it prepares, like a matador in the bull ring, to lunge in with the sword when the victim is bled weak.

The British have stood up magnificently—a nation of "47,000,000 Churchills"—but they have been accumulating

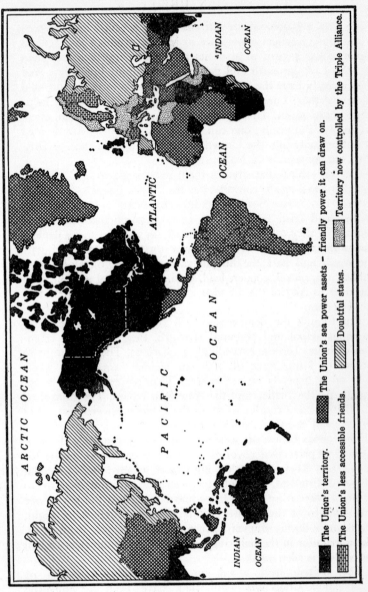

Legend:
- The Union's territory.
- The Union's less accessible friends.
- The Union's sea power assets – friendly power it can draw on.
- Doubtful states.
- Territory now controlled by the Triple Alliance.

CONTROL OF THE SEA KEEPS THE WORLD FREE

strain and losses. An unlucky break, a base betrayal, a heart-rending appeal to us, a heartbreaking answer, the sudden moral and material collapse that can come when friend and foe alike prove too hardhearted, a rightabout change in Cabinets, a bitter revulsion in British popular feeling toward America as there was in French feeling toward Britain, a Nazi threat of unspeakable vengeance against the families of sailors if the fleet is not surrendered—and then what?

We can safely assume that Hitler will stop at nothing to get the world control that possession of the British fleet can give him any time before our two-ocean navy is completed in 1946.

If We Lose the Sea

If we lose the sea, then we lose catastrophically to dictatorship. Then the remaining democracies can be cut apart, lose essentials they need to gain control of the air, be conquered one by one. Then we race after powers who have in their hands far greater plant capacities than we have to build both planes and ships.

Then we must back out of the Pacific to protect our vital North Atlantic seaboard. We must abandon to Japan, Australia and New Zealand, and perhaps Alaska. We can still form a Union with Canada, but the Monroe Doctrine falls for much of South America, and in the Caribbean the "good neighbor" may be driven into imperialism.

When we lose the sea we lose abruptly most of our trade. Some prices tumble, others soar. Chaos in factory and farm brings panicky demands for dictatorship from within. All the while the fear of foreign autocracy leads us to clamp on ourselves a regime of increasingly long hours of labor and heavy taxes, of endless borrowing, centralizing, regimenting.

And though we repulse invasion, this regime remains with us, gnawing away our freedom from inside, not for a year or two but interminably, as long as the threat of military or economic invasion remains. And it will remain until autocracy is uprooted overseas and democratic world government is securely planted there and here. But how and when shall we uproot the one and plant the other . . . once we have lost the seas? How

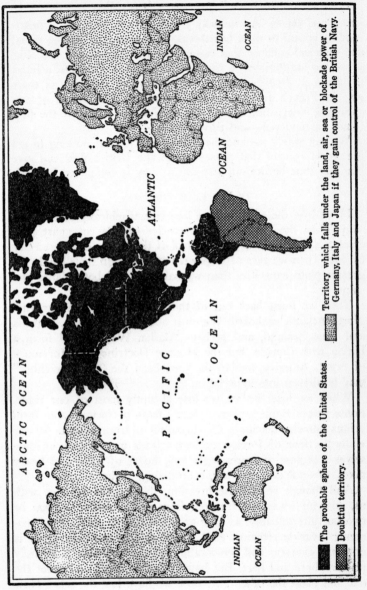

ARCTIC OCEAN

ATLANTIC OCEAN

PACIFIC OCEAN

INDIAN OCEAN

INDIAN OCEAN

The probable sphere of the United States.

Doubtful territory.

Territory which falls under the land, air, sea or blockade power of Germany, Italy and Japan if they gain control of the British Navy.

WHERE WE ARE WITHOUT THE BRITISH FLEET

long can we preserve meanwhile our own democracy and Federal Union?

We are now in the position of a people who, to quote de Tocqueville, "present today a terrifying spectacle . . . their fate is in their hands, but soon it will escape them." We still "have it in our power to begin the world over again," as Tom Paine put it—but we can lose that power suddenly, even before we see the need of using it.

We face now the danger of losing, in the consequences of a single blow, not only the hope of democracy and Federal Union in the world but also, for all practical purposes, the reality, the blessings, of Federal Union where it already exists—here in the United States of America as well as in Switzerland, Canada, Australia and the Union of South Africa.

Union Needed to Win the War

When *Union Now* was published our basic problem was to win the peace we had failed since 1918 to secure. Because we continued to put off this problem we are now saddled with two other problems. They are inextricably bound up with the original one, and they are even more urgent. Here is the full task we face now:

1. To halt tyranny's onward march and save America from invasion.
2. To win the war.
3. To win the peace.

Every one of these is primarily a problem in inter-state organization, and the answer to each of them is Union now with Britain. We not only need Union now with Britain to secure enduring peace; we can no longer reasonably hope either to win the war or even to halt dictatorship without it. For us to keep out of the war, Britain must not merely continue to hold Hitler and Mussolini enough in check to keep Japan and Russia out, but also defeat all comers, combined, without us. That is no longer a reasonable hope; it is but wishful dreaming.

It is disunion that involves us in this war. Had *Union Now* never been written, were no one now working for Union with Britain, our entry in this war would only be the more inevitable.

The majority of Americans, according to the Gallup and

Fortune polls, have gradually grown ready to aid Britain even at the risk of war. This policy of aiding Britain without Union has long had more adherents than our policy of Union with Britain, now or later. Yet suppose that no one in America were working for any kind of aid to Britain. Suppose that all we Americans had from the start shut the British from our minds and hearts as completely as the most ardent neutralist, anti-British or pro-Nazi agent could desire. Our involvement in this war would then remain not only inevitable—assuming this policy had not already led to the conquest of Britain and the invasion of the United States of America—but we would then be in very grave danger of defeat.

When *Union Now* appeared in 1939, the great majority refused to believe that our situation had already become so dangerous that we needed The Union at once as a peace measure. Many even now remain unconvinced that we need The Union for peace. Similarly, the great majority refuse to believe that we need Union now with Britain as a defensive measure, a war-and-peace measure.

The majority's disbelief and inaction will not lessen this need. They will simply worsen the danger and sharpen the need until we are flung into the war. Nor will this insure that we shall then adopt the Union policy. It will insure only that we shall enter the war in much worse conditions and lose more lives than necessary. The only question is whether we shall be the first democracy to see in time these truths, or whether we, too, will see them only after we can no longer save ourselves. Unhappily, it is our entry into the war that we have already made inevitable—not the establishment of The Union.

Even those who do not agree that our entry in the war is inevitable may readily agree that we *may* become involved in it any day by forces beyond our control. They may agree that before this happens the situation of Britain and ourselves will have become much worse and that we shall then need to do the very best we can to win. They may agree that we shall then be fighting on the same side as Canada, the United Kingdom, and the other democracies of the British Commonwealth. They may agree to these facts, too: We shall then have to organize ourselves somehow with these British democracies. Failure to organize ourselves effectively with them will cost dearly in American lives. It will prolong and worsen the worst there is in war. It may cost us victory. It can lose us the peace even though we win the war.

THE EUROPEAN OR THE AMERICAN WAY?

Agreement on all this, however, leaves us facing the question: How shall we then organize ourselves with the British?

Shall we combine with them again as an associate in the old European alliance way—improvise another Supreme War Council, another batch of inter-allied committees? Or shall we invite them to unite with us in a rough-and-ready Federal Union—keep Washington's advice to avoid entangling alliances and continue in the way our forefathers gave the world when they invented the American Constitution? That is the choice we shall have to make, willy-nilly, the moment we enter the war.

If we leave this question till that moment, it will only too probably be answered the worst way—the way that will again cost us the victory after we have bought it dearly. The British and the French left this question to the last minute. And they combined as an alliance.

Shall we begin back where the British and French began in September, 1939? Or shall we learn by their experience, and begin where they left off, with the offer of a Federal Union?

They faced the most unified power on earth, the Nazi totalitarian dictatorship, and so they combined in the most unified alliance ever made. We must be prepared to face, in much worse conditions, the world's three most unified aggressor powers, the Nazi, Fascist and Japanese governments all allied against us. But we cannot make a tighter alliance to defend ourselves from them than the British made with the French against the Nazis. For the British and the French went the limit then.

They combined their defense forces. They put both armies under a French general, both navies under the British Admiralty. They combined their foreign policy in solemn pledges by both governments never to make peace separately. They practiced constant consultation on all questions of foreign relations. They combined their war supply, shipping, economic, financial and monetary power under joint committees of the two governments, and then combined these in a Joint Co-ordinating Committee under a single chairman, Jean Monnet. They went so far that many Americans called the combination a "Union," but it was never that.

The British and French combined as far as they possibly could without combining themselves in a common citizenry governing these common affairs through representatives they elected to one common government. Had they gone this one step further they would thereby have changed the alliance into a Federal Union—into the same relationship that the British and French enjoy in Canada. But in Europe the British and the French trusted in each other's government instead of in each other, man to man. So they stuck to the old way of Europe and combined together, government to government.

They made the strongest alliance possible . . . and at the test it proved pitifully inadequate.

As it crashed, the British saw where the defect lay. In frantic haste they begged the French to go that one step further, turn from the European to the American way, change the alliance into a Federal Union. They were just too late. The French government hesitated . . . and declined . . . 13 votes to 10.

Had the British and the French united in a Federal Union, then the French sea, air and land forces, like those of the British, would have become the defense forces of the Union, and only the Union's officers and government could then have surrendered any part of them. The French government then could have no more surrendered even a fraction of these forces than the Pennsylvania government could surrender any forces of the American Union when Lee invaded its territory. This is one of the great differences between a Union and an alliance.

Had the British and the French formed a Union, there could have been no separate armistice, no Vichy government, no tragic battles between French and British. Had they done this, even though too late to save France itself from occupation, all the French colonies, all the French navy and air force, and much of the French army would have continued to be live assets of an Anglo-French Union government. But the British and the French did not unite our way. And so we Americans now face the alternatives they faced.

Shall we, too, try the European alliance way once more? Shall we go back to where the British began with the French? Or shall we start where they left off, and unite with the British in the American Union way?

And shall we, too, make the mistake they made from the start—declare what we are fighting *against*, but fail to declare what we are fighting *for*? Shall we, too, encourage our foes to fight the harder against us by asserting we are out to smash them, by lamenting our failure to go on to Berlin in 1918, by promising to "cut their country up in pieces this time," by speaking so vaguely of the "new order" our victory will bring the world that we make even friendly peoples suspicious of our aims?

AMERICA UEBER ALLES?

Shall we do even worse? Shall we follow the advice of all those Americans who tell us never again to fight for any ideal, but to fight only and always for ourselves, and as selfishly as we can? Shall our practice pervert the good there is in the sentiment, "America First," until we convince mankind that what we are really fighting for is *America Ueber Alles*? Or shall we take our stand with Lincoln when, on his way to defend the Union at Washington, he stopped to say these words at Independence Hall:

I have never had a feeling, politically, that did not spring from the sentiments embodied in the Declaration of Independence.

I have often pondered over the dangers which were incurred by the men who assembled here and framed and adopted that Declaration. I have pondered over the toils that were endured by the officers and soldiers of the army who achieved that independence. I have often inquired of myself what great principle or idea it was that kept this Confederacy so long together.

It was not the mere matter of separation of the colonies from the motherland, but that sentiment in the Declaration of Independence which gave liberty not alone to the people of this country, but hope to all the world, for all future time. It was that which gave promise that in due time the weights would be lifted from the shoulders of

all men, and that all should have an equal chance. This is the sentiment embodied in the Declaration of Independence.

Now, my friends, can this country be saved on that basis? If it
can, I will consider myself one of the happiest men in the world if I
can help to save it. If it cannot be saved upon that principle, it will
be truly awful. But if this country cannot be saved without giving
up that principle, I was about to say that I would rather be assassi-
nated on this spot than surrender it.

. . . this is wholly an unprepared speech. . . . But I have said
nothing but what I am willing to live by, and, if it be the pleasure
of Almighty God, to die by.

Shall we now disavow Abraham Lincoln and put to shame
the Founders of this, the first of Federal Unions? Or shall we
add new grandeur to their work by answering,

> *We are coming, Father Abraham, one hundred thou-
> sand strong!*

as they who kept the name, *American,* for us all answered
then?

We can answer now in a way that will speed catastrophe over
there and over here, and be remembered to our everlasting dishonor. Or we can give an answer that will encircle the earth
in a flash with a force as omnipresent, never-resting, invisible
and acceleratingly powerful as gravity itself, a force that no
army can keep out, that no dictator can put his finger on, and
that yet comes sweeping on as does an avalanche. We can give
an answer that will sow confusion and revolt among the enemies
of freedom, and put new, invincible life in its beleaguered defenders. We can again give "hope to all the world." We, too,
can answer in a way that will go shining through the ages to our
undying honor, as the answer that turned lightning-shattered
darkness into enduring sunny light for all mankind.

A Limited Provisional Union First

To work this wonder we need but call out in time to the
British:

"Hold the fort, for we are coming—coming with the thing to
end this loathsome horror for good and all. For we bring you

now The Union of the Free. We invite you British, Irish, Canadians, Australians, New Zealanders, South Africans, to unite with us at once, not in any brittle alliance or feeble league, but in a powerful Federal Union, as the nucleus of the United States of the World, the Commonwealth of Man."

Why take unnecessary chances? Why run the risks of breakdown? Let us give each other and all the world every guarantee by not waiting till the war is won to start this newer, better world. Let us start this Union *now,* do as our Thirteen States did, start by forming a provisional Congress, a solid common government instead of a fragile Supreme War Council. If we must fight, let us fight and win the war *as* a Federal Union of ourselves . . . for a Federal Union of mankind.

Let us give this emergency government much the same powers that those Thirteen States gave their Continental Congress, as regards foreign affairs, trade, currency, and communication services. Let each of our democracies give the others the effective guarantee against any separate surrender which the Thirteen mutually gave when, in the Articles of Confederation they agreed:

> "The United States in Congress assembled shall have the sole and exclusive right and power of determining on peace and war * * * * appointing all officers of the land forces, in the service of the United States, excepting regimental officers—appointing all the officers of the naval forces, and commissioning all officers whatever in the service of the United States —making rules for the government and regulation of the said land and naval forces, and directing their operations."

Since there can be no effective Union without common citizenship, let us follow, too, the example of the Thirteen when they established such citizenship in the Articles of Confederation.*

* Article IV of the Articles of Confederation provided: "The better to secure and perpetuate mutual friendship and intercourse among the people of the different states in this union, the free inhabitants of these

What men could do so long ago in wartime, we can surely quickly copy now—and improve upon. We need not make the costly mistake they made at first of having their common Congress represent the state governments, and operate only through and on them. This mistake prolonged the war for years, for, as John Fiske has pointed out, "Had there been such a government that the whole power of the thirteen states could have been swiftly and vigorously wielded as a unit, the British, fighting at such a disadvantage as they did, might have been driven to their ships in less than a year."*

Before it ruined them, the Thirteen corrected this mistake. They made Congress operate on and through the citizens in the new Constitution (our present one), in the few fields where it operated at all, and they apportioned representation in Congress according to the number of Union citizens in each state. They made Congress represent the citizens equally instead of their state governments, while effectively safeguarding the people in the smaller states from domination by the more populous ones. Let us not prolong the present war and risk ruin before we, too, adopt these basic Federal Union principles that have proved so successful. Let us from the start base our new Union Congress directly and equally on the population.

The old Continental Congress issued a Declaration telling the world just why the Thirteen States had united in it. Let us have our Inter-Continental Congress do this, too—proclaim at the outset that we have united not to gain territory, nor to promote any American or British or English-speaking imperialism, nor to force our way of life on others, but to defend those same principles of equal freedom for everyone which the Declaration of 1776 proclaimed:

---

states, paupers, vagabonds and fugitives from Justice excepted, shall be entitled to all privileges and immunities of free citizens in the several states; and the people of each state shall have free ingress and regress to and from any other state, and shall enjoy therein all the privileges of trade and commerce, subject to the same duties, impositions and restrictions as the inhabitants thereof respectively. . . . Full faith and credit shall be given in each of the states to the records, acts and judicial proceedings of the courts and magistrates of every other state."

* *Critical Period of American History,* Houghton Mifflin Company, p. 56.

"We hold these truths to be self-evident: That all men are created equal; that they are endowed by their Creator with certain unalienable rights; that among these are life, liberty and the pursuit of happiness; that to secure these rights, governments are instituted among men, deriving their just powers from the consent of the governed; that, whenever any form of government becomes destructive of these ends, it is the right of the people to alter or abolish it, and to institute new government, laying its foundation on such principles and organizing its powers in such form as to them shall seem most likely to effect their safety and happiness."

Since our Democracies do depend on each other for this freedom let us say so honestly, and call our new Declaration the Declaration of Inter-Dependence and Union.

A Broader Permanent Union Later

Let us declare also at the outset our intention to assemble, as soon as we can, another Federal Convention—perhaps in Independence Hall—to work out a permanent Federal Union of the Free. Let us model it on the United States Constitution and the Canadian, Australian, South African and Swiss federal unions. The Constitution of The Union raises many perplexing problems. They require the most careful study and discussion by a specially chosen assembly of delegates. We cannot safely either do without this or wait for it. Let us therefore make our Union irrevocable only after we have had time to try out Union in practice and hold a Constitutional Convention—and then only after the people in each democracy have carefully considered the resulting text and solemnly ratified it. Thus we can all avoid the dangers inherent in hasty action, just as we avoid, by quickly establishing the provisional Union, the dangers of uniting too tardily or too loosely.

Finally, let us make abundantly clear that we make our Union as the nucleus of a world government of, by and for the people—a Union to which outside and colonial peoples could and would be admitted to full and equal statehood as states are admitted to the United States of America. That means that each application would be decided on its merits, with no people barred and each required to give the same democratic guarantees as the other members of The Union, including proof of their ability to make good their guarantees.

It is dangerous to try to force outsiders to accept our way. It is dangerous, too, to keep outsiders out. But we can steer between these dangers. Though circumstances lead us to start The Union with only English-speaking founders, we can counteract any fears this may rouse by admitting at the earliest opportunity democracies of other languages.

For Union in Peace

Let us also state from the outset that our Union is prepared to negotiate at once armistice and peace terms with any government attacking any territory of The Union on these conditions: No indemnities, reparations, occupations or annexations by anyone, and arbitration of disputes on details. These terms, it is true, fall far short of smashing dictatorship. They let each nation keep its prewar system of government as long as it desires. They leave the dictators not only in power in their own countries but with their armed forces intact.

Though Britain alone could not wisely make this offer now, our much stronger Union could afford to, for it could stand peace without victory better than its foes. We cannot safely offer the Axis substantially more than this, and it is highly doubtful that the dictators would accept even these terms.

So let us make it harder for them to refuse, and easier to encourage revolt if they do. To this end we could give certain key peoples stronger pledges than the general pledge to outside peoples. First, let us expressly guarantee to admit to The Union, as soon as circumstances permit, those peoples which have already long governed themselves democratically. Without naming any of them, we could draft a pledge so that each of the western European democracies would know at once that it applied to them, and insured their admission to The Union as soon as dictatorship no longer occupied or surrounded them. Second, let us similarly guarantee to admit to The Union such peoples as the Germans when, by successfully ending autocracy at home, they prove their devotion to the basic principles of The Union, their ability to practice them, and their desire to end this war.

If this is our answer, then, instead of helping totalitarian propagandists to sow suspicion of us everywhere and crush the spirit of the captive democracies, we shall be rousing millions to run the risks of passive resistance and active revolt. Instead of giving the misguided zealots of Hitler and Mussolini cause to fight desperately, we shall be giving them cause to hesitate, more and more, to fight at all.

We shall then have planted something in Germany and Italy that is far more dangerous to Hitler and Mussolini than all their fifth columns will be to us. For then we shall have planted in the heads of these dictators *fear of revolt* and *suspicion that the other dictator will make a separate peace*. These two ideas, once planted in their heads as only this Union policy will plant them there, can make them lose their heads more swiftly than they could lose them in revolt. They are already peculiarly susceptible to both these ideas. They were afraid of free speech at home even before the war began. And not only do Hitler and Mussolini deeply distrust each other already, but so do the German and Italian peoples.

If dictatorship will not accept our peace terms, then we must overthrow it over there, lest it overthrow freedom over here. Either we must overthrow it with a tremendous expeditionary force or we must overthrow it from within, by the just and generous policy of *Union Now*. How can we overthrow it sooner, more enduringly, with less loss of life than by this policy which would (1) unite our military power to stop its war machine, (2) tightly blockade it by sea, and (3) from the air cut its land communications and destroy its production . . . while (4) encouraging its victims to undermine and overthrow it themselves?

Union How?—Action in Congress

But how is this to be done? How is it to be started? Where does one begin? The starting power is in each of the citizens of the seven proposed founders, and most of all in us Americans. The first thing to do is to make one's will for Union known, and keep on making it known to those in power. The next thing is to act, individually and collectively through the Federal Union organization, to persuade others to make their will for Union known, to spread, and keep on spreading, the good news that we can save ourselves by Union.

For this public opinion to take effect, there would have to be action by the President and Congress of the United States to initiate it formally. This action would preferably take the form of a Joint Declaration and Resolution by Congress authorizing the President to invite the democracies of the British Common- wealth to unite with us in a provisional Federal Union for such ends and in such ways as the Resolution itself would set forth.

We must always keep in mind that we are dealing with a rapidly developing, not a static situation. It can make yesterday's impossibility possible today—and impossible again tomorrow.

The contents and exact terms of the Resolution would be taking shape gradually in the discussion that would be develop- ing among leaders as the tide of Union opinion rose and danger made action more urgent. This discussion has already begun informally. It will spread among statesmen in this democracy and in the others, and between them. Its object must be to secure a text for this Resolution of invitation to Union which will be reasonably sure of acceptance, not only by Congress but by the British democracies.

Disaster may not leave much time for negotiation. The greater the pressure of events becomes, the more it will be necessary for the Resolution itself to provide the broad ma- chinery for the provisional Union government. When enough informal agreement has been reached, or when the situation has become so dangerous as to precipitate action, the Resolution would come up for formal discussion and adoption in Con- gress. Once adopted, the President would extend the invitation to Union to the British democracies. The provisional Union could come into being as soon as the United Kingdom or Canada formally agreed to the American offer.

One can argue that the Joint Declaration and Resolution should be kept very short, confined to setting forth broad prin- ciples and providing a minimum of machinery. On the other hand, the American people and Congress must have certain guarantees before they will make any Union offer; the fewer

and vaguer these guarantees are the more reluctant they will
be to make the offer. Moreover, to leave too many basic questions for the new Congress to work out is to risk having it
spend on constitutional matters time it should be devoting to
winning the war.

All real thinking on this whole problem must always keep in
mind (a) that the circumstances which make it possible to start
the Union are certain to be circumstances of much greater danger than we have yet experienced, and (b) that we are setting
up a Federal government that, like the alternative, an Inter-
Allied Council, is strictly provisional. Many things considered,
it would seem wise—certainly at this stage of the discussion of
so momentous a decision—to aim at having the Resolution cover
all the constitutional ground that can reasonably be covered,
while basing the new government squarely on the broadest degree of popular consent that can be *quickly* obtained.

THE UNION PROGRAM IN OUTLINE

In this spirit, and by way of summary and clarification, it is
suggested that the Joint Declaration and Resolution should:

1. *Declare* the end sought in establishing the Union, namely,
   to secure equally for all mankind individual freedom, peace
   and prosperity, reasserting, in this connection, the basic principles of the Declaration of Independence and the last words
   of Lincoln's Second Inaugural, and listing the chief Rights
   of Man—such as freedom of speech, press, association, religion—which are to be safeguarded.
2. *Provide* the means of attaining this end in the form of a
   Federal Union, modeled broadly on the U. S. Constitution
   and designed clearly to grow peacefully from a nucleus into
   a universal world government in two basic stages, (a) immediately and provisionally, and (b) later and permanently.
   A. *Immediately but provisionally:*
      1. *Set up* as the supreme Government of The Union an
         Inter-Continental Congress of either one or two
         houses, with each Member Democracy represented in
         proportion to its self-governing population by repre-

sentatives holding office for a fixed term and responsible directly to the *people* of that democracy instead
of to its *government*.

2. *Set up also* Executive and Judicial organs, or alter-
natively, *authorize* the new Congress to do this.

3. *Give* the Union certain specific powers, notably sole
or supreme power over war, peace, foreign affairs,
currency, trade and communications between members, democracies or with the outside world, the
admission of new citizens and states to the Union,
and the government of all the present nonself-governing territory of Member Democracies; and also power
to tax and borrow, to enforce its laws on individuals
through the courts, and to settle peacefully disputes
between member democracies.

4. *Stipulate* that all other powers and rights remain in
the hands of the Member Democracies, or of the people, and whenever necessary guarantee these powers
the more surely by specifying them.

5. *Grant* to the citizens of each Member Democracy
citizenship in The Union, entitling them to move freely
about its territory and enjoy the rights of citizenship
in every member democracy.

6. *Provide* for the Union government to begin functioning, as regards members accepting it, when these include, besides the U. S. A., the United Kingdom or
Canada.

B. *For the later, permanent stage:*

1. *Require* the Union Assembly to convoke a Constitutional Convention as soon as possible to draft a definitive Constitution for The Union, to be binding on
a Member Democracy only after it has been ratified
by its people.

2. *Make clear* that The Union is designed to grow gradually into a universal Federal Union, by the peaceful
admission of outside and colonial peoples to full and
equal membership as rapidly as this will safely promote the end for which The Union is established.

3. *Strengthen* the preceding pledge, as regards certain

peoples of primary importance to the early success of
The Union, without naming them and thus offending
others, by providing expressly for the admission, as
soon as circumstances permit, of those peoples who
have already long governed themselves democratically
or who, by successfully ending autocracy at home,
prove their devotion to the basic principles of The
Union, their ability to practice them, and their desire
to end this war.

C. *Allow* each Member Democracy to withdraw from the
Provisional Union only in the event it has either ratified
the definitive Constitution and entered the Permanent
Union, or has rejected a definitive Constitution which had
secured enough ratifications to go into force.

3. *Recommend* that the new Union Congress offer at once to
negotiate armistice and peace terms with any government at
the time attacking any of its territory, on these conditions:
no indemnities, no reparations, no occupations or annexations
of foreign territory; and arbitration of disputes on details
that cannot be settled by direct negotiation.

The Alternative, an Alliance—Its Dangers

Obviously this program has many problems to be worked out,
many difficulties to be overcome. Some will therefore assume
that the program makes the problems and the difficulties. The
reverse is true. The program is there because of the problems
and the difficulties. It does bring them out more sharply, but
that is an advantage—a great advantage since it puts them in
order, in perspective. It allows what in reality is vast and complex to be seen more as a whole. It provides a broad plan for
handling it, supplies a guiding line all the way through. The
alternative to this roughly mapped and roughly cleared wilderness is a jungle of problems, a terra incognita of difficulties, an unguessed tangle which has no terrors till one is caught
within it.

To consider concretely the problems and difficulties of the
Union program is to begin to solve them and to appreciate
better the tremendous advantages this program has over others.

For example, some will gasp at the difficulties involved in organizing the new Union government. But what is the alternative? It is that we continue to govern our relations with the British on the present government-to-government basis. If we enter the war on this basis we go in as an ally. We have to organize a new inter-allied government, set up again all the machinery of the Franco-British alliance that collapsed at Hitler's first blow. Is it going to be easier for us to make this alliance machinery work than it was for the British and French, easier than to copy our own successful Federal Union system?

Certainly our alliance would be more complicated than the Anglo-French one. The latter could be limited practically to two governments, representing about equal populations, the United Kingdom and France, for the war then was centered in Europe. But the war we enter will be world-wide rather than European.

ALLIANCE MEANS SIX VOTES TO OUR ONE

The British Dominions will certainly play a much bigger role in it and will have to be represented in the Supreme Inter-Allied Council. The government-to-government system guarantees each state an equal vote, regardless of population. We have already accorded this equal status to the British Dominions in various international conferences. Only recently we set up a Joint Defense Board in which we gave Canada, which has about the population of New York State, the same representation as all our forty-eight states together. Consequently, if we extend this policy into an alliance with the British, the 70,000,000 self-governing people of the British Commonwealth of Nations would have six votes, and the 130,000,000 citizens of the United States would have one vote.

There would be this six-to-one setup in every one of the inter-allied committees that would have to be organized to co-ordinate the work of the seven governments on economic matters, war supplies, finance, and so on. It would exist also in the Supreme Council which would have the unenviable task of trying to coordinate all these sovereign co-ordinators. Will this machinery be simpler and easier to organize than a single Federal Union government? Will it not be much harder to operate successfully? And the fact that an alliance allows us Americans only one vote in seven during the war and at the peace settlement—does not that raise dangers for us, as well as problems and difficulties that we avoid by Federal Union?

ALLIANCE MEANS NATIONAL DISUNITY

An alliance raises many other dangers. Nothing short of conquest by foreign dictatorship could so endanger American democracy as would our entry in the war on any government-to-government basis. For this is bound to augment fearfully two internal dangers that the American people deeply dread: The centralization of power in the hands of one man, and bitter partisan division of the people. These two dangers have already reached disquieting proportions. That was shown by the violence of the recent presidential campaign, the closeness in the popular vote, and the earnest, ephemeral attempts thereafter to restore unity by words.*

Words cannot produce unity when facts give one man war-time power over 22,000,000 persons who voted against giving him any power at all over them, many because they feared this very thing. When millions of these voters already—however wrongly—distrust this man and suspect him of dictatorial ambitions, something much stronger than appeals to unity is urgently needed. A free people is certain to undergo terrific internal strain when anything results in giving practically 100 per cent power over 100 per cent of the people to any President elected by only 55 per cent of the people, and elected by them to a position of limited power only. Going to war on any alli-

---

* When President Roosevelt delivered, January 6, 1941, his Message to Congress on American policy as regards the war, Mrs. Roosevelt wrote in *My Day*: "I was not only astonished but saddened to notice that the applause came almost entirely from the Democrats and only a few noticeable exceptions on the Republican side raised a hand in approval at any point. It looked to me as tho these members of Congress were saying to the country as a whole:

" 'We are Republicans first. We represent you here in Congress, not as citizens of the United States in a period of great crisis, but as members of a political party which seeks primarily to promote its own partisan interests.'

"This is to me shocking and terrifying."

Her words did not lessen the danger of partisanship in a critical period.

ance basis would be sure to result in this, no matter who the President was.

ALLIANCE GIVES ONE MAN ALL OUR POWER

The President already has the most extensive powers any President ever had in peacetime. Already by executive action, without the advice or the consent of Congress, he has committed us to defend Canada, set up permanent machinery to execute this, and given a belligerent power fifty destroyers in return for a ninety-nine-year lease on naval bases. By continuing in this course—as we are under the "Lend-Lease" Bill—we enter the war as an ally, and thereby virtually give the President total power, as regards not merely internal affairs—our lives and our business—but foreign relations, too.

It will be the President who will then decide, as far as we are concerned, the exact nature of the Inter-Allied government which must then be organized—just as it was for President Wilson to decide without reference to Congress such far-reaching questions as whether or not the American Expeditionary Force should be under French command. It will be the President who will name all our representatives in the Inter-Allied government. They will be responsible to him and hold office only so long as they please him. He will name and remove at will not only our generals, admirals, production, transport and other "czars," but our peace negotiators.

After the victory is won the Senate has always . . . hitherto . . . been able to reject the peace that the President negotiates —but what good does that do us, has that done us? For all practical purposes the President's voice is supreme—as far as we are concerned—both as regards the conduct of the war and the negotiation of peace. If we go to war again *the alliance way* we shall be putting all our hopes in one man, this time far more than in the past. We shall be using the method of dictatorship to gain the ends of democracy.

ALLIANCE MEANS PARTISAN WAR

And we shall be fighting another partisan war if we go to war again *the alliance way.* Of course, everyone will agree that the war should be nonpartisan. The President will earnestly

attempt to make it nonpartisan. The war may even seem nonpartisan to many for a while . . . until the first Congressional
election comes, or the armistice. But the President is the head
of one party. The fact that he picks some collaborators from
the other party does not offset the fact that he is the one that
picks them. They become his personal representatives. They
draw their power from him, and remain in office at his discretion. No matter how much the President tries, he cannot make
the war nonpartisan. Surely the head of the Republican party,
Wendell Willkie, made this clear when, in his radio talk of
Nov. 11, 1940, he said:

In Britain some opposition party leaders are members of the
government and some say that a similar device should be adopted
here. That is a false conception of our Government. When a leader
of the British Liberal Party or of the British Labor Party becomes
a member of the Churchill Cabinet, he becomes—from the British
parliamentary point of view—an equal of Mr. Churchill's.

This is because the British Cabinet is a committee of the houses
of Parliament. It is a committee of equals, wherein the prime minister
is chairman, a lofty chairman, and yet a chairman. The other members are his colleagues.

With us the situation is different. Our executive branch is not a
committee of our Congress. The members of his Cabinet are not his
colleagues. They are his administrative subordinates. They are
subject to his orders.

An American President could fill his whole Cabinet with leaders
of the opposition party and still our Administration would not be a
two-party Administration. It would be an Administration of a majority President giving orders to minority representatives of his own
choosing. These representatives must concur in the President's
convictions. If they do not they have no alternative except to resign.

Clearly no such device can give us in this country any self-
respecting agreement between majority and minority for concerted
action toward the National welfare. Such a plan for us would be but
the shadow—not the substance of unity.

In these circumstances the danger of the war, and especially
the peace, becoming a partisan issue would seem to threaten
us even more this time than the last time . . . if we go to war

*in any way that centers all power in the President, as does an
alliance.*

Worse still, we shall then again fight the war and make the
peace through a President, Congress, and party that we never
elected for those purposes. Each party recently gave a great
many citizens the impression that by voting for it they could
keep America out of war—while also aiding Britain, stopping
Hitler, and defending the United States and all Latin America.
Many leaders conceded privately that we could not have our
cake and eat it, too. Members of both parties have predicted
that no matter which party won we would be in the war a few
months after the election was over. But neither party dared
contemplate publicly even the possibility of our being flung
into the war, and so the campaign issues could not include such
basic questions as how to organize our relations with the
British in the event that we went to war.

If we were electing a government expressly for the purpose
of fighting the most dangerous war in our history—and that
is what this war will be when we enter it—we would surely have
the common sense to disregard party politics and pick the best
men in the land to govern us during the emergency. Instead we
have wishfully decided that words could keep us out of war,
and have therefore indulged in the luxury of a bitterly partisan
campaign. We have thrown away our chance to confide the
safety of the Republic into the hands of the best men we could
find in both parties—in the event we do go to war any time in
the next four years . . . . the alliance way.

*But we still have that chance if, when we go to war, we
organize our relations with the British in the American Federal
Union way, instead of the European alliance way. For the
source of these dangers to our freedom lies not in fighting for
freedom—as many confusedly assume—but rather in going to
War as an ally. If, instead, we fight as a member of The Union
of the Free, we can avoid these dangers.*

Who Would Compose the Union Congress?

If we form a Federal Union with the British, we no longer
divide 130,000,000 Americans more bitterly than ever by making one man their only and all-powerful voice. For then we must

choose a number of citizens, each responsible only to us, to represent us in the new Union Congress. We authorize each of them equally to speak and act for us in it on all those questions of war and peace which the other system would leave to the President's spokesmen in an Inter-Allied Council. Then we *can* confide the safety of the Republic into the hands of the best men in both parties. For then we do establish and elect a government expressly for the purpose of carrying us through a most dangerous emergency.

This is true no matter whether we decide to establish a two-house or a one-house Congress, whether we constitute a Union executive or leave it to the Congress to establish one. There are good arguments for all these solutions. But for present purposes let us suppose that the Joint Resolution provides the simplest solution—establishes a one-house Congress and authorizes it to set up its own executive.

Suppose, too, that the Resolution provides that each member democracy shall have one representative in Congress, plus one additional representative for every 5,000,000 of self-governing population, or major fraction thereof. That would result in a Congress of forty-nine members, of whom twenty-seven would be named by the United States, eleven by the United Kingdom, three by Canada, two each by Australia, New Zealand, the Union of South Africa and Eire. And, in accordance with one of the essentials of the Federal Union system, no member of the Union Congress could continue to hold any office in his home democracy.

The emergency would not allow time to elect the first members of this Congress by popular vote. The American members, for example, would have to be named at the start by the existing government, presumably appointed by the President with the approval of the United States Congress, or perhaps elected by Congress from a long list nominated by the President. Even so, their status would be quite different from that of presidential appointees to an Inter-Allied government. It would be comparable instead to that of a United States Senator in the days of Daniel Webster, when Senators were elected by the state legislatures, instead of by direct popular vote.

The twenty-seven American members of the Congress of The

Union would each hold office for a set term. It could be arranged that the first ones would hold office only until a popular election could be arranged—say, six months—and that thereafter they should sit for, say, three years. No doubt most, if not all, of those originally named to this Congress would be confirmed in office at the first popular election. The point is that, whether they were named originally for six months or for three years, they would each be responsible, not to the President or the American Congress, but only to us, the American people. We, and no one else, would have the power to remove them—to refuse, that is, to re-elect them.

Three facts would insure that the twenty-seven American representatives would really represent the American people, and the best that is in them, regardless of party and petty politics: (a) the fact that we the people had the ultimate power over the members both of the Union Congress and of the United States Congress (which would, of course, continue to govern the United States in all except the few fields transferred to The Union), (b) the fact that we the people had by our public opinion obliged the United States Government to help establish The Union and transfer some of its powers to the new government, and (c) the fact that the emergency, which made all this possible, would be a very grave one.

To create this Union, the American people must return to the level of 1776 and 1787—and it will be while we are at this high level (and not at the miserably low level of today) that our twenty-seven spokesmen will be chosen.

Think of the galaxy on which we could draw. Surely we would want Franklin D. Roosevelt in the new government. And surely we would want Wendell Willkie to be one of the twenty-seven, and Alfred Landon, Herbert Hoover, Al Smith, John W. Davis, James Cox, Charles Hughes—all the men who have been President of the United States or runner-up could serve us then. We could then deal with both war and peace on a genuinely nonpartisan basis.

There would still remain 19 voices left to speak directly for the great variety that is America's great power. Whom would we want to speak them for us? Here is space to write in your

own nominations: ——————, ——————, ——————,
——————, ——————, ——————, ——————,
——————, ——————, ——————, ——————,
——————, ——————, ——————, ——————,
——————, ——————, ——————, ——————.

Would you not include the outstanding members of the U. S. Cabinet, Senate and House, whether Democrat or Republican, Federal Unionist or Isolationist? Would you not want all major viewpoints represented by their leading champions? Isn't that democracy? And would you not want to draw on our industrial leaders, labor leaders, farm leaders, publishers, religious leaders, women leaders, diplomats, university presidents, scientists, Nobel prize winners, youth leaders?

There are so many interests and viewpoints to be represented, so many good men and women whose ripe wisdom and unique experience could help us through the crisis—perhaps we had better arrange a ratio of representation that would allow us forty or fifty equal spokesmen, instead of only twenty-seven.*

Remember how our Continental Congress, when once established, drew to it the greatest men in every state. The greatest men and women in each of the seven democracies would gravitate as naturally from them to the new Union government. It takes some effort to keep in mind that when we form The Union, we transfer supreme war power to it, and, since the leading statesmen are bound to be where the power is, they will follow it from the national government to The Union. If we want to keep these statesmen where they are now, then we form an alliance, not a Union.

In this Union Congress our picked men would not be dealing with the representatives of His Britannic Majesty's Government. They would be dealing with the leading men whom the British people had similarly named to speak for them, and with those whom the Irish, Canadians, Australians, New Zealanders and South Africans had respectively chosen. No doubt they, too, would all pick their best men to speak for them on this

* Though it would seem unwise to make the total membership of Congress too large and cumbersome, still it might safely have, all told, say, 100 members.

common problem of life and death. They, too, would each seek to have their major interests represented by leaders. Whom would the British send to the Union Congress? ——————?
——————? ——————? ——————?
——————? ——————? ——————?
——————? ——————? ——————?

——————? And the Canadians? The Australians? The New Zealanders? The South Africans? The Irish?

WHO WOULD BE THE UNION EXECUTIVE?

And what of the executive? What of the hard fact that the Union plan requires the present executives of the democracies, and particularly the President of the United States and the Prime Minister of the United Kingdom, to renounce the tremendous powers that their office would assure them in an Inter-Allied Council? Well, let us assume the worst. Let us assume that the men now in these posts really aim to keep all this power centered each in his own hands, and consequently will be reluctant to sacrifice any of it. If that is true, it is a highly dangerous fact and the Union proposal will be doing democracy a great service in making this evident before such dictatorial love of power has had time to become a hard-and-fast dictatorship.

Fortunately, however, all the men occupying the executive posts in the seven democracies are in them because they have already given the great majority of their countrymen convincing proof that they have no such motives and are sincere defenders of democracy. And this is particularly true of Franklin D. Roosevelt and Winston Churchill. There is no doubt whatever that the democratic world looks upon these two men as the two greatest living champions of democracy.

Because they occupy so outstanding a position in the whole democratic world there cannot be the slightest doubt that both these men would be called on to continue to play the outstanding roles in the new Union government. They would really be moving up to a position of greater though less dictatorial power—in the sense that the mayor of the city of New York has a much greater power for good than had any of the tyrants of the ancient Greek cities, simply because he heads a far greater body of men. And they would be moving up to a much higher position in history. Many a man has already been President of the United States, Prime Minister of Britain. No man has done before what Franklin D. Roosevelt and Winston Churchill can do by Union now.

But which would head The Union of the Free? Surely both could not head it? Why not? The Roman Republic grew in power for centuries while headed by two equal consuls. There are, of course, disadvantages in this system. It would not seem wise to adopt it permanently. But we are concerned only with a provisional emergency arrangement now. True, in grave emergencies Rome named a single "dictator" for a briefly limited period of office. But it is also true that, as Rome spread afar, some of the difficulties in having two consuls, even in time of war, were solved by the custom of dividing the powers of the consuls so that one remained at Rome administering at the center, and the other was posted at the danger zones on the periphery of the Republic's territory.

This would obviously fit in remarkably with the immediate needs of the *provisional* Union. The capital of The Union would have to be on this side of the Atlantic—either in the United States or Canada—for this would be the most secure and central place for it. At this capital would sit the Congress which would govern the whole Union and elect its two Consuls—or perhaps it might call them Tribunes, Chairmen, or something else.

If this Roman model were followed, Chairman* Roosevelt might stay at this capital, administering the Union's territory on this side of the Atlantic and in the Pacific, including Australia, New Zealand, Singapore, Hong Kong. Chairman Churchill might keep his headquarters for the present in London and have charge in the provisional Union's territory in the British Isles, Africa, the Mediterranean, the Near East and India. Or India might be handled specially.

Who doubts that the citizens of The Union would welcome Chairman Roosevelt enthusiastically when the Union Clipper set him down in Britain to confer with Chairman Churchill?

* I do not mean to urge adoption of this title but adopt it here merely to simplify and stimulate discussion by making it more concrete.

Who can imagine their welcome to Chairman Churchill when he came here to the Union capital to meet with Chairman Roosevelt and report to the provisional Union Congress, as he now reports to the British Parliament?

There would be the danger of a tie? That could be settled by one Chairman having the deciding vote one year, and the other one having it the next year. And it could be arranged, if desired, for the one with the deciding vote to have the functions of titular head of the provisional Union, while the other had the functions of a Prime Minister.

Such is one possible solution of the problem. Another solution would be to have the Congress elect a Board of Five as proposed in the original *Union Now* Constitution as the Union executive. Or this could be reduced to a Board of Three during the provisional period.* The third member might be Mackenzie King, in view of Canada's unique relation to both Britain and the United States. Or he might be de Valera, and there would be good arguments in favor of others,—of, say, an Australian, or a Frenchman, or a German. The three could take yearly turns as Chairman of the Board. Or Congress could make one of them Chairman for the full term. Or this could be done by lot.

If, on thorough consideration, it is found that any form of plural executive would be unwise, Congress could elect a single executive. Would not the great majority of citizens of The Union, whether American, British, Irish, Canadian, South African, Australian or New Zealander, easily accept either Mr. Roosevelt or Mr. Churchill as President of the Union?

If it were left to a popular vote of all the 200,000,000 citizens of The Union—and that might well be the eventual solution —who could foretell which of these two would be elected President? The majority of the voters, it is true, would be Americans, but Mr. Roosevelt has many American foes . . . and many British admirers. Mr. Churchill has won the hearts of many Americans . . . and is half-American by blood. Are American nationalists to count Mr. Churchill's mother as less important than his father? It would be strange if American women took

* Some Geneva (N. Y.) Unionists suggest that Messrs. Roosevelt and Churchill be authorized to choose from anywhere on earth the third member of this Board.

this narrow view. They are responsible for ending the ancient practice whereby a wife automatically took the nationality of her husband.

Certainly many voters of The Union in every member democracy would be very embarrassed if they had to choose between Mr. Roosevelt and Mr. Churchill to head The Union. Whatever they decided was the best constitutional setup for the long run, they would want both Mr. Churchill and Mr. Roosevelt to lead them through this emergency. They would feel confident that this team, at least, could and would work together for them.

What a government, what a Congress, this Union of the Free could have! Here would be an assembly of leaders who could be compared to the Continental Congress with its Jefferson and Adams; to the Federal Convention with its Washington, Franklin, Madison, Hamilton, Mason; to the Parliament that knew Burke and Fox and Pitt. What an inspiring demonstration of democratic faith and practice this Congress could be and would be, once we decided to go the Union way, and cure the evils in democracy as they always have been cured—by more democracy.

Here would be a spectacle of seven democracies meeting the challenge of totalitarian autocracy by putting their trust in a Union Congress with 200,000,000 men and women as the free and equal dictators of its fate and theirs. That would be a proof of sincere, mature democracy that would shake the whole world from the first day it was given . . . even from the day that it was seriously contemplated. Nothing could long withstand 200,000,000 men and women capable of creating this Union of the Free.

THE ALTARS OF DABBLE AND DAWDLE

In freedom's age-old relay race with slavery, has mankind come this far only to have our generation stumble, fall and fail? Are you and I to lose the race because we kept our feet on the ground so much that we could not go ahead—or kept our eyes on the clouds so much we failed to see that we had reached the homestretch?

By acting at the time I write we can gain tremendous advantages. Our best hope of keeping Japan, despite its alliance with Germany and Italy, from making war on us is to take the initiative now—while we can unite the world's two greatest navies—and boldly form a Federal Union with Britain as the nucleus of an eventual United States of Man. If this will not give the Japanese government pause and its people hope, then nothing short of Union can.

This Union policy is likewise best calculated to check Hitler and Mussolini by its immediate moral effect on Russia, Turkey, the French Empire, all Europe, and particularly the Italian people. If the Union policy should fail in all these respects, then any lesser policy would not only fail even worse, but fail without the great saving advantage of Union now with Britain: it allows us to start sooner to prepare with all our power to meet the worst. Here is a policy that meets every acid test.

First, it gives the maximum guarantee of keeping dictatorship out and stopping its war machine, whether by peace or war.

Second, it gives the only reasonable promise of overthrowing dictatorship where it is already entrenched. It offers the only real hope of doing this without need of any great American expeditionary force whether in Europe, Africa, Asia or Latin America. For it is the only policy capable of destroying Hitler with his own master weapon, the one that raised him from the crowd, the weapon of words, ideas.

Third, Union now gives the only practical promise of ending dictatorship and war for good and all, ending the world statelessness and lawlessness that produced these evils, enduringly winning the peace while winning the war.

Here is a policy that meets every acid test, if only we adopt it in time. Events now are moving so fast that even before these words can reach your eyes some of the advantages we would gain by Union *now* may have been sacrificed already. How much more shall we sacrifice to Dabble and Dawdle, those gorging gods whose altars we have fed so long with blood?

We are threatened by two dangerous groups, both inside our country: Those who lack the sense to see the truth, and those who lack the courage to say the truth until it is trite. I find more of the latter. Time after time I have been told, privately by prominent leaders and publicly by ordinary citizens, "The world will have to come to Union, of course, but the mass

of people will have to suffer badly before they will accept it."
The people must suffer—which means in words of one sound:
They must be hurt, lose their jobs, lose their legs, arms, eyes,
lose the ones they need and love the most . . . . suffer. And so,
as if the suffering of millions must of itself turn to good and
not to bad, they sit back and wait, these common men who have
no faith in man, these leaders who to save from sorrow the
humble folk who trust them need but speak out what they
whisper.

A debate in which both sides are wrong still fathers American
foreign policy, as it has for twenty years. It can no more lead
to good than we can curb the smallpox by debating whether to
leave each one free to do as he pleases or to quarantine the
victims only for an hour a day. We Americans have been trying
to choose between guides who think their blindness vision, and
guides who seek to blindfold us. One side would have us build
no house at all because the cave was good enough for father.
The other would wheedle us into laying a brick here and there,
and now and then—either building aimlessly, or afraid to let
the owners see the plan.

No wonder there is such a sense of disillusioned frustration
in America. For twenty years we have been cursed with the
delusion that the only practical choice is between impractical
alternatives, between a policy of always nothing and one that
falls forever short—short of peace and short of war, short of
honesty and honor, short of courage, faith and hope, shortsighted, short-winded, short-lived, always short, never enough
of anything to get anything really done.

Shall We Repeat the Errors of 1917-1920?

And now? Shall we go on down to doom? Go on wobbling
between policy (a) that would risk losing all the British fleet
and naval bases to Germany and Japan rather than help Britain
seriously, and policy (b) that would give Britain enough war-
ships and planes to weaken us should Britain lose, but not the
aid Britain needs to win? Go on helping dictatorship sap away
the power of both of us? Go on aiding Britain in a way that
gives us no voice in the peace terms should Britain win, yet
forces us to keep aiding Britain increasingly the more the war

goes against her, and leaves us more and more dangerously exposed to swift attack if Britain should collapse? Go on governing our relations with the British in a way that centralizes all power in the hands of the President, gives 11,000,000 Canadians the same weight as 130,000,000 Americans, leaves them, like every member of the British Commonwealth, free to go to war in Europe when they please, but practically forces us to help them when the war goes against them?

If we continue in this weak and wobbling way we are certain to plunge into the war after piling up the odds against us, and then repeat all four of the major mistakes we made in the last war:

1. We shall then enter the war again as an ally or associate, and throw away our best opportunity to get the British to accept our Federal Union system as the basis for world government.

2. We shall then get neither from our allies nor from our own government any definite commitments at the start—when we can get them most easily—regarding how victory is to be converted into peace.

3. Once in the war we shall then be led again into continuing to neglect this basic problem of peace. Those who tell us that we must not imperil aid to Britain by insisting on Federal Union now, will argue then that it is too late for Union. They will say then that we have lost our powerful position as regards Britain and our own government, and must henceforth concentrate on winning the war. With wartime emotion to help them, they will argue that we must not imperil victory by insisting on setting up a Federal Union and knowing just what kind of peace we are fighting for. They will urge that we leave all that to be considered after the war is won.

4. And when the war is won at far greater cost than we needed to pay, then we the people will slump as we did in 1919. While the British indulge in another "Khaki election," in the United States the cry will again go up, "get the boys back home at once," and "return to normalcy," regardless of the peace settlement. *Having nothing to hold us to our allies except a common enemy, our hold on them will break when we break the enemy.* We shall then suddenly awake to find that we have only one voice among many at the peace conference, with no

more control over our allies than they have over us. And once more we shall botch the peace treaty at the conference, pour out on it, in the Senate and election, all the partisan feeling pent up in the war, render all our wartime sacrifices vain by losing the peace again. . . . And so to war again a few years later.

Shall the continuance of our present policy have no worse results than that? Already it has made our situation far worse than in 1917. Then France, Belgium, Italy and Japan were on our side. We have already let Germany overcome the first two, and line up the second two against us. Shall we go piddling on till Japan, finding Britain bled white, no longer fears the united power of America and Britain and jumps in the war for its share of the British Empire? Or shall we wait a little longer, till our waiting convinces Stalin that he had better jump in, too, and secure an Iranian-Indian window on the Indian Ocean? Shall we piddle away every chance of keeping both Russia and Japan on the sidelines, and wait till we face a coalition of all four autocracies in control of the whole continental mass of Europe and Asia? Half the world against the other half?

Already our calamitous policy has placed us in the most dangerous situation in our entire history. Already we are threatened for the first time in our history with the danger of attack from both East and West. Already we have let the war reach a stage where it affects the fate of all our species as none before ever did.

Previous wars were not fought on so gigantic a scale and in a way so ruthlessly destructive. They did not directly touch so much of the earth's surface, so many of its inhabitants. They could not directly and indirectly affect so quickly and incalculably all the earth and all mankind as this war does; the means of communication were never so good before, nor nations so interdependent.

The Crusades could not disturb the Incas. We often say that civilization hung in the balance at Marathon but we forget that the rise and fall of the Persian, Greek and Roman empires jarred civilization in China no more than the wars in China disturbed civilization in Egypt, Assyria and Babylon. But civilization everywhere on earth is already endangered in this war. Already the whole human species is threatened with a suicidal catastrophe such as it has never faced before.

VISION AND VIGOR MADE AMERICA AND BRITAIN

We Americans and British now have not only a responsibility, but an opportunity such as we have not had before. We know no more than other men how long we have to live, but we do have the privilege of living in one of those great periods when every man can make his life count for more than he could otherwise, when each of us can live and taste of life as men rarely can. For a fleeting moment we have an opportunity to make an epoch—to open a Golden Age for all mankind, to do in the nick of time, against terrifying odds, one of the great things that men have always longed and failed to do.

We have a further privilege. We can found this New Age on the free principles which made Britain and America. With the great British invention, representative government, men of vision and vigor solved the problem of how to make democracy work effectively for human freedom. They brought that invention here, and round the world, to many nations. With equal vision and vigor now, we and the British can unite these representative democracies through the great American invention, Federal Union, which solved the problem of how to make free peoples work together. The time has come to carry our constitutional system across the seas as it was carried across this continent. With these two great instruments, *Representative Government* and *Federal Union,* we can now build the Great Republic, the Commonwealth of Man.

In 1775 Virginia was much farther from the Bridge at Concord than we are from London Bridge. So, too, were other colonies. There were many men among them who said, "This is not our affair," or sided against "those damned Yankees." But the bulk of the people from Georgia through New England quickly saw that the cause of Massachusetts was their own. They gave an example of far-flung solidarity for freedom such as the world had not seen before. Yet each of the Thirteen Colonies was quite unprepared for war.

The men of the Thirteen Colonies had never worked together

before. They had never realized that they depended on each other for their freedom. They had jealously kept their governments independent of each other and dependent only on the British Crown. They kept up this folly until an invading army almost twice their strength lay off New York City.

Then they united in their great Declaration. And they gave sole power over war and peace to a common government—the Continental Congress. They lost Boston, New York, Philadelphia. But not one state surrendered. None could surrender separately. In the end they all won their freedom—and they then preserved it by uniting still more tightly, recognizing still more openly their dependence on each other.

What the men of the Thirteen States did then, we men of the seven democracies who speak their language now can and must do today. To save all that they then won for men, someone must raise somewhere soon their old standard of the Union of the Free. Let each of us 200,000,000 equals join in raising it now. If we do not raise it now, who will? Who can?

Who wants to live in Hitler's nightmare world where no people can depend upon another? Where no man can trust his neighbor? Already our easy American confidence in each other is being undermined, shot through with suspicion of fifth columnists, or fear that one may be oneself suspected.

To escape that nightmare world we need awaken to the old truth that free men do depend and must depend on each other for their freedom. Only by declaring our interdependence can we keep alive the faith in which freedom roots—the sublime faith of free men in each other.

How much freedom has been lost already because we and the British, French, Scandinavians and others sought too long to be free alone, and learned too late how deeply we depend upon each other?

Now we Americans know in our hearts that we do depend on the men and women of the British Commonwealth holding on and on. And they know that they depend on you and me. Why not say so, all together?

"You can depend on me."

"I do depend on you."

Nothing warms a man's heart more than to hear or say these

words. Why not fire 200,000,000 hearts with these words, today?

WE WHO EMBODY ALL MANKIND

We who speak the English language speak the language of the Rights of Man, not the language of one race alone. Our pride is that our speech and thought and blood came from no single fraction of mankind, but from many races. Our line, like our language, stemmed a thousand years ago from Celts, Romans, Vikings, Germans, French.

A pioneering line, it has gone on opening its frontiers more and more until it numbers now citizens of every religion, nationality and race, black, brown, red, white and yellow. It is unique; there is no other line or language that embodies, as ours does, *all* humankind. It won its rights for *every* man, and against tremendous odds. It never fights so well as when the goal is high and the fight seems hopeless. Since our line was born a thousand years ago it has never once been conquered, except by those who spoke its language of freedom.

We all together form this people of the Seven States that rule the Seven Seas. And none of us can be conquered now and the cause of freedom lost, except through our disunion.

Those who speak Hitler's tongue are now reunited. So are those who speak the tongues of Mussolini, Stalin, and Japan. We, the 200,000,000 who speak the language of the Rights of Man,—we remain with our power divided now when disunion means disaster, and when the cause of our disunion has been replaced with greater cause for union than we ever had.

The whole English-speaking world has long since adopted the basic principles of 1776. All the larger British democracies have gone still further and established for themselves Federal Unions modeled on the Constitution of the United States of America—whose framers had turned to the British Constitution to solve some of their hardest problems. Prime Minister Churchill's offer to form a Federal Union overnight with France has shown how ready the British are to accept such an offer from Washington.

Since men began speaking English they have ended in reunion all their civil wars but one. The civil war they began in 1775 is the one exception. It has not yet ended as did those between Parliament and King, between North and South. Milton and Hobbes have not become aliens. Grant and Lee remain fellow citizens. But children are still taught to regard as foreigners Franklin and Faraday, Burke and Hamilton, Shelley and Whitman.

We face today not George the Third but Adolf the First. To end war, we must first end this civil war by uniting our seven democracies in The Union of the Free. To achieve Federal Union of the World we must first of all achieve Federal Union of ourselves.

Before we can conquer anything in others, we must each first conquer the pettiness, narrowness, meanness, the prejudice, injustice, and shortsighted selfishness in ourselves. But the more we conquer ourselves, the more certain is the triumph of democracy everywhere.

What men have done, men can do. Lincoln has shown that, even in the throes of civil war, men can still strive on, "with malice toward none, with charity for all, with firmness in the right, as God gives us to see the right . . . . to do all which may achieve and cherish a just and lasting peace among ourselves and with all nations."

We, too, can attain that nobility of soul. With it, and with the Union principle he lived by and kept alive, we *can* achieve Lincoln's goal. Together, we can found the "Great Republic" he foresaw "for man's vast future." *We* can be the ones to bring to our confused, aspiring species what men have sought since at Babel they began the building of "a city and a tower whose top may reach unto heaven."

Chapter 2

Union vs. Alliance (Diagramed)

> Look here, upon this picture, and on this.—*Shakespeare,*
> Hamlet, *III:3.*

Diagrams* may help clarify the alternatives we face.

Figure 1 shows how nationalism—the current dogma of absolute, unlimited national sovereignty—organizes the world on a
government-to-government basis, inevitably centralizes power
in the national executive, and leaves the citizen out in the cold.
This system forces you, in your relations with your fellow men
in other nations, to take the weary, dangerous road through (a)
your government, (b) your chief executive, (c) the more or
less secret and tortuous channels of diplomacy, (d) the chief
executive of the other man's nation, and (e) his government
before you reach John Q. Citizen.

Under this system you have to get your government's consent in the form of a passport before you can even pay the
other man a neighborly visit. When you arrive you have to
submit to ignominious search, seizure and questioning by the
minions of his government—and then when you come back you
have to submit to all this again at the hands of your own government.

To write him a friendly letter you must pay double postage,
and often let a government censor pry into your private life.
You can hardly send him a decent Christmas present without
forcing him to make a Christmas present to his government in
the form of customs duty.

To do business with him you must change your money to
the kind his government ordains, often at the value it sets. To
buy and sell and trade with him, you must pay tribute to your

* The diagrams were done by our son, Pierre.

government and his—if they consent at all to your particular transaction—and then suffer vexation and delay at each frontier.

This government-to-government system is the old king-to-king system disguised as a sacred "sovereign-to-sovereign" national system. It produces the diplomatic understandings and the alliances that entangle you in war. You do not get away from it by organizing the nations as a league. The League of Nations experiment showed—and it is the best thing ever done by nationalism—that a league not only operates on a government-to-government basis but it keeps intact all the old paraphernalia of diplomacy, alliances, national armaments, tariffs, and so on.

So long as the world is on a predominantly government-to-government basis, the best of leagues is helpless to prevent this setup from continuing to divide and victimize the citizens of every nation with the pestilential products it inevitably exudes—propaganda, poisoned history, trade walls, lies, prejudice, ignorance and chauvinism.

Figure 1, to simplify this complicated mess, reduces the world to seven nations. Since there are nearly seventy nations in the world, one will get a truer picture of the nationalistic world we live in by multiplying this sketch by ten. To get the whole tangle, one should also make allowance for the relative power of the different nations—there are only seven great powers—and for the fact that they range in variety from autocracies where the executive is the whole government to democracies where the government has more or less control over the executive.

Figure 2 shows how Federal Union reverses this situation and centers the whole world in you, the citizen, no matter what your nation is—so long as you make your nation a member of The Union. By Federal Union you crack the whip all along the line, instead of having the whip cracked on you.

By this system you govern your relations with men in other nations on the man-to-man basis on which you govern them with your fellow citizens in other towns and counties. You make world government depend directly on you, to exactly the same degree that your town government does. You yourself choose the men to govern your world interests just as you

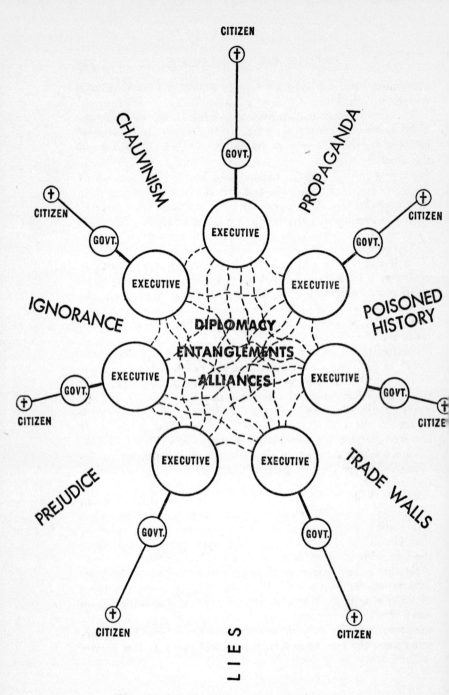

How Nationalism leaves you out on the Rim

choose the men to govern your town, county, state and national interests.

In The Union you give each of these sets of employees his special field to cultivate for you. You fire him if he tries to usurp the field you allotted to another or fails to do his job

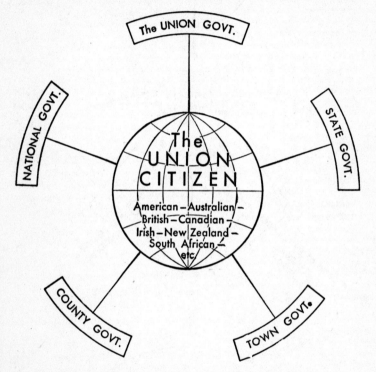

How The Union makes you the Hub of the World

well. You shift your employees from smaller field to larger field as they prove their merit. You take from one field and add to another from time to time as suits your interests. Federal Union, in a word, makes you the boss, from start to finish.

This is equally true whether you live and exercise your far-reaching power at the voting booth in County Cork or Lafayette County, in London or Chicago. It is just as true whether

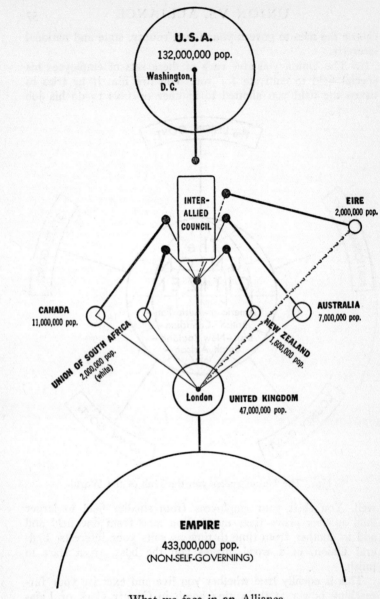

U.S.A.
132,000,000 pop.

Washington,
D.C.

INTER-
ALLIED
COUNCIL

EIRE
2,000,000 pop.

CANADA
11,000,000 pop.

UNION OF SOUTH AFRICA
2,000,000 pop.
(white)

AUSTRALIA
7,000,000 pop.

NEW ZEALAND
1,600,000 pop.

London **UNITED KINGDOM**
47,000,000 pop.

EMPIRE

433,000,000 pop.
(NON-SELF-GOVERNING)

What we face in an Alliance

you cast your ballot in Spanish in the state of New Mexico, in Afrikaner in the Transvaal, in French in the Province of Quebec, or in English in South Australia. And it remains true whether you call yourself American, British, Irish, French, German, or by any other national name—so long as your nation is in The Union.

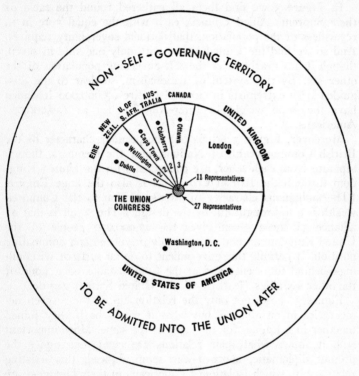

What we get in a Federal Union

By this Federal Union system you keep your national servants from becoming officious and self-important, and from interfering with your freedom instead of serving it. You brush them away from the things that most concern you, and handle these things yourself, directly, man to man with the other fellow. You do business with him or pay him a friendly visit without asking any of your officials any longer for permission. By Federal Union you sweep away this cluttering, meddling, excessive bureaucracy and make the whole world gradually your workshop and playground.

Figures 3 and 4 show the difference between an alliance and a Federal Union of the seven English-speaking democracies.

In Figure 3 we find them all gathered round the table of their Supreme Allied Council, each with the equal vote in it, regardless of the population, that national sovereignty requires. And so we find the United States with only one vote in seven, though it has nearly twice the self-governing population of the other six. By this system of nationalism, so dear to the misguided Irish extremists in our midst, Eire's 3,000,000 Irishmen have the same weight in Inter-Allied policy as 130,000,000 Americans.

Moreover, Figure 3 brings out the peculiar character of the British Commonwealth of Nations, how the members, though separate from each other, are connected with the United Kingdom through the British Crown, as is also the huge Empire. (The ambiguous character of Eire's relation to the Commonwealth is also brought out by the design.) The result is that an alliance of these seven gives the 47,000,000 people of the United Kingdom an undemocratically privileged and dominating position. It permits this government to do all sorts of wirepulling—behind the scenes and at the Council table—that none of the other six allies (least of all, the United States) can do.

Figure 3 shows not only the relationship of these seven democracies in an alliance, but what it would be if they joined together in a league, for the setup is the same. More important still, it shows what their relations are *right now* under the present diplomatic, short-of-war setup. Indeed, this existing relationship, which isolationist Americans in their blindness are so determined to maintain, increases rather than decreases the favored position that the British government enjoys in an alliance or league.

Figure 4 shows how different the relationship among these same seven democracies will be once they form The Union. Here we find each member democracy as independent as before in its home affairs. Each still rules itself from its own national capital. But these capitals no longer have anything to do with governing the common relations of the people of the seven, or with governing their nonself-governing territories. All these are governed, instead, by the central Union government.

In it each of the 200,000,000 citizens of the Union has a direct and equal voice, the representation of each democracy being roughly proportioned to its population.

In a two-house Union Congress the American people would elect a majority of the members of the House, while the people of the British Commonwealth would elect a majority of the Senate. For simplification, Figure 4 is based, however, on the suggested one-house Congress in which each democracy would have one representative, *plus* one more for each 5,000,000 self-governing population or major fraction thereof. This formula insures that the smallest member will have at least two votes in the Congress. It thus helps to strengthen and safeguard the position of the less populous member in a single chamber, just as the Senate does in a two-chamber Congress.

Finally, consider how solid is the setup in Figure 4, how fragile the one in Figure 3. In the alliance there is no strong connection at the center, and the pull is *away* from the meeting place. And so, as in the Franco-British Alliance, the outward pull helps break Allies apart in time of greatest stress. Only by Federal Union can one reverse this and get the strong structure of the circle that centers on its axis and whose parts are pushed together, not pulled apart, by outside pressure anywhere.

Chapter 3

"First in Peace, First in War"

> This Constitution will be much read and attended to in Europe.
> —*Benjamin Franklin in the U. S. Constitutional Convention.*
> The plain truth is that peace and order always depend . . .
> upon there being overwhelming power behind just law. The only
> place where that power can be found behind the laws of a liberal
> and democratic world is in the United States and in Great
> Britain, supported by the Dominions, and in some other free
> nations.—*Lord Lothian's Last Address.*

Aid to Britain short of war is neither a peace policy nor a war policy. It is both together—a peace-and-war policy—as are also the Draft, the "two-ocean navy," "no foreign war-ism," "America first-ism" and Union now with Britain. This last is not a "warmongering" policy any more than the others are; it stands much higher than the others as a peace-planning policy.

Union now with Britain is far more effective than alternative policies—both as a peace measure and if war comes.

UNION AS A PEACE POLICY

Union now with Britain is infinitely more effective as a peace policy than are all these other policies put together. They cannot possibly bring us peace—unless we consider peace to be nothing better than our present state. They can prolong this condition of trembling truce, but the nearest they can come to "peace" is to give us an indefinite period of feverish arming. The backers of these other policies ask the greatest sacrifices ever asked of Americans. They have fastened on us, for example, that Prussian innovation—compulsory military service by our young men in "peacetime" as well as wartime, and their policy would keep it fastened on us interminably. But, unlike the Prussians, they want no man to risk his life until the lives of his women and children are endangered, too. They cannot bear to think of an American air force jumping off from Britain to bomb the Bremen shipyards or the Berlin humbug hive. This they call a "foreign war." They offer us instead the bombing of American homes when, some starry night, their "peacetime" crashes suddenly into war.

Even should these policies result in Britain defeating autocracy as effectively as we all together did in 1918, they still leave us exposed to another Versailles, another League, another period of ungoverned recrimination, rivalry and racketeering among sovereign nations who admit no law except their own. They reward us not with peace but with another depression, another arms race, a more hideous Hitler, a worse cataclysm.

Suppose the war should result by a miracle in some United States of Europe being formed—in this favorite dream of those who think there can be peace without full American participation. There would still remain the problem of its relations with us, and with Russia and Japan. World War I reduced the number of great Powers from eight to seven. For World War II merely to reduce them from seven to four or five, by consolidating this time instead of cutting up, cannot possibly bring peace. It can bring only World War III.

The Flaw in "Pax Britannica"

It is true that after Napoleon's defeat there was not another world war for a hundred years. But that was because his defeat left Britain ruling most of the earth and all the seas, and dominating the business and financial world—dwarfing all the other powers. World War I came on when this *Pax Britannica* resulted in a more equal distribution of world power among a bevy of strong sovereign nations, each struggling for more power so as to remain a law unto itself. World War I redistributed world power, but continued this roughly equal distribution of it among several great sovereign rivals who remained each a law unto itself, and so quickly resulted in World War II. And World War II is bound to result soon in World War III if it continues this basic cause for world war—as it must, if it fails to result in the creation of The Union of the Free as the *sole* Great Power on earth, towering above all others from the start and growing gradually and peacefully into a universal world government.

The flaw in *Pax Britannica* that ended it was this: British preponderance of power, on which this peace depended, could be maintained only by the conquest of outsiders or by their peaceful submission to the British Crown. The British Empire failed to develop any practical principle of growth through mutual equalitarian inter-state agreement, as did three nations —Italy, Germany and the United States—that did not figure in the Congress of Vienna, but rose to great power rank in the "British century."

Powerful free principles had given the British their hegemony, and had made the nineteenth century the greatest century human freedom yet has known. But when growing freedom fails to make for a wider union, it inevitably makes for greater anarchy. Lacking the principle of free and equal union (except as regards Scotland and England), British freedom turned against itself. It became a disintegrating force, both in the world as a whole and inside the British Empire. It was helping build up power in the outside world while it was holding the Empire together only by dividing its freest, strongest parts with tariffs, currencies and other paraphernalia of misguided sovereignty. Meanwhile, all the rising outside powers—France, Germany, Italy, Austria, Russia, Japan and the United States— were each engaged in removing these sovereign attributes from a wider and wider area, either by force or by free agreement.

If mankind could be saved for a century from world war by British preponderance of armed and economic power, its peace can be saved more easily and completely, and for a much longer period, by the greater preponderance The Union of the Free would have. For Federal Union preserves this *Pax* from the flaw in *Pax Britannica*, and endows it with the principle of natural, vigorous, peaceful growth that the latter lacked. It allows The Union to add to its preponderance without any outside people suffering the humiliation of conquest or of cowardly submission.

Pax Americana OR *Pax Dei*?

Federal Union gives immediately to every man in the latest state admitted to The Union a voice in its policy equal to that

of any man in The Union's founder states, and an equal chance
to attain the highest Union office. It requires The Union, moreover, to admit to equal statehood in it, as rapidly as it wisely
can, more and more of the peoples in its own nonself-governing
territory and in the outside world.

This increases The Union's preponderance at the double-quick.
Each nation admitted to it reduces the danger of attack and
strengthens defense. The Union speeds this process most at the
start, in our time, when we need it most. It must aim to admit
first the nations that are most advanced in civilization. These
are its most dangerous enemies while they remain outside it,
but their strength counts for it once they are in it. The day
Germany is admitted to The Union, the problem of world disarmament is practically solved. And Federal Union continues
this healthy process of growth to its present natural limits—all
mankind.

(I speak of The Union's *present* natural limits, for who can
imagine what its limits may be when mankind has achieved
World Federal Union? We must always keep in mind that the
tremendous expansion in the natural limits of mankind, achieved
in the first century and a half of the democratic era, are likely
to seem small indeed after even fifty years of The Union of the
Free.)

The peace of The Union would be a peace, not of power alone,
but of power harnessed to liberty, equality, fraternity, justice,
moderation and kindliness—power harnessed to them so effectively that these abstract words would become active principles.
They would bring the world then the enduring, creative, pro-
ductive, abundant, living peace that only Federal Union has
ever brought to the sovereign states of man.

Federal Union having been invented by Americans, *Pax
Americana* might become the name of this peace that passeth
understanding now. It might well be called *Pax Americana*,
since it can come only if we Americans take the lead in making
it, only if we risk our all to offer mankind this Union of the
Free. We ourselves remember long and lovingly those who acted
in the past with great gallantry, generosity, and wisdom, who
saw far, spoke truly, did nobly, and won when all seemed lost.
We need not fear that men will ever forget America if now

this dream, deep in the heart of every normal man, comes true through us. America cannot perish in that attempt.

But when we have so great a thing behind us, we shall be too humble, and too thankful for the privilege we had, too aware of how we must have failed had we been alone, too grateful to others and to Providence, to want this peace called *Pax Americana.* And when The Union has become universal, men may call its peace, *Pax Dei,* remembering that it is "the peace of God which passeth all understanding," as St. Paul said. For that to come about we must remember now the Apostle's next injunction:

Finally, brethren, whatsoever things are true, whatsoever things are honest, whatsoever things are just, whatsoever things are pure, whatsoever things are lovely, whatsoever things are of good report; if there be any virtue, and if there be any praise, think on these things.

Those things, which ye have both learned, and received, and heard, and seen in me, do: and the God of peace shall be with you.

To Begin Peace Negotiations

But we are now far, far from that peace. We are in the midst of a war unleashed by those whose answer to these sentiments is to cry "Jewish propaganda" and invade their weakest neighbors without warning. There is no use trying to persuade in English men who know no English; one must speak to them in terms they understand. One must translate the language of freedom into terms of force for those who talk only in the latter language, if one is to make them understand, and keep them from imposing their language on one permanently. All except the small minority of extreme pacifists admit this.

The real question facing us is how to end this war, with the least actual resort to force ourselves, in a peace that will give us the minimum security we need and have at least a gambling possibility of enduring and growing.

Even Senator Wheeler has conceded that, for peace to have a chance, Germany must completely evacuate France, Belgium, Holland, Denmark and Norway.* To leave Hitler in control of

---

* In urging peace negotiations in his broadcast, December 30, 1940, Senator Wheeler said: "A working basis for a just peace might involve

this area would be not only unjust and immoral but equivalent to replacing with a "phony peace" the period of the "phony war," and loading it heavily in favor of Hitler. He could then assemble without danger of bombardment all the equipment he needs for invading Britain, and attack with the force of surprise that bowled over Denmark, Norway, Holland, Belgium and France. If this "phony peace" caused the British to relax, their complete and quick destruction would be certain.

To get the other side to accept the principle of no annexation or occupation of western European territory, which is a *sine qua non* of peace, the British position must be far stronger than it now is. To ask Germany, as Senator Wheeler would, to relinquish her conquests and accept arms limitation in return for such chicken feed as her previous colonies and internationalization of the Suez Canal is to show a naïveté that does not characterize the Senator in domestic political negotiation.

The British position must first be vastly improved. We shall have to wait a long time for this to be achieved by positive military defeat of the Germans. The longer it takes the harder it will probably be to make a real peace. A much more reasonable preliminary for peace negotiations is to improve the British position tremendously without a tremendous military victory. The United States alone can do this by throwing its weight into the balance.

We cannot do this by the present method of slipping another pound of support on the British side whenever Germany knocks two pounds off it or adds weight on her side of the balance. This "short of war" method has not been succeeding. It should be clear now that it cannot bring us enduring peace.

We can strengthen the British position much more by noti-

---

among other factors the following: 1. Restoration of Germany's 1914 boundaries with an autonomous Poland and Czecho-Slovakia; 2. Restoration of independent France, Holland, Norway, Belgium and Denmark; 3. Restoration of Alsace-Lorraine to France; 4. Restoration of German colonies; 5. Protection of all racial and religious minorities in all countries; 6. Internationalization of the Suez Canal; 7. No indemnities or reparations; 8. Arms limitation."

With characteristic isolationism, the Senator calls for "protection of all racial and religious minorities in all countries" and "arms limitation," but says no word about how these are to be attained and maintained without establishing an effective world government. This prerequisite of peace he omits entirely.

fying Germany and Italy that, if they refuse peace on terms we consider just, we shall enter the war as Britain's ally. But this would not be enough to secure that peace, or even negotiations for it. We threaten Hitler, after all, with nothing more than an alliance, and he has already smashed in France the strongest alliance that could possibly be made. We would be a stronger ally than the French in some important respects, but not in trained soldiers and officers equipped, ready for action, and on the spot.

The master of the blitzkrieg may well rate our potential power lower than we do and reject our peace offer. We shall then have to prove that his rating of us was wrong by going to war. But by fighting on the cumbersome alliance basis we give him the advantage. And when, after great loss of American lives, we prove him wrong, our alliance gives us no better guarantee of peace than we had at Versailles. It does give us a voice in the settlement, but practically bars us from organizing the sure peace of Federal Union. For had we really believed in Federal Union we surely would have united in one with the British instead of allying with them. Once we have ourselves opted for the old European alliance method, we can hardly offer the Germans and Italians anything better, by way of enduring peace, than the system of collective alliances and League of Nations that has already left so sour a taste in their mouths.

Were you a German or Italian, would you consider another League peace offer to be another Anglo-Saxon trick to keep the British and American nations top dog, and Germany and Italy underdog? Or would you be so enraptured by it that you would risk your life to overthrow your dictator if he refused it? If it would not rouse you to revolt, you cannot expect it to rouse them.

There remains the Union policy. It makes the position for peace not a British position, but something new, a Union position, backed by Americans, British and others acting as one people, and tremendously improves it. We confront Hitler with all the power of an Anglo-American alliance, but we unite it much more tightly. A Union adds enormously to the material power of an alliance by centralizing and co-ordinating the control, and removing waste effort, duplication, friction, cross-purposes, and diffusion. By removing, moreover, the sovereign right of Britain or America to make a separate peace, our Union takes from Hitler the hope of breaking our combined power in two, as he did with Britain and France.

Were you a German or Italian, would you fight the harder if you could gamble on winning the war once you conquered the British Isles, or if you knew that even if you conquered them you would still have to fight a Union that controlled one-third of the world?

On the moral side, too, Hitler and Mussolini would have far greater cause to fear this Union than an alliance. For The Union would be offering their people, not a few crumbs from the imperial table, as Senator Wheeler does, but the same seat at the table that Britain and America have. And it would be offering them admission to an infinitely richer market than the colonies—to the great free-trade market formed by Britain, America and the other self-governing members of The Union.

It would be offering them genuine relief from armaments—not another Geneva conference on armament limitation—and real security from war. It would be offering them a new world where they would stand on a level with the highest in dignity, power, opportunity and freedom. In return The Union would ask no more of them than it had already received from Britain and America—the transfer of some of their sovereignty to it, and the effective guarantee of the common rights of man.

If they preferred nationalism and dictatorship to Union and democracy, this Union policy would not attempt to force the latter on them. It would face them with no humiliating "do-as-we-say-or-else" proposition.

The Union government in announcing its formation, would simply say to Germany and Italy, in effect:

"We represent a new Federal Union, called The Union of the Free. Enjoying the usual Federal powers, it has sole charge of the foreign relations and defense of all its members. These include Britain and the United States. When The Union was formed, you were at war with Britain, but you were at peace with the United States. It is for you to decide whether you will extend to all The Union your peaceful relations with the United States, or extend to all The Union your war with Britain.

"The Union, for its part, offers you peace. It recognizes that all the nations are responsible for the present calamitous conflict. It is ready to open negotiations for the establishment of normal relations with you on the principle of no annexation or occupations of foreign territory, no reparations and no indemnities, and settlement by arbitration of the original causes for the war, as well as any subsequent differences that cannot be settled by direct negotiation.

"The Union is so peacefully inclined and friendly in spirit that it is ready to admit you—should you so desire—to full and equal membership in it at no greater price, in effective democratic guarantees and renunciation of sovereignty, than its founder members have already paid. It is, indeed, the hope and desire of the founders of The Union that it should thus peacefully grow into a universal Commonwealth of Man. They seek nothing more than to save our common species from the present calamity and secure all mankind enduringly from the curse of war.

"If, however, you reject peaceful relations with The Union, refuse to prove your peaceful intentions toward us by evacuating the foreign territory you have seized by war, and attack any of the territory of The Union, if, in short, you insist on war against any of us, we must warn you that you will be at war then with all The Union united as one man, and determined to defend its whole people. You are bound to win if you now take the road of peace with The Union—and the sooner you take it, the more you will win. You are bound to lose if you take the road of war—and the more you make The Union cost us, the more it is bound to cost you, too, in the end. You have our offer. We await your answer."

UNION AND THE JAPANESE ALLIANCE

This Union peace policy has another considerable advantage. It gives the best hope of breaking up or pulling the teeth of the Triangular Alliance. It leaves Germany, Italy and Japan as the ones exposed to the fatal defect in any alliance—the power each ally keeps to save himself at the expense of his allies by making a separate peace. The autocrats cannot avoid this danger by making a Federal Union, too, for a Federal Union is possible

only among men who practice democracy, the thing the autocrats oppose most bitterly. Nor can Hitler accept Mussolini
as his *fuehrer*, or Mussolini—even if he should so desire—get
the Italians to accept Hitler as their *duce*.

Even without a premium being given the one that first makes
peace with The Union, both Hitler and Mussolini are bound to
suspect the other will either accept the Union offer, or be
forced to do so by his people. Each, in deciding on his own
policy, must face the danger of being suddenly left out on the
limb alone if he decides for war. Moreover, since The Union
did not exist when the Axis was made, each can reasonably
and honorably argue their alliance does not bind them to make
war on it.

Then there is the Japanese angle of this Triangle. Since
Japan depends on sea power, it would have even more urgent
reason than Germany to fear the war power of The Union. It
would also have cause to hope for a fairer deal from The Union
than from the continuation of the prewar system of power
politics. Japan is aware of the existing mistrust between the
German and Italian rulers and peoples. It would have especial
reason to fear being the one left out on the limb if it went to
war against The Union.

But the United States by entering the war as an ally of
Britain helps Germany and Italy to represent it as an attack on
them, with Japan therefore honor-bound to come in on their
side. It also tends to divert much of the American war effort
toward Japan. The Americans who now argue that we should
not send so many weapons to Britain but keep more for our
own defense, would then insist on concentrating on Japan as
our part of the war, and leaving the British to shift for themselves. No doubt the Nazi agents here would make the most of
this "me first-ism" to wrap the American flag around them
here—and the British flag around them in Britain. For the
more they diverted us toward Japan, the more they could hope
to conquer neighboring Britain before we could conquer distant
Japan. And if they did, they would have won the war for
Japan, too, since our fleet would then have to leave the Pacific
for the Atlantic. If we practice "me first-ism" till Britain falls,
we cannot expect to inherit the British navy.

Contrast this with the Union policy. Tokyo has already made clear that it considered itself bound to act under the alliance only if the United States attacked—and if Germany and Italy rejected The Union's offer, they would be the attacking party. Should the United States adopt the Union policy, we could hope that both interest and honor would persuade Japan that its alliance did not apply to so new an element as The Union, whose peace offer could not be construed as an attack on Germany and Italy. For Tokyo to split away would make Berlin and Rome fear all the more a split between themselves. It would make them fear defeat even if they both decided to fight, for it would allow all the armed power of the United States to be concentrated at once on them. So helpful and friendly a Japanese policy toward The Union would certainly encourage a similar attitude toward Japan, it would serve to improve transpacific relations incalculably, and in the way that must be done before real peace can be made there on any basis.

Could Hitler Accept the Union's Peace?

It would be for the dictators, of course, to puzzle out which would be the least dangerous to their personal rule—to accept the Union peace offer or to attack The Union. True, neither would be safe for them. But can we go substantially farther than this offer goes to make the world safe for autocracy?

Acceptance of the Union offer would not in itself involve the end of dictatorship in Germany or Italy nor loss in their armed power. Consequently, Hitler and Mussolini have nothing to fear from it, unless they fear that the attraction of membership in The Union would be so strong as to lead their people, once peace was restored, to overthrow them, in order to enter it.

The Union offer, furthermore, gives Hitler the safest basis he can hope to get for withdrawing from Norway, Denmark, Holland, Belgium and France. So long as Britain or the United States remains unconquered, his occupation of these countries remains a source of danger to him. Once The Union is formed, this danger becomes very serious. The occupation then drains his power and affects morale in many ways.

Hitler quite possibly may think that he can survive the Union peace better than The Union can. He may calculate that The Union is like concrete—to solidify it must first be held together from the outside. He can reason that The Union came into existence only through the outside pressure he supplied, and that if he removes this pressure by accepting the peace offer before the Union concrete has had time to harden, the span bridging the chasm between London and Washington will slop to the ground. As a master of the art of propaganda, he can hope to separate the Americans and British under peace conditions by preying on their prejudices against each other, on their mutual jealousies, on the passionate eloquence and emotion of the Irish, and so on.

In the atmosphere of embittered disillusionment that would follow any such collapse of The Union, it would be child's play for Hitler to repair the great mistake he has already made in this war, when he dealt his knockout blow to France instead of Britain. Once The Union had broken apart he could count on suddenly knocking out Britain by surprise before France had had time to recover, or the United States had finished its two-ocean navy. And thus he would secure the keys to world control.

If Hitler is as shrewd as he often seems to be, and as confident in the superiority of his system over democracy as he professes to be, he will think along these lines and accept the Union peace offer. This proposal, which allows him to remain in office with his military power intact and merely requires him to evacuate conquered countries, is not without real danger to the Union's continued existence. But if the American and British peoples gain the evacuation of the European democracies without war, simply by forming The Union, and then destroy The Union themselves—well, then no policy can save them and they deserve all the punishment they get.

For my part, I have enough confidence in the internal strength of democracy to be willing to run the risks of peace by offering to end the war on these terms before The Union has had time to solidify from outside pressure. But what if Hitler and Mussolini should agree—as is only too possible—that The Union can stand this peace better than they can? What if they should therefore try to destroy The Union by War? What then?

IF WAR COMES

If we cannot secure peace without war by this Union policy, we cannot hope to keep out of the war by any policy short of it. We may, of course, defer the war. We may avoid fighting it in Europe. We may fight instead in the chill of Iceland, Greenland and Alaska, where a wound means death; or in tropical Latin America where disease will be as dangerous as battle. Or we may fight on our own soil where our families and homes will suffer, too. But if we cannot escape the war by the Union policy, we cannot escape it at all.

The truth is that, whatever policy we Americans now follow, the odds are against its keeping us out of this war. Consequently, the best peace policy is the one that, should it fail to do this, still leaves us in the best position to win the war. To face this situation is not war mongering; to refuse to face it is defeat-mongering.

The aid-to-Britain-short-of-war policy is doomed to bring us in the war in the worst conditions. It is cursed by the fact that it is known over here and over there that this aid stops "short of war." That handicaps it, first of all, in the thing on which it most depends to win without fighting—in the production of weapons for the British. A democracy that gears production to a short-of-war spirit cannot rival Germany, where production is on a total war basis, and the government is staking its existence on victory.

There is no better way to encourage the Germans and Italians to continue fighting than to tell them that, whatever happens, the "Yanks are not coming." The more seriously we threaten "short-of-war" to make America a real arsenal for Britain, the more we spur Hitler to smash the British before we can make good our threat.

As for the British, the more we speed production and lease or give them weapons "short-of-war," the more we convince them that they are fighting our war for us. We make them ask themselves more and more—even though they do not ask us openly—"If we are defending a common cause, why should we be the only ones to risk our lives while the Americans risk only property?" The more we help the British "short-of-war," the more we help the Nazis attack their morale as they did that of the French—"Britain will fight till the last Frenchman." The Nazis, who exploited so effectively the relative smallness of the British Expeditionary Force, are bound to put our policy in the worst possible light* They will broadcast to the British that "short-of-war" means "America will fight till the last . . . Englishwoman—and then take over Canada and all the Empire it can safely take." And Goebbels will be delighted to have prominent Americans chorus, "The Yanks are not coming."

Putting the accent on "short-of-war" means entering the war when the British Commonwealth is much weaker than now, when we have lost most, perhaps all, of the weapons we have sent to Britain, when Germany has possibly captured many of them, and when the British fleet will be a question of much greater concern to us than it is already. Failure of the "short-of-war" policy means that we shall have to send out great expeditionary forces, either to the British Isles, to bolster the line there, or to Africa, the Azores, Latin America, Asia. We pay

---

* In *The Chicago Daily News*, Jan. 10, 1941, Wallace R. Deuel, its Berlin correspondent, reported on his return home:

". . . possibly the most shocking and stupefying of all the things that are happening is this—that filthy pictures have been used as weapons for the conduct of hostilities.

"It is the Germans who used them. They used them as part of the most gigantic, the most systematic and the most skillful attempt the world has ever seen to shatter the nervous systems and wills to resist of whole armies and whole peoples. . . .

"Postcard size, the pictures were beautifully drawn and printed in four colors. At first sight, they looked innocent enough. All they seemed to show was a picture of a wounded Poilu lying amid the ruins of a town, sketched in the lower left-hand corner. The rest of the picture was blank, except that across the top there was printed the question, 'Where are the Tommies?'

"But when you held the picture up so that light came through from the back, a scene appeared in the blank space, the picture of a triumphant, well-fed Tommy courting a French woman—with a photograph of the Poilu hanging on the wall behind the couple. . . .

"The Nazis printed hundreds of thousands of these cards, they produced a special type of trench mortar, and they shot the cards over the French lines for the Poilus to find.

"The French authorities made it a court-martial offense for the Poilus to keep the cards. . . . But the Nazis found cards, nevertheless, on tens of thousands of the prisoners they took in May and June." (Reprinted by courtesy of *The Chicago Daily News*.)

dearly in years of war for the months of "peace" that "short-
of-war" gives us now.

The Successful Wilsonian War Strategy

Suppose the Union policy also should fail to keep us out of
this war. If Germany and Italy refuse the Union's peace terms
and attack its British member, then the Union policy allows
us to use at once the wartime strategy that President Wilson
used so effectively. We need to distinguish thoughtfully between the Wilsonian war strategy and the Wilsonian peace
strategy. The former was sound and amazingly successful. The
proof is that it quickly and completely achieved its purpose—
the winning of the war. It was the Wilsonian peace strategy
that was faulty. The proof is that it failed to win the peace.
To avoid losing this time both the war and the peace we need
to follow the policy that succeeded, and correct the one that
failed.

What was the basic American war strategy in 1917-18? It
was to move simultaneously with all the power then possible
along two parallel and mutually supporting lines, the one military and the other moral (it could be called political or psychological). The cry, "We are too unprepared, there is nothing
we can do now," did not deter us then. We declared war when
we were far more unprepared on the military side than we are
now. Two facts will tell the whole incredible story:

"When war was declared in April, 1917," Col. Leonard P.
Ayres says in the official United States "statistical summary,"
The War With Germany, "the United States had two aviation
fields and 55 serviceable planes . . . 51 of these airplanes were
obsolete and the four obsolescent." The army then had "only
four machine guns per regiment," although the Secretary for
War, in successfully urging Congress in December, 1916, to
order 4,000 more, pointed out, "Perhaps no invention has more
profoundly modified the art of war than the machine gun. In
the European War this arm has been brought into very great
prominence."

We decided then that, since we still had the ocean between
us and the enemy, the safest and quickest way to arm was to
throw all our potential power into the balance at once and put

production immediately on a war basis. Within a year after
production began we had 4,939 airplanes. When war began we
were producing 4,000 machine guns a month; within five
months we were making 35,000 a month; by the end of 1917
we had 227,000.*

When we went to war in 1917 the outlook for the democratic side was dark, too—that was the real reason why we
went to war then. The revolution had then weakened the Allies
on the Russian side. There had been mutinies in the French
army that winter. Then came the submarine campaign, threatening to bring down Britain. The underlying situation was so
bad that, six months after we had thrown our weight into the
balance, there was Caporetto—and a year after American
troops began arriving in France the Germans were able to reach
Château-Thierry. It was only then, in July, 1918, that our
troops became a real military factor. What must have been the
collapse had we waited as long that time as we have waited
now? Had we not told our hard-pressed European friends when
we did, that they could count on us to the limit?

The fact that we were determined to stop short of nothing
began working powerfully for us the very moment we an-
nounced that determination. It kept on working incessantly for
us, night and day, every hour thereafter. It was putting new
life into the Allies, preventing further panic and mutiny among
them, while insidiously discouraging and demoralizing the other
side—quadrupling the strength of our friends, quartering the
strength of our foes.

From the start we backed this with a still more powerful
moral factor. We raised the whole plane of the war; we made
it turn on the basic constructive issue of organizing a better
world for everyone. We captured at once the imagination of
most of mankind by fighting, not for ourselves alone, but for
all mankind. We gave ourselves and friends something more
worth dying for—and so we began to capture gradually the
imagination of the Germans and Austrians, too. We began to

* These figures are from Col. Ayres's book (published by the U. S.
Government Printing Office), to which the reader is referred for a mine
of information on what the United States can do when it acts short of
nothing—and how long it takes us to prepare in certain essentials even
on this basis.

give them something worth dying for in revolt against their masters.

Result: The wavering democratic line held firm during the year we needed to prepare on the military side; the morale on the other side declined. And when we finally did need to go into serious military action, we required less than five months of heavy fighting to end the war in overwhelming victory.

We won the war by this parallel use of our military and our moral power, and by getting all the value we could from both as soon as possible. Had we waited with our moral power till our military power was ready, we would have lost. Had we sought to win by military power alone, without the promise of a better world, victory would have cost many more American lives. Had we sought to make peace without being willing to fight for the peace we wanted, and strong enough to halt the German war machine at Château-Thierry and throw it back, we would have lost. It was the close combination of our moral and the military factors that won the war, and it was our decision then to abandon this combination—drop the moral, political factor and depend entirely on the army, navy and ocean for our future security—that cost us the peace.

No Great Expeditionary Force Needed

Now, how can this strategy be applied to the present war? First, on the military side. The sooner we proclaim we will back the Union policy with all the men that we may need wherever they are needed most, the less we shall need to send an expeditionary force overseas. How many we may need to send depends almost entirely on how soon we adopt the Union policy and how well we use the moral force it gives us. These latter are so powerful that it is quite possible that we shall not need to send a single soldier overseas to war, even though we may be technically at war for a while.

The first critical period will be when the Union announces its existence and its peace terms. We can count on that announcement rocking the world, but we can hardly expect immediate acceptance of its terms; we must foresee a short period in which the issue hangs in the balance. It may be said that we shall be at war during this period. But if we think of war in

terms of men instead of words our position, for all practical purposes, will be about the same as it was before, except
that we shall have begun to intensify production. Even if Hitler
answers with war, the Union offer may cause a break in Italy
or elsewhere on the Continent. The Union may thus end the
war in the rather long period that must elapse before we shall
be able physically to bring our material power to bear in
Europe. But though The Union gives us the brightest hope
of this, we had better not count on such good fortune.

Yet, even if the war continues, we should not need to send a
great expeditionary force to Europe. Because such a force was
needed in 1918, it does not follow that we need it to win this
war. From the military standpoint, this war is quite different
from the previous one. The better we keep this in mind the
safer we shall be from the mistakes the French general staff
made. There is no western front in this war now, and no need to
send a great expedition from America to help defend the British Isles. To do so would be to send infantry instead of arms
to a fort that is already strongly garrisoned but short of arms
—it would be folly indeed. The circumstances of the war are
such as to restrict the American contribution mainly to the air
and naval sides, and, of course, to war supplies.

As regards the last point, Major D. S. Babcock, 19th Field
Artillery, U. S. Army, sends me this stimulating proposal,
which shows some of the myriad possibilities that open to us,
once we form the provisional Union:

> "Many people are against aid to England for finan-
> cial reasons. Already it is evident that England alone
> cannot finance her complete rearmament and must get
> credit from us. The tremendous rearmament required
> for total defense may well dislocate our economic sys-
> tem. Many appeasers fear an all out effort because it
> will wreck capitalism. With England doing the fighting
> and the U. S. doing the financing many peoples (Dutch,
> Belgians, etc.) are making a negligible contribution
> toward their own salvation. All this could be rectified,
> in my mind, by the following procedure: . . .
> "Let the setting up and *financing* of a *common de-*

fense be the first business of The Union of the Free. We can then advance credits to The Union rather than Britain. We can then produce planes and guns for The Union, rather than Britain. We can equip and man fighter squadrons for The Union rather than for Britain or for ourselves. . . . We can confiscate enemy shipping in our harbors in the name of The Union. It will be the Union armed forces which will finally defeat Hitler.

"All nations can raise and equip troops for The Union without committing themselves as nations. And the tremendous effort involved can be financed equitably instead of being borne by a few. Moreover, with Hitler vanquished, the title to much of the vast flood of armaments which will result will rest with a Federal Union and not with any one country. It will take a deal of working out but I am convinced that there is an answer to many of the obstacles now blocking an all out effort here."

It is difficult to discuss Union war strategy before knowing the conditions existing at the time of its formation. But, as things now appear, the wisest policy for The Union would be to use its land forces very sparingly and seek to win mainly with its sea, air and moral forces. This would mean keeping the army on the defensive in the British Isles, while training— as we are already doing—a great army in America, so as to be prepared for the worst. It would mean using the navy to apply a much tighter blockade than was possible in 1917-18, when goods could leak through the European neutrals. This should allow the navy to divert more power to anti-submarine work. Another naval task would be to clear the Mediterranean, where Italy is already naturally exposed to sea power.

The air superiority which American factories and flyers should soon give The Union would allow something new in warfare—the blockade of the chief land communication lines of a continental power. Even before The Union was strong enough to take the offensive against the German air force, it could begin doing much more than the British now can do to destroy German production centers and harass their communication lines everywhere. The Union would have a much smaller area than the Nazis to defend against attack. The vast area they occupy would force them to disperse their forces as The Union air power grew, or leave them open to attack. This advantage would be a very considerable one, once The Union was strong enough to drive the Nazis from the air. And once The Union controlled the air, the "air blockade" would seriously endanger Germany.

In such conditions the great Nazi army might well become a millstone around Hitler's neck. It would have no front on which to fight and should become more and more exposed to the moral forces of The Union. As for Italy, it surely could not stand out long after The Union controlled completely the air as well as the Mediterranean. The Union's offensive weapon, in short, would seem to be the air force, not the army.

It would seem wise, however, to send some American troops to the British and Irish Isles, for the powerful moral effect this would have. Volunteers could easily supply all that would be needed. These volunteers might well be specialized troops, for these would seem more likely to be needed in Britain than infantry. Among the very first troops that the Allies asked America to send over in 1917 were eight regiments of railway engineers. These were all quickly filled with volunteers—even though the volunteer had to produce two letters of recommendation to prove his engineering experience before he could enlist.

I speak from experience, having joined the regiment that was recruited on the Pacific Coast—the 18th Engineers Railway. Hardly six weeks after we civilians were organized as a regiment, we were on our way to England and France, being among the first 30,000 Americans to arrive over there. The first American soldiers to be seen "somewhere in France" can testify how much the morale of hard-pressed people is stimulated by flesh-and-blood evidence that America is really with them.

THE MORAL FORCE OF UNION

The Wilsonian strategy, however, went far beyond inspiring one side and demoralizing the other by promising unlimited military support and giving early evidence of it. This strategy derived its greatest force from its purely moral or political side, its promise of a new world, something better than anyone else promised. The Union policy allows us to use this force again. To be effective we must give a much more substantial promise than President Wilson did. The Union policy alone does this; it goes far beyond the Wilsonian offer while keeping its good points and eliminating its faults.

The primary faults in the Wilsonian promise were its vaguenesss and its failure to tie either us or our allies to it from the start. Just as I want us to avoid these mistakes now, I wanted us to avoid them then. I was then a student at the State University of Montana, editor of the college paper, *Montana Kaimin*. On April 4, 1917, a big mass meeting sent President Wilson a telegram promising him the "enthusiastic support" of a "united student body." I was among the handful who voted against it. The next day I explained my reasons in the *Kaimin* under the heading:

BLIND DEMOCRACY

I have been asked why I voted against sending the telegram to President Wilson which was to say that the University students "stand behind him in whatever he undertakes." I was opposed to it because I object to all-inclusiveness of the wording which I have just quoted. . . .

Instead of being a "glittering generality" the telegram should have said something definite. If it had said, "We are behind you in every move you make to aid the cause of democracy against autocracy, and we urge you to make the entrance of the United States into the war dependent upon the definite agreement of the allies to establish a league to enforce peace after the conflict is over and, while overpowering the German government, to oppose dismembering and economically crushing that nation and thus sowing the seeds of future warfare"—if the message had been of that order, I would have been among the first to say aye.

The United States today has the opportunity of

doing great service to the cause of democracy. The
allies need our help, they are dependent upon us for
munitions and other supplies. They are fighting the
cause of democracy, but at the same time so many
racial passions and other issues have entered into
the war that it is doubtful whether the furtherance of
democracy or the commerce of the allies will be upper-
most in the minds of the men who gather around the
council table when the war is over. We had a Platt*
amendment before we went into the Spanish war to
keep us to our purpose of making Cuba independent.
We can do equal service for democracy and world
peace if we make the condition of our entry in the
war as definite as outlined above.

There is even greater need now than there was then to bind
our friends *and ourselves* to a definite program before we go to
war. For now we must overcome the disillusionment and distrust caused by our omission of these precautions then. From
this omission resulted the all-round failure at the Peace Conference, and from it resulted a psychological reaction among
ourselves, among our friends and among our foes, which has
powerfully contributed to bring on the present war.

The result was that we felt the British, French and Italians
had let us down at the Conference by insisting on an objection-
able treaty. The British, French and Italians felt that we had
let them down—that we had got them to make various important concessions by promising to come into the League and
guarantee the Rhine frontier, and had then refused to do this.
The Germans, who had surrendered to President Wilson, felt
that everyone had let them down—the Allies by the terms
of the treaty, and we by our refusal to enter the League where
we could have softened the application of these terms.

The ill feeling this created has, of course, since led to worse
feeling all round. Time had deepened each people's self-pity
and hardened their hearts against those who "let them down."
Take our own case. By refusing to enter the League we deprived the Versailles Treaty of its safety valve and helped

* It was not, however, the Platt amendment; that came afterward.

make matters worse in Europe. This deterioration made some Americans work the harder to bring us into the international picture, but it seemed to justify to others our rejection of the League.

Result: We signed the World Court protocol, and then refused to enter it; we made possible the Young Committee which set up the World Bank, and then refused to enter it; we got everyone to sign the Kellogg Pact, and then refused to implement it; we sent our representative to the League Council table in the Manchurian conflict, and then refused to let him say anything; we invited the British and French premiers here in 1933 to help restore financial confidence, and then went off gold while they were at sea; we sent Secretary Hull to the London Economic Conference, and then blew the ground from under him and it.

Having begun by giving all the Europeans dramatic cause to feel that we had let them down, we have continued for twenty years to build up the feeling that we Americans cannot be depended on to do what we promise or start to do, that we let down those who take us at our word. Meanwhile, of course, the British, French Italians and Germans by *their* acts confirmed for us and for each other the belief that they, too, could not be trusted—that they didn't pay their debts, or they didn't pay reparations, or they didn't disarm, or they didn't execute treaties or the League Covenant—that they let down those who took them at their word.

For the present purpose we need not concern ourselves too much with their reputation; we need to look to our own. For the purpose is to save the lives of Americans in wartime by making the most of the moral force at our command, as President Wilson did. In doing this now we are handicapped by the reputation we have acquired in the world since we disavowed him. Our first task, if we are to get results in the field he tilled so well, is to restore confidence in us. The British, French, German and Italian peoples should keep always in mind that their governments are deeply mistrusted here, and they should seek to remedy this. But we need to remember that Europe no longer has the confidence it had in our government, especially our Senate, and that before we can get real results we must remove this handicap.

And those who form our government—especially the Senators and President—need to keep in mind that a great many of us citizens do not have the confidence in them that we had in 1917. This is perhaps especially true of the younger men and women, whose confidence is most essential to any government in wartime. For years misguided men have been teaching them that unscrupulous or naïve politicians, propagandists and profiteers duped the American people into a futile war in 1917, that it was a horrible case of the government selling out the people and an excellent example of economic determinism, and that we got nothing for our sacrifices.

The parents of these youngsters, the men and women who were their age in 1917, know that this is a dangerously distorted picture of what really happened. But many of us parents join our children in insisting this time that we shall get what we fight for, not win the war only to lose the peace, not sacrifice in vain. Indeed, it is easier to go to war oneself at twenty-one, than to raise a boy to manhood only to lose him at the threshold; easier to be the sister than the mother of a soldier.

Many of us parents realize now that, whereas it takes only a majority of Congress to declare war, it takes only one-third of the Senate to prevent peace. A great many of us, both parents and children, are willing to risk our all for a better world, but we want a stronger guarantee this time that no handful of peevish Senators can destroy in the hour of victory what they sent the boys to die for.

To Reassure Us and Everyone

To get now the precious results that President Wilson proved could be had through moral or political force, there must be, in short, much greater guarantees than were needed then:

First, guarantees to ourselves. We the American people need to be reassured not only by the British but by our own government and ourselves, that we shall not lose the peace in winning the war.

Second, guarantees to our friends. The British,

Canadians and others need reassurance that we will not withdraw once they agree to organize peace on the lines we propose.

Third, guarantees to our foes. The Germans especially need to be reassured that if they overthrow Hitler as they overthrew Wilhelm, we will carry out our promises, and let no one take advantage of their trust in us.

We cannot hope to reassure ourselves, or anyone, or have any moral power, if we go to war for any purely selfish, "me-first," national interest, or if we go to war again as an ally or associate. No matter how noble our language—and can we be loftier now than President Wilson was in 1917?—this will not give us, or our friends, or our foes, any better guarantee than the one that proved insufficient then. We can rouse no enthusiasm or faith anywhere, at home or abroad, if we keep to generalities now, or promise nothing better than the League we promised before.

We can do better with an alliance if we promise Federal Union at the peace conference—but even that will not give us the moral force we need. For American parents and sons will know that we shall then enter the peace conference as we did in 1918—as a sovereign power, with only one voice among many, with no real guarantee that, if we get what we want at the Conference, a minority in the Senate will not destroy it for partisan purposes. The British, French, Dutch, Belgians, Norwegians and others will know this, too. And this sickening fact will come back to them most, as it will to us, just when a tonic is most needed.

The Germans and Italians will know this, too. When our glowing promises of a future Federal Union reach them by radio and airplane and begin to cause difficulty for the dictators, Goebbels will remind them of the "future music" they heard before from America. He will ask them, "When did the Senate ratify the Covenant?" and answer:

> The devil was ill, the devil a monk would be,
> The devil was well, the devil a monk was he.

Would you really blame the most democratic German for being a Missourian, for wanting to be shown that the United States is actually in the Federal Union that it offers Germany, before he risks dropping the first monkey wrench into the war machine?

There is only one basis on which we can hope to win with little if any loss of life. That is the basis of Union now with Britain. By forming this provisional Federal Union at the outset we safeguard ourselves, and our friends and foes.

We bind ourselves and our Senate and the British to the mast of Union before a single American risks his life for it. We give the British the best assurance that this time we shall carry on through the peace. We get from them the best assurance that they will carry on through the war. We give the French, the Germans and the Italians and others the reassurance that they must have before they will run the risk of passive resistance and revolt. Everywhere we give men the tonic they are thirsting for.

The sooner we couple to our military power the world-stirring moral power of a Union of the Free—no longer a dream but a living, growing, kindly giant—the sooner we shall have peace. First in peace, first in war, Union is bound to be first in the hearts of civilized men.

Part II
GUIDE OF THE FREE

He who blesseth himself in the earth shall bless himself in the God of truth . . . . For, behold, I create new heavens and a new earth. — Isaiah, 65: 16-17.

The Workingmen of Manchester, England,
To President Lincoln, Dec. 31, 1862:

Since we have discerned . . . that . . . victory . . . in the war which has so sorely distressed us as well as afflicted you, will strike off the fetters of the slave, you have attracted our warm and earnest sympathy. We joyfully honor you, as the President, and the Congress with you, for many decisive steps toward practically exemplifying your belief in the words of your great founders: "All men are created free and equal . . . ."

We implore you, for your own honor and welfare, not to faint in your providential misson. While your enthusiasm is aflame, and the tide of events runs high, let the work be finished effectually. Leave no root of bitterness to spring up and work fresh misery to your children . . . .

Our interests, moreover, are identified with yours. We are truly one people, though locally separate. And if you have any ill-wishers here, be assured they are chiefly those who oppose liberty at home, and that they will be powerless to stir up quarrels between us, from the very day in which your country becomes, undeniably and without exception, the home of the free.

President Lincoln in Reply:

I know and deeply deplore the sufferings which the workingmen at Manchester, and in all Europe, are called to endure in this crisis [which by cutting off cotton caused unemployment] . . . Under the circumstances, I cannot but regard your decisive utterances upon the question as an instance of sublime Christian heroism which has not been surpassed in any age or in any country.

Chapter 4

Guide of the Free

As nations can not be rewarded or punished in the next world, they must be in this. By an inevitable chain of cause and effects Providence punishes national sins by national calamities.—*George Mason in the U. S. Constitutional Convention.*

I also believe that without His concurring aid we shall succeed in this political building no better than the builders of Babel: We shall be divided by our little partial local interests; our projects will be confounded, and we ourselves shall become a reproach and bye word down to future ages. And what is worse, mankind may hereafter from this unfortunate instance despair of establishing Governments by human wisdom and leave it to chance, war and conquest.—*Benjamin Franklin, urging prayer when breakdown threatened the U. S. Constitutional Convention.*

There are men who would take some other man, some infallible Fuehrer, as their constant guide. We Americans as a people placed our faith instead in each man equally; we took Conscience as our guide. Twenty years ago our generation turned against it. Since then we have tried to deny it or appease it. We have now a bad conscience. There is no denying or appeasing it. We must face it honestly and do its bidding.

We have no excuse for not doing well. Our generation began well. We proved at the start that we could do great things. We began by gaining mankind's highest prize—its confidence. Some twenty years ago we won the world's leadership to a degree never before attained.

We had one unique advantage, which we have not ruined yet. America has been for centuries the Old World's secret hope, the dream child of its masses. "The people in Europe are friendly to this country," Benjamin Franklin long ago reminded members of the Federal Convention when they sought to have the Constitution discriminate against the alien born. "Even in the Country with which we have been lately at war, we have now, and had during the war, a great many friends not only among the people at large but in both houses of Parliament. In every other Country in Europe all the people are our friends. We found in the course of the Revolution that many strangers served us faithfully—and that many natives took part against their Country."

Long ago America entered the hearts of mankind as no country ever did before, or may again. We represent an opportunity given civilized man for the first and last time on earth. No undiscovered continent now remains. Ours was the New World where men could start afresh and do things better, right ancient wrongs and solve for all mankind its time-toughened problems.

Who can measure the longing that led millions to our shores, generation after generation, and from every religion, nationality, class and race? Who can estimate the longing with which millions more who stayed behind followed in their hearts the loved ones who had gone to make the New World? Who can deny that the American people is the child of all mankind, its favorite child, the one from whom the world has expected most?

Some twenty years ago it seemed the Old World's dream was coming true, that America had come of age and was about to justify hopes that were growing gray. I read those hopes in shining eyes when the great masses of the Old World first saw in the flesh an American President, Woodrow Wilson. Our generation then had the world in its hands . . . and what did we do with it? How did the long-awaited American champion justify the faith of all those millions, living and dead, in the Old World and the New? . . .

The fawning yes men who are the curse of kings have been flattering you and me for years. For we the people are the kings of America. On our favor depends the fortunes of politicians and preachers, journalists and other writers, commentators, businessmen. A horde of them seek every day to gain our favor in the old, old way—by telling us that what we want to believe is always so and always right, that we the American people have done no wrong and can do none. *Had*

*we not better begin to see ourselves as others see us before
history does?*

There is one way to escape paying dearly for one's mistakes.
It is to admit them and repair them before it is too late.

They who made our language long ago drew from the phrase
at one the word *atone*. They gave in these three words the vast
idea that we must all atone when not at one with Truth, whether
in a religious, political, scientific or other sense.

For God to bless, for God to spare America, we, its governing generation, must first confess the truth. We must avow
our error before we can achieve at-one-ment. So it is with us
each in everything, and so it is with us all when bound together
as a people; this must be done, and there comes a final time in
which to do it.

I believe that we as a people now face our final time. I fear
we have already passed the point when we could erase our
wrong without our tears and blood. And even suffering can
save no one by itself. It can only lead a man to do what he
could have done without suffering—confess the truth and seek
atonement. The Almighty atones for no man and no nation.
He requires each to take one step alone, the first one. That is
why this is the hardest step. He does help those who help themselves. . . .

We are not the only people who are in the wrong. But let us
leave the British, French, Germans, Italians, Russians, Japanese and others each to write this chapter for themselves, to
see and say the ill that they have done, and right it. No one
can right the wrong that we have done except ourselves.

Others are already being punished for their faults—punished so disproportionately that the world has taken on the air
of a medieval torture chamber. The French sought to lord it
over Germany—though not so arrogantly as Hitler—and how
cruelly the French have been humiliated. To keep the right to
bomb a few marauding tribes, the British blocked Geneva's ban
on all air bombardment—and to London the bombers have
come back to roost by thousands.

When such are the ways of God with man, what lies in store
for America? We who threw away the world for a mess of isolationism, are we already doomed to taste what isolation from

mankind really is? Are we to have a brutal lesson to teach us
how we do depend upon other peoples for our happiness and freedom? Our generation remains to this late hour smug and selfish. It is hard to hope that we can still escape the human
suffering we have been piling up. But we can at least lessen that
suffering and turn it to great good, if we begin now to amend
our ways. Our generation can yet redeem itself.

We started more splendidly than many a generation before
us. Other Americans had made this hemisphere safe for democracy. We set out to make the whole world safe for it.
We were the first soldiers of the United States of America to
cross the Atlantic to fight for human freedom. We sailed overseas when we ourselves were far removed from danger and
badly unprepared for war. We took up the cause of democracy in Europe only when its defeat seemed almost certain. No
people has reached a higher level than ours did when, almost
unanimously, our generation declared that President Wilson
spoke for us in giving these as the reasons why we went to war:

We are accepting this challenge of hostile purpose because we
know that in such a Government, following such methods, we can
never have a friend; and that in the presence of its organized power,
always lying in wait to accomplish we know not what purpose,
there can be no assured security for the democratic Governments of
the world . . . We are glad, now that we see the facts with no veil
of false pretense about them, to fight thus for the ultimate peace of
the world and for the liberation of its peoples, the German peoples
included: for the rights of nations great and small and the privilege
of men everywhere to choose their way of life and obedience.

The world must be made safe for democracy. Its peace must be
planted upon the tested foundations of political liberty.

We have no selfish ends to serve. We desire no conquest, no
dominion. We seek no indemnities for ourselves, no material compensation for the sacrifices we shall freely make. We are but one of
the champions of the rights of mankind. We shall be satisfied when
those rights have been made as secure as the faith and freedom of
nations can make them. . . .

The right is more precious than peace, and we shall fight for the
things which we have always carried nearest our hearts—for
democracy, for the right of those who submit to authority to have a

voice in their own Governments, for the rights and liberties of small nations, for a universal dominion of right by such a concert of free peoples as shall bring peace and safety to all nations and make the world itself at last free. To such a task we can dedicate our lives and our fortunes, everything that we have, with the pride of those who know that the day has come when America is privileged to spend her blood and her might for the principles that gave her birth and happiness and the peace which she has treasured. God helping her, she can do no other.

These words, Senator Lodge himself said at the time, "expressed in the loftiest manner possible the sentiments of the American people." And President Wilson's great adversary, Theodore Roosevelt, was among the first to say: "The President's Message is a great state paper of which Americans in future years will be proud. It now rests with the people of the country to see that we put in practice the policy the President has outlined."

We put this policy in practice so well that within twenty months after we declared war, we won overwhelming victory. Not a single one of the ancient hereditary dictatorships of Europe remained. The Romanoff, Hohenzollern, Hapsburg and Ottoman dynasties, all were uprooted. Immature democracies began to build up republics modeled on the United States of America. The masses of Europe everywhere welcomed our President as the "Apostle of Humanity."

Our actions confounded then the enemies who had said that Wilson's noble words in 1917 were only window dressing to mask the real "dollar-loving American." Had our motives been economic, our deeds must have betrayed them at the peace settlement. Instead, we still asked nothing for ourselves, no conquest, territory, indemnity, material compensation, economic advantage. We sought, instead, to curb the appetites of others, to lessen the burden on the vanquished. Hard as the Versailles Treaty nonetheless remained, it inflicted on them no such indignities and hardships as its greatest critics, Hitler and Stalin, have since then made even their own people suffer.

Moreover, thanks to President Wilson's tenacity, the victors did carry out our promise of a "concert of free nations." True, we got them to model it on our old American Confederation, the League of Friendship, which had failed to work even with Thirteen States that all spoke English. True, we made no attempt to organize the world, when we had it in our hands, on the model of our own Federal Union—we turned our back completely on our own Constitution which had solved so successfully this problem in inter-state organization. Even so, our victory *did* establish, for the first time in man's long history, a living world government.

Such was the result our generation achieved after fighting less than two years to do what men had never done. And then, abruptly, we quit the struggle and roughly refused to have anything to do with the new world order. Not because it was a League instead of a Federal Union. Though we were the ones who got the world to adopt an unworkable system, we never yet have attempted to get the world to change to a workable system—Federal Union. We have offered no alternative. We have simply found fault.

At the first peacetime obstacle we encountered we quit the great task to which America has so long been dedicated. We followed then false prophets, and have followed them ever since. They taught us to think only of ourselves and to insist on remaining a law unto ourselves. They persuaded us that, no matter what happened to the rest of mankind, we would be all right if we only stayed at home once war began. *They got us to adopt their dogma that the United States is not a part of the world but a world apart.* They appealed to all our lower instincts—or was it not, rather, that we let our lower instincts get the upper hand? . . .

Our children were taught either to sneer at those who risked their lives to make men free, or to treat them as the dupes of propagandists, profiteers, and hypocrites. Our children's minds were poisoned with the miserable maxim—"If you can't make the whole world safe for democracy in two years you are entitled to quit and blame the failure on everyone but yourself." History was perverted to persuade our children that the things men really die for are mainly economic, that, from the time we made our Constitution on through the Civil and World Wars, Americans had professed high ideals only to disguise their greed—that the belly was always our master, not the heart or mind or soul. If our children form the first American generation to be soft and waste their lives on paltry things, they will have to take the consequences themselves, but whose will be the fault?

Twenty years ago the majority of us began to wreck the new world order for which all of us had fought. Now there is nothing left of it to wreck. In those twenty years of isolationism our prosperity has sagged, while our unemployment soared. Our policy has brought upon us the gravest economic, social, monetary, political and moral dangers Americans have ever faced. Our generation which began so gallantly and generously has since written the most shameful and calamitous page in all our history.

You and I are the first Americans to see a decade pass in which the standard of living of great masses of our fellow citizens has gone down, and in which democracy and human rights have been thrown in dangerous retreat all through the world. *We are the first Americans to lament that our dead have died in vain.* And we are also the first Americans of whom it can be said that they abandoned in the hour of victory the cause for which their dead had died.

Are you proud of the twenty years of American history that opened with the "Harding gang" under the banner of "dollar diplomacy"? Do you suppose that they will be remembered as one of the great periods of America—these twenty years when *you* helped form America? And if you find our record good, do you think it safe for us Americans to be the only ones who do? How much of the opinion of mankind does the Almighty find testifying in our support?

We each admit that as individuals we often make mistakes and do things we are ashamed of later. Why is it so hard, then, to admit this of the nation we compose and govern? Who would be proud of a shameless nation? We all dislike men who are always finding perfidy in others and perfection in themselves. Why, then, insist on making one's nation what none wants to be himself—insufferable? We each admire a man who freely admits, repents and repairs his errors. Why not let one's people, then, thus earn one's admiration, and that of all mankind? It is time that men required their nations to be men. It should be a satisfying thing to have one's nation be the first to "put away childish things."

Would you yourself hope to gain anyone's respect by organizing Vigilantes in a lawless Western camp, and then refusing to take any risky role, and announcing you would be neutral no matter how flagrantly the camp's unwritten code was violated?

To follow the advice that we have been getting as a nation, we should no longer give our medal to the man who risks his life to save a stranger. For we are told on every hand to emulate the man who calculates:

"If my neighbor loses in this fight it will go hard with me and my way of life, so I'll sell him anything he wants that I don't need, so long as he will come and fetch it and pay cash. And if he runs short, I'll restore his credit, and even give him what he needs and deliver it myself. He has many faults and is fighting his own battle more than mine, but my sympathy and interest are both on his side; I'll aid him all I can to save his life—short of risking mine until he loses his."

You yourself would not admire such a man. Yet that is precisely how we are treating our fellow freemen in Britain today. Do you expect your God to let off lightly a nation of such men?

"Can it be that Providence has not connected the permanent felicity of a nation with its virtue?" George Washington put this question to us long ago.

Some concede our faults and agree that we should begin setting our own house in order—and then they make even this virtue serve the very vice that they profess to mend. For they would set our house in order by continuing our worst fault until we have corrected other faults whose correction involves less risk for us and promises more selfish gain. Each nation has its peculiar faults, but this blind selfishness, this concentration on national affairs, this refusal to contribute what each must contribute if effective government is to replace world chaos—this is the one great fault all nations have in common. It is here we Americans have gone wrong the most, and anything that keeps us in this road is wrong itself. How much longer shall we continue deceiving no one but ourselves?

Enough of this dreaming that world government will ever fall easily into our laps. Enough of this blathering that so great a good can be had without risk, without time and toil and tears. And enough of this wasting of our lives on the tawdry and the mean. Let us now begin to live by opening our eyes to the great opportunity of the present, admitting our share of the blame for the past, learning from our mistakes and taking our part of the risk "for man's vast future." There is no other course for honest men and women in a democracy that gives each an equal responsibility for it, as well as an equal chance.

No man, of course, can be a hero all the time, and neither can a nation. When nations reach a high moral level or undergo intense emotional strain they seem bound, like men, to slump immediately, and for a much longer time than individual men.

An hour in the individual's life may be likened to a year in a nation's. Judged by the moral standards that nations had then actually attained, we reached a dizzy level in World War I. Twenty years to recover from two years of such high and dangerous endeavor are perhaps not disproportionate. But now we must resume the struggle, or we shall lose all we achieved, and all that previous generations did.

Those in the prime of life some twenty years ago now have the least time left to save the enterprise they then began in the grand line of our tradition. We who were youngsters then and took the heavy share of risk that youth has always boldly taken at each great step in that tradition—we have now entered that prime age when the responsibility for continuing that enterprise reposes most on us. And those who were born some twenty years ago must now begin to play the part of men and women in carrying on a grand tradition.

None, old or young, knows when the Almighty will cut short his moment of maturity. Now is our generation's time to redeem itself. Those twenty years will be forgotten as the moment when the champion rested before his final effort—if we now do what we set out to do. We can do it now, with the help of God we can form The Union of the Free. And once we decide to try our best to do it, no matter what the cost, we can be sure that God will bless our people.

Part III

LANGUAGE OF FREEDOM

In contemplating a subject that embraces with equatorial magnitude the whole region of humanity it is impossible to confine the pursuit in one single direction. It takes ground on every character and condition that appertains to man, and blends the individual, the nation, and the world. — Thomas Paine, Rights of Man.

Chapter 5

Our Entangling World

What marvel could be more astonishing than a plant that brings Egypt so close to Italy that Galvinus and Babilius, both prefects of Italy, could go from the Straits of Messina to the port of Alexandria, the former in seven days, the latter in six? And last summer, did not Valerius Marianus, Roman senator, reach the same port from Pouzzoles in nine days, though the wind was very slight?

Thus, an herb can carry us from the Pillars of Hercules, from Cadiz to Ostia, in seven days, from eastern Spain in four days, from Narbonne in three, and from Africa in only two days, even with a moderate wind, as was proved by Caius Flavius, lieutenant of the proconsul Vibius Crispus.

O peak of Man's audacity and perversity! He sows seeds in the earth to garner at sea the winds and storms!—*Pliny the Younger celebrates the invention of sails and the beginning of sea power*, Historiarum Mundi, *Liber XIX*.

Wall Street's Crash Brought Us Hitler

The Atlantic Ocean will never be so hard to cross in our time as it was in 1491. Even then it failed to prevent the invasion of America. All their oceans, arms and science failed to save the Aztecs. Their gold and gods and human sacrifices proved of no avail to the Americans who enjoyed every advantage a millennium of isolation can provide.

Since courage, vision and machines gave men power over the oceans, those who have had the most sea power have had their way in America as in Europe. This has not changed because the machines have changed. To the ships that plow the waves have been added ships that fly above them faster, and radio towers that flash across them man's most disruptive, constructive and easily hidden power—a simple idea. The new machines have made sea power only more important.

The better and faster the machines, the more they entangle us in what the Old World does, while entangling Europeans, Asiatics, Africans, and Australians just as much in what we do. Colonel Lindbergh is wrong when he blames politicians for a process of entanglement which he has brought about much more than they. He is engaged in a tragic enterprise when he seeks to undo the consequences of his 1928 flight by proving his own blindness to them.

The machines that have now entangled all mankind have enlightened mankind even more. Who can help but glory in these marvels made by men as Pliny gloried in the early sailing ship? Our instinctive fellow-feeling with this ancient Roman tells its own story. The good that man's machines have done so far outstrips the bad that no one in his senses in 1941 would restore the world of 1491, or the world that Pliny knew.

But many men today are in a fearful, unreasoning mood. They seem less desirous of enlightenment than afraid of entanglement; they shy at the word, "entanglement," and press on with the machines that have already produced its substance.

I am as much concerned as anyone with keeping our people from becoming entangled in the policies of foreign governments over which we have no control. But I have never been shown anyone who kept out the smallpox by saying, "I'm not going to get the smallpox because I don't want to get it." Nor anyone who kept it out by saying, "I'm going to be neutral; I'm not going to have anything to do with this smallpox epidemic; it's too dangerous to take sides even with the doctor or the victims." I have never been shown anyone who kept out the smallpox by carrying a rabbit's foot and mumbling when he saw a victim:

> European, European,
>   Fly away to war,
> For I'm a better democrat,
>   Better than you are.

I have been shown people who kept out the smallpox by being vaccinated, by facing beforehand the danger outside their control and bringing it under their control, instead of waiting for the disease's hidden web to entangle them.

We Americans now have even less control over what the British government will do tomorrow than the British government had over the French government in the June debacle. We have no control whatever over what the German, Italian and Japanese governments will do. Yet should the British government be forced to surrender its fleet to Hitler, we would be inextricably and horribly entangled in the result.

Senators once denounced President Roosevelt for hinting that our frontier was on the Rhine. Yet when the blitzkrieg swept across that river they were so entangled that they promptly voted thirteen billion dollars for defense. They initiated conscription here in peacetime just as promptly when Hitler ended conscription in France.

We can blame the Europeans with some right for the way their actions are interfering in our lives. We can blame them as righteously as we please. That will not change the fact that we share the responsibility for the condition all mankind is in today. Here is one example of how we entangled others in it:

When *The New York Times* first assigned me to Geneva in January, 1929, there was no shadow of war then either in Europe or Asia. Franco-German relations were never more friendly this century than then. It was at the Assembly of the League of Nations that September that Briand held his famous luncheon at which—as he smilingly told us reporters when he came downstairs—he laid the cornerstone for his plan for a United States of Europe. No European foreign minister supported him more in that plan than Stresemann did. The two of them were fast liquidating the injustices of the Versailles Treaty. Not only debts were being paid, but reparations too, and the world was buying American goods as never before.

Only a few days after that happy Assembly dispersed there came the crash in Wall Street. We can hardly blame that on the Europeans or the Japanese, their hatreds, "love of war," and all that. For ten years we had been following a policy of strict isolationism. We had decided that by this policy we could keep out of the dangers we saw in the Versailles Treaty and in the League of Nations. We were "big enough to go our own way alone"; we had oceans around us. We were also an economic law unto ourselves. We were no longer subject even to old economic laws; we had entered a new era all our own. In those days our leaders told us, "The future destiny of America is in our hands, and is not dependent upon other nations."

We were not, of course, alone responsible for the bubble that burst in 1929, but we could hardly have done more than we did to make it a 100 per cent American bubble. And then what did we do to the rest of the world?

After Wall Street crashed, we began reducing our purchases from abroad. While Briand's Committee was seeking to stave off the effects of that crash by uniting Europe in a tariff truce, we raised our tariff higher to reduce still more our imports. We insisted more than ever that the Europeans pay us gold instead of goods, and, of course, factories began to close abroad, and unemployment began to rise, particularly in Germany which was working on the smallest margin. And as unemployment rose there, something else rose with it.

Through the 1920's Hitler had been talking his anti-Semitic nonsense and denouncing the Versailles Treaty, and he hadn't got to first base even when the Versailles conditions were at their worst. What even the Ruhr occupation failed to do for Hitler, our Wall Street crash and subsequent policy succeeded in doing. In the Reichstag of September, 1929—elected in 1928—Hitler had only 12 deputies. In the first Reichstag elected after our bubble burst—just a year afterward—he had 107 deputies. Two years more of depression, and on July 31, 1932, Hitler elected 230 deputies. Six months later he began his reign.

Hitler rose to power with the hard times and unemployment that burst on the world so dramatically from America. That is how the German people, after ten years of resistance, became entangled in racial fanaticism and in a highly centralized totalitarian dictatorship. And as the Germans got entangled in all that, we have been getting entangled in it, too. Not only on the war side.

IDEAS CAN INVADE US, TOO

The ocean and all our armaments have not proved big enough to keep our country uninvaded by that most un-American of all the Nazi doctrines—the doctrine that denies that "all men are created equal," and that condemns and discriminates against them, not because of anything they have done, but because they happen to have been born Jewish. The ocean and all our armaments have not saved us from the Nazi trend toward centralization. Germany, too, was a federal republic before Hitler came. Long before we ourselves had reached the point of doing business abroad by barter as Nazi Germany does, we had necessarily reached its prerequisite—we had put the government into business, making millions of cotton growers, hog raisers, wheat farmers, businessmen and workmen (both employed and unemployed), dependent on the central government.

Despite all our efforts and our wishes we have not been disentangling ourselves from any of that. Even while we have kept from being entangled in the war that all of this resulted in, we have been getting more and more entangled in these other un-American creepers.

And some of us still talk as if the only danger that our freedom faces, no matter what side wins in Europe, is conquest by an invading army. They talk as if they did not know that we are in much greater danger from an invading idea, that no barriers have yet been found that will keep out an idea, that an idea with enough success behind it needs no Trojan horses. They talk as if they did not know that the Italian and German peoples lost their liberties to no foreign conqueror. We, too, can lose within our state what we made it for. Should we lose our freedom to a home-grown autocrat after letting the British lose theirs to a foreign one, shall we be the better off? And shall we be the less entangled and entangling?

We are all living now in the same world, and none of us has been governing the world we live in. Our situation was well described by President Ernest Wilkins of Oberlin College when he called it "ruination without representation." We are all living precariously at the mercy of fearful powers beyond our control.

All the means we had developed to govern our common world have broken down. We failed to get agreement in time to be of any good either from the old prewar diplomatic machinery on which we Americans relied exclusively, or from the more advanced League of Nations machinery. The agreements we did

succeed in getting by these means in the period just after World
War I—the League Covenant, the Nine-Power Pact, the Peace
Pact—we could not keep inviolate except by going to war
against Japan, Italy, Germany. We didn't want to do that, nor
did the British, nor the French, nor the others, and so the
agreements were not kept. We lapsed back into a condition of
no law and no government, of anarchy and the rule of force—into
World War II.

When there is anarchy in a community, whether it be composed of individuals or nations, one of two things is bound to
happen. Either some strong man tries to unite the others under
him by force, to dictate his law to them. Or the law-abiding
people unite of their own free will in establishing self-government, democracy. And usually they haven't sense enough to do
it until the dangers of anarchy or of dictatorship are very near
and great.

Doesn't that describe what has been happening in the world?
First, we have seen Japan uniting great areas of China under
its law by war; Mussolini uniting the Italians and the Ethiopians
and Albanians under his law by force; Hitler uniting under
him by force the Germans, and Austrians, Czechs, Slovaks,
Poles, Danes, Norwegians, Dutch, Belgians, French, Rumanians.
And then we have seen Hitler unite Mussolini and Japan with
him in the Triangular Alliance. But while all this has been
going on, the other movement has been going on, too. The old
democracies have been edging closer and closer together as
their number dwindled. They have realized better with each
disaster that, as old Benjamin Franklin put it, either they must
stand together or hang separately.

All mankind must choose now one of these:

1. Continuance of world anarchy
2. Submission to world dictatorship
3. Formation of free world government.

World-statelessness, the lack of world government, is the
underlying cause of this World War and of the world depression and World War I that came before it. Only when peoples
have no contact with each other can they possibly enjoy endur-

ing peace without effective government. Indeed, when they do not even suspect each other's existence, they will not—as Columbus proved—leave each other alone.

The need for world government rises for every people not simply from their geographical contacts with others, but from an inescapable two-way movement: their own outward movement into the world, and the world's inward movement into them. The American opening of Japan, which ended that country's long attempt at hermithood, showed that no people can by itself govern both these movements.

The closer and more frequent the relations between men become, the more each man's freedom, prosperity and peace depend on the establishment of some trustworthy means of governing his relations with the others. Except on penalty of hard and bloody times, we cannot possibly have such things as world prices and world markets, and yet leave ungoverned all the complex human relationships whose existence is attested by such terms as "world prices" and "world markets."

To bring this ungoverned, entangling, fear-stricken world under law and order is the problem of world government. It affects, directly or indirectly, the food, shelter, health, liberty and life of every person on earth. It is truly the vital problem of today.

Chapter 6

What the French Did for Freedom

Liberté Egalité Fraternité.—The French Republic.
Humble because of knowledge; mighty by sacrifice.—*Rudyard Kipling,* The Islanders.
On what do the destinies of empires hang? . . . If instead of the expedition of Egypt—I had made that of Ireland . . . what would England have been to-day? And the Continent? And the political world?—*Napoleon, at St. Helena.*

WHY FRANCE FELL

The reasons now generally given for the fall of France omit one simple factor that was, I think, decisive. It needs attention if we are to learn in time why it is essential to democracy that we make the world safe from war. In my judgment the French fell primarily because they are a democratic people—one of the most democratic I have ever lived among—who had to meet war's greatest danger for democracy, the first onslaught.

This opinion is not hindsight. In the months before the blitzkrieg, when the French and British were so confident and public opinion polls reflected American optimism, I was on speaking tour in the United States. In answering questions then I often expressed the view that the French and British would suffer disastrously once the war really started. I mention this now because this forecast was based entirely on the fact that France and Britain are democracies, and so it may show better the importance of this factor.

I had no foreknowledge of fifth-column work in France. Instead, I shared the then general belief that the morale of the French was high. I accepted the view then widely held by experts outside Germany that the conditions of modern war gave the advantage to the defense, and so I assumed the French defense psychology was sound. I was not aware of the Sedan flaw in the Maginot Line, nor of the mental rigidity in the French general staff. Nor had I foreseen the use which the Nazis made of tanks, parachute troops and Stuka bombers— even though, as *New York Times* correspondent, I had watched the German air force at the Zurich aviation meetings in 1936 badly outclass the French and other armies in "hell-diving."

In short, I expected disaster for none of the many reasons now generally held responsible for it, though rarely mentioned by any critic before the event. I would readily agree that all these other factors contributed to the disaster, and made it much swifter and completer than I foresaw. But I believe that most, if not all of them, really rooted in the democracy of the French, and were consequences of this primary cause.

Here is the reasoning that led me to this conclusion: The more democratic a people is, the higher the value it therefore sets on each individual's life and the more it therefore gives each individual a free and equal voice in policies that involve his life. But the more this describes a people, the more that people is then exposed to wishful thinking* on war, and also to the swarm of politicians, generals, journalists, ambitious mediocrities, "practical" men and sentimental idealists who pander to this weakness. And the more this is true of any people, the less effectively it can prepare for war and the more likely it is to be taken by surprise. Result—war is likely to begin disastrously for the more democratic side, though there are exceptions that prove the rule.

The noblest thing in democracy—the high value it sets equally on each individual's life, liberty and happiness—exposes it dangerously to sudden attack and makes it most vulnerable in the early stages of war. This is the profound truth in Woodrow

---

* As late as May 28, 1940, even President Roosevelt was reported in the press as saying that "there was no reason for the country to become 'discomboomerated' in apprehension of what may come to pass. The women of the country would not have to give up their cosmetics, lipsticks and chocolate sodas in consequence of the preparedness program. It was the intention not to upset the normal trends of American life any more than necessary. Mr. Roosevelt underscored his observation that the present defense program was not to be compared with that of 1917 when the nation was attempting to raise an army of 4,000,000 men. There was no thought in government today to revive the draft system, whether of men or money."

Wilson's words, "The world must be made safe for democracy," and in his attempt to make it safe by setting up a world government to eliminate the danger of war.

In our ungoverned world, the vital defense problem of democracy is, consequently, to survive somehow the initial disasters it is almost bound to suffer once war begins. If it can do this, then it is fairly sure to win in the long run, for then the great virtues of democracy assert themselves more and more powerfully, while the vices of autocracy are enfeebling it. Democracy gives a people greater enduring and inventive powers and makes for better morale than does autocracy, because it gives each citizen a direct and equal interest in the war. It is his war, not his ruler's war, and this stimulates him to feats of courage, ingenuity, resourcefulness, and to more fruitful teamwork. The more democratic a people is, the more it can harness, in its time of need, the most powerful, perhaps, of natural forces—individual enterprise. But it takes some time for any democracy to unharness this power from peaceful work and harness it to war.

Conversely, autocracy to win must make its initial blows decisive, and not merely disastrous. It must gamble to win in a war's early period. For then it is at its peak because of its very nature—its disregard for human life and honor, its ruthlessness and terrorism, its secrecy and concentrated power. Dictatorship is a sprinter, not a distance runner, and it must keep the race short if it is to win.

HITLER'S GREAT BLUNDER

That, briefly, is the reasoning that led me to expect disaster —but not decisive defeat—for the French and British this time as in World War I, once Germany attacked. The only questions in my mind were, which of the two great democracies would Hitler seek to knock out first, and how swift and great would the disaster be.

Here my guesses were wrong. I underestimated the speed and the extent of the disaster, and yet I overestimated Hitler. For I thought he would go for Britain first. Napoleon had already proved that one could conquer the Continent and yet lose because England remained in control of the seas. Hitler had played his cards so shrewdly that it seemed prudent to expect him to profit from this experience. His Scandinavian campaign pointed in this direction, for it opened the way for invasion of Britain from Scapa Flow to the Channel. It did not fit into an attempt to knock out France first.

When, after the break at Sedan, the Germans headed for the Channel and not toward Paris as in 1914, I felt dismally sure that Hitler was shrewder than Wilhelm and Napoleon. Then he took Calais, Boulogne, Dunkirk, held all the Channel ports, and left me aghast at the possibility he had gained of sweeping on through Britain. So amazingly efficient and thoroughly prepared an army would no doubt have shallow shipping ready to swarm across the Channel.

And then, on June 5, Hitler turned and spent on France his surest knockout blow. I still wonder why. Whatever his reasons, history may well find that France diverted him into the decisive blunder that cost him his best chance to win the war and gain the keys to world control.*

Had Britain or the United States occupied the place of France there seems no reason to suppose that the disaster would have been less. For the test showed not simply that the French were unprepared to withstand the initial onslaught, but that the British were still less prepared for it and that we Americans were far behind the British.

The 1940 showdown showed that all the old democracies, great and small, European and American, were tragically unprepared for war and vulnerable to attack—despite the huge amounts each had spent for defense. It left the people of no democracy in position to blame other democracies. Those that still survive need to say instead, "There, but for the grace of God, go I."

* After this book went to press, I found confirmation of this view in the interview Lord Halifax gave the press Jan. 25, 1941, the day after his arrival in Washington as Ambassador. *The New York Times* of Jan. 26 reported him as saying:

" 'I believe that when history comes to be written, it will be said that Hitler lost the war in June, 1940, when he failed to take advantage of the situation after the French collapse and the withdrawal from Dunkerque.'

" 'Do you mean that Hitler could have taken England at that time?' a reporter asked.

" 'I think he had a better chance then than he ever will have again,' the Ambassador replied."

It showed, too, how sound was the supposition that the democratic philosophy itself exposes a people dangerously to the wars of aggressive autocrats. The democracies were vulnerable in different ways, but none was in position to withstand in May, 1940, the surprise that Hitler was able to deliver then. The democracies that remain, remain because they did not have to suffer then, as the others did, the full shock of his onslaught. The billions we Americans have spent and the millions we have drafted, since France fell, show with brutal frankness how much we had been relying on French taxpayers and their sons to defend America in defending France.

It is no reflection on the magnificent fortitude and daring which the British are showing to recall that they did not have to bear the brunt of the assault as did the French, and that they did have an opportunity to steady themselves which the French never had.

Could the British have been saved by their Channel and their chins had Hitler, when he reached Calais, concentrated everything on following swiftly through to London? He had already captured on the Continent practically all the armament of the British army. Sir Walter Layton, of the British Ministry of Supply, told the Associated Industries of Massachusetts, October 17, 1940, that Britain "had thrown in the land battle all that she had of trained men and equipment. When, therefore, the men of Dunkirk arrived in England with nothing but what they stood up in the cupboard was very, very bare indeed." An American army officer in position to know has told me that the British then had "hardly a full division" in condition to defend the Island, and that its beach defenses against invasion at that time were extremely weak.

No doubt the R.A.F. and the British navy would have made invasion cost the Germans dear. But Hitler has shown how ready he is to sacrifice the lives of others—and the cost of invasion is increasing all the time. Surely his best hope of securing surrender of the British fleet was a stunning, swift invasion then of England. Control of the seas would have closed a prison door on the French army and at the same time would have opened to Hitler the door to an unprepared America. But Hitler, when he reached the Channel and had to make his tremendous choice, chose to give the British and not the French the time every democracy needs to begin to fight.

Here is one of the great mysteries of this war—one about which a whole shelf of books may well be written. Why did Hitler make this blunder? Had Hitler completely failed to learn from Napoleon and World War I? Had he planned all along to knock out France first? Or did he have a plan to strike at England first, but was diverted from it at the crucial moment? If so, what diverted him? Or who?

In discussing these questions recently with the American army officer to whom I have already referred,* I learned that he, too, and some other high military authorities believed that the original German plan was to knock out Britain first. They, too, were amazed when the Germans turned from the Channel back toward Paris. According to my friend's information, Hitler himself was directly responsible for this sudden change in plan. That would seem plausible. Even so, the reason remains guesswork.

WHY DID HITLER TURN ON FRANCE?

No doubt a number of factors, some apparently contradictory, entered into Hitler's decision. Perhaps he did not realize how bare the British army cupboard was. Certainly the splendid work of the British navy and the R.A.F. at Dunkirk did much to hide this poverty and to remind him that the Channel was

---

*I submitted this chapter to this officer for his comment and criticism. He replied:

"I have no fault to find with the article except in one respect. While basically you may be right as to the fall of France, to me the biggest single factor in the debacle was not so much the democracy of the people with their highly individualistic attitude, but was essentially based upon the *defense* psychology of the people, as a whole, and their leaders. This, coupled with a mental rigidity, or, perhaps, more properly speaking, a lack of adaptability, caused the other factors, such as you mention, to have a much more devastating effect than would have been the case otherwise.

"Aside from the foregoing, I think the article is fine."

To me, this rigid defensive psychology is but another of the weaknesses to be expected in any democracy when war begins. This type of military mind seems almost certain to be in command then in a democracy. In peacetime a democracy and its politicians are bound to fear the strong, aggressive, adventurous type of soldier and sailor, and give the highest posts to the officers who fit in best with the defensive psychology which naturally dominates a democracy in peacetime.

not the Rhine or Meuse. Quite possibly Hitler himself was not prepared for so smashing a success, had not expected to reach the Channel so soon, had not prepared to assemble there so early the boats and planes needed for invasion.

Perhaps Hitler could not resist the temptation of humiliating the French when he found their resistance less than anyone expected. After all, France was Germany's "hereditary enemy" and Hitler's early hate. Its army had much greater military prestige than Britain's, and here was a long-dreamed-of opportunity to crush it ignominiously—an opportunity that was much too good to last long. Every people has its moments of weakness and of panic, but few have shown such resiliency and powers of quick recovery as the French—the only people who have both won and lost an empire three times over in the last two hundred years. Given merely time to catch their breath and recover from the shock, the French were capable of swiftly reorganizing their army into a formidable force on Hitler's left flank. The British were infinitely weaker than the French in the very elements that need the longest preparation—in numbers of trained officers, soldiers and reserves. If Britain was potentially the greater danger to Hitler, France was a much more immediate danger.

Of course, these French assets would not matter much if Hitler quickly gained control of the seas—but could he gain it quickly enough, if he left a reviving French army on his flank? And what if he failed to gain control of the seas even by invading Britain?

On the other hand, perhaps Hitler was so drunk with success when he reached the Channel and so contemptuous of both the French and British that he thought he could safely take time out to fell the former first.

It seems more probable to me, however, that respect for French powers of recovery rather than contempt diverted Hitler from London to Paris. Had Hitler found the French army as weak as it is now the fashion to believe, he would hardly have made the efforts he was making at this critical time to persuade Mussolini to stab France in the back. We forget too easily that while the Germans were closing in on Dunkirk, June 2, they were also air-raiding down the Rhone Valley to prove their ability to support an Italian attack. It hardly seems likely that Hitler would have sought to share with Mussolini a victory he believed that he could quickly win alone. The psychological weight of Italy entering the war just when it did can hardly be overestimated, in trying to judge now why men, caught in a torrent of events, acted as they did.

If so much of the British army was rescued at Dunkirk, it was not only because of the British naval and air forces, but also because of the actual and potential pressure of the French on the German flank—pressure so great as to divert German planes from Dunkirk even to the Rhone.

AN OCEAN OF RESPONSIBILITY

The great and not-to-be-forgotten services that the French rendered democracy were these: (a) they sustained the first shock of the onslaught, and then (b) when the Dutch, Belgian and British armies were practically all *hors de combat* and Hitler held the Channel, the French still threatened Hitler's flank enough to make him decide to remove this threat before invading Britain.

We need to remember, too, that the French paid for the common victory of democracy in 1918 immensely more in men and property than we or the British did. In battle deaths the French Empire then suffered per capita more than any other people—thirty times more than we did, eight times more than the British Empire. We need to keep in mind these words from the speech, already cited, of Sir Walter Layton:

When German militarism last broke loose 26 years ago and threatened to overrun Europe, the French and Russian army and the British navy held the Kaiser's forces at bay for two years while the British Empire steadily built up and equipped almost from nothing a great army, which ultimately exceeded 90 divisions. When the United States entered the war three years later, she too had a year's grace in which to prepare while the Allied Forces continued to hold the front.

This time the pace is very much faster. The task of holding the Western front imposed too great a strain on the resources of France. . . . Yet those eight months [September, 1939 to May, 1940] gave us in Britain an invaluable respite in which to call up and train our rapidly growing army, and to crank up and set in motion Britain's war machine. I hope that no Englishmen will ever forget that France first stood in the breach and, by so doing, kept Hitler's air force within Germany's own frontiers during those vital months when we were so ill prepared. The development of America's war industries has inevitably started many months later than our own. The sailors and airmen of England are giving American industry the respite it needs to get under way. But the pressure is severe, and we must expect that the attack will develop with redoubled force in the spring.

Certainly it would seem fair to say that without the French army the fate of democracy would have been sealed only too probably in June, 1940. It was the French who gave the British and us the time democracy must have to steel itself for war psychologically and materially.

Put in another way, we enjoy an advantage over the British which they enjoyed over the French, the advantage of being separated from autocracy by a wider barrier. Where the French had a river and the British have a Channel, we have an ocean.

Without the sacrifices which the British have been making with such admirable courage, we would have no time to unite the remaining democracies or complete our defense against invasion. We owe to Britain now the kind of debt that we and the British owe the French—that democracy everywhere owes anyone who risks his home and life anywhere for it.

France's fall can teach us that if a neighbor's sudden collapse would endanger us, we cannot safely let him bear more of the common burden than he can stand, even though we can make him overstrain himself awhile. The sacrifices of the French and British will be in vain if we Americans fail, with the time they have gained for democracy, to save it from this attack . . . and from the danger of another war.

Our ocean now is an ocean of responsibility for man's freedom everywhere.

Chapter 7

The Language of Freedom

English-speaking peoples are all free-speaking peoples. Their Union would not be so much an English-speaking as a Free-speaking Union. English has long been the language of freedom, as of union. Indeed, English is a language in which *freedom* and *friend* have the same root. That root began before America or England did. It began when Man began—in the Sanskrit word for *love*. To quote *Union Now*:

"As a child sometimes sees deeper than a man, so Man, when he was making words for those ethereal solid things that he has never touched and always reached for, saw into them more deeply than we do, and he made his word for *love* his word for *free*. We have too long forgot that we began to *free* . . . with *love*; we have yet to learn that . . . from the very nature of things stem together *friend* and *freedom*."

English Speech Is Free Speech

This war is at once a culmination of the anarchy in the world, and a struggle between the dictatorial and the democratic ways of ending it by uniting men under a common government. It is a war between two ancient adversaries who both seek now to set up something never before achieved on so grand a scale. The ambition of Darius, Caesar and Napoleon, swollen now into a darker cloud, seeks to blot out the vision of Isaiah, Socrates and Lincoln. This is a war in which the issue is: Empire of the Earth or Man's Great Republic?

As Hitler said, December 10, 1940: "Two worlds are in conflict, two philosophies of life. . . . One of these two worlds must break asunder. . . . This fight is not only a struggle for the present; it is especially a fight for the future." He pretended then—this cunning champion of the "monumental lie"—that the issue is between "gold versus labor," with America and Britain upholding gold and Germany upholding labor. The true issue is:

119

Shall Man's future be governed by the principle—not of labor but of slavery—that Hitler flaunts through Europe: *Du bist nichts, das Volk ist alles—thou* (yes, you yourself), *thou art nothing, the nation is everything?* Shall men sink back with the misery-making autocratic principle that governed the world for ages, and now trumpets as its war cry, *Ein Reich, ein Volk, ein Führer—one empire, one nation, one ruler?*

Or shall Man's banner be: *One union, many nations, a myriad equal rulers?* Shall he press on with the richest political principle he has ever found, the principle that the state, the nation, is made by men to secure equally their individual lives and liberties, that *you yourself are the end, the nation but the means?* Shall the future relations of men be governed by this principle which English colonists in America first declared to be the basis of all government, and toward which mankind had been moving rapidly for a hundred and fifty years, with America and Britain in the van—until we ourselves refused to carry it forward, from the nation to the world?

There can be no issue that concerns both Americans and British more directly and deeply than does this one. It goes to their roots. For seven hundred years, since Magna Carta, the Rights of Man have been proclaimed first in the English language. These free-speaking peoples do not need to be convinced that no community, small or large, can long continue in a state of anarchy, or enjoy freedom, peace and plenty unless it has dependable government. Nor need they be persuaded to choose democratic government and reject dictatorship.

Through many generations they have proved their preference. Century on century they have shown a quicker and steadier reaction against autocracy than have others. They disdain dictatorship now as a child disdains a helping hand, once it has learned to walk alone.

Each of the great languages of mankind can be identified with some great field of human striving, in which the men who used it led the way for many others. Thus, Latin can be identified with law, Greek with knowledge, Hebrew and Arabian with religion, Hindu with philosophy, Persian with poetry, Chinese with wisdom, Italian with the Renaissance, Spanish with exploration, German with the Reformation, French with logic and reason, and Russian with economic collectivism. Similarly, the English language has become identified with freedom and union.

English was the native tongue of the two fundamental creations of modern democracy, from which many others stem. One was created by the British, the other by us Americans. The British worked out for us and for every other nation the basic machinery of every democracy today—representative government. We Americans solved for the British and the world, as well as for ourselves, the problem of how to govern the relations between these democratic states. We provided the machinery of inter-democracy government—Federal Union.

Whether they are Englishmen, Americans, Scots, Welsh, Irish, Canadians, Australians, New Zealanders, or South Africans, the people who speak English present this double phenomenon: *They are most jealous champions of local government—and yet, they are most zealous advocates and builders of inter-state government.* They cling to the town meeting while they reach toward the Commonwealth of Man, these free-speaking peoples, every one of them.

Conflicts between local and general government stud their histories. Characteristically, both have won in substance—and in the substance that most deserved to win. This has been true from the wars that ended in creation of the United Kingdom, through the Boer War's creation of the Union of South Africa. The American Civil War is only the most clear-cut and bloody of these conflicts. It is also the most impressive example of victory serving ever after to keep local and central governments from belligerently encroaching on each other.

WE AND THE BRITISH ARE TOWN-AND-WORLD-MINDED

One might argue that, as between the British and us Americans, the genius of the former leans toward state government, while that of the latter leans toward inter-state government. But one might easily dispute this, too.

It is true that we Americans have been the great innovators and leaders in the field of representative inter-state government. We have brought half a continent and 130,000,000 men of all nationalities and races under such a government. The largest representative government the British have established remains an island of 47,000,000 people. Nor have the British ever tried to unite the continent nearest them. While Frenchmen from Henri IV to Briand, and other Europeans from Kant to Coudenhove-Kalergi dreamed of European union, the British produced no such proposals. They practiced, instead, *divide and rule.*

It is not surprising that many feel that this maxim has become second nature with the British. Fiske has pointed out that "under the government of England before the [American] Revolution the thirteen commonwealths were independent of one another, and were held together, juxtaposed rather than united, only through their allegiance to the British crown . . . with no telling how long they might have gone on thus disunited," had they remained British. The government in London similarly holds together now, like spokes of a rimless wheel, the Commonwealth of Australia, New Zealand, South Africa, Canada and Eire. It has never sought to unite them with it in a common representative government. It still keeps Newfoundland separate from Canada. Not so long ago it proposed to solve the Palestine problem by dividing even those few acres into separate Arabic and Jewish states.

But if all this is true, it is just as true that the British have brought under one government more people and land and water than any empire ever did before. They have united more than three times the land and people we Americans have united. They rule a far more polyglot population and widely scattered territory than ours. The British have held this vast empire together longer than we have held our territory. They have done it with an army far smaller in proportion than that of any other empire. And, with all their shortcomings, they have developed self-government and human rights within it more than has any comparable regime.

Some of the many faults of the British Empire are doubtless unique—as are some of the faults of our American Federal Union. Most of the faults of the British Empire, however, have been the faults of all empires. The criticisms of the Empire (and it is significant that the most telling attacks on it have been

made by English-speaking people) are based more on comparisons with the ideal than on comparisons with other empires,
past or present.

It is true that we Americans have been the great champions
of human equality in rights and status—with such exceptions
as negro slavery which the British abolished long before we
did. It is also true that in World War I the American people
broadened the aim of the democratic side from the rights of
small nations to the establishment of world government. It is
noteworthy that an American led in making each of the four
experiments in world government that followed: Woodrow
Wilson, the League of Nations; Samuel Gompers, the International Labor Organization; Elihu Root, the World Court;
and Owen Young, the World Bank.

But, on the other hand, the United States refused to enter
any of these institutions. We shared with Bolshevik Russia the
distinction of being the only great powers to greet the infant
League with a scowl and sneer. One of our Presidents and
many of our Senators rejoiced in the early twenties at periodic
reports of the League's "death." We continued to practice the
old, narrow principle that each nation is a law unto itself while
pre-Nazi Germany, pre-Fascist Italy and pre-Manchukuo Japan
were loyally practicing the new Wilsonian principle at Geneva.
Even Soviet Russia finally joined the League, leaving the
United States as the only nation on all the earth that never once
tried to make the Covenant work.

In fairness, we must also admit that it was mainly British
support that enabled every one of those four invaluable experiments in world government—League, Court, Labor Organization, and Bank—to be made real, and not left on paper. And
much as one can criticize the League policy of the British government, the fair American critic must always add that our own
government's policy was fundamentally as bad, if not worse,*

* This is true even as regards the Manchurian conflict where—by one
of the triumphs of our own American brand of self-propaganda—many
Americans have now the fixed conviction that "we got out on the white
horse and the British let us down." This myth was made by centering
attention on our policy of January, 1932, when Mr. Stimson did take
the lead—to the exclusion of our record during the previous four months.
Having been *The New York Times* correspondent at Geneva during the

and that no people gave the League such warm support as did the people of the United Kingdom.

Whichever way one strikes the balance, the facts remain: America and Britain have each been the world's outstanding supporters of both local and general government. No other people has proved quite so parochially-minded as each of them has been. No others have done so much to bring about world government as we Americans and British have. No others are so qualified by experience in this field, and so likely to succeed in bringing all mankind the boon of a government that will safeguard equally the individual, local, national and world rights of every man and woman.

We English-speaking people have shown such long abhorrence of anarchy and dictatorship, such preference for, and such skill in making and maintaining democratic government, both small and vast in scope, that only one course is left us today. It is to try once more to form a free world government. The League has failed, but there remains the better way of Federal Union. Will pettiness and pride keep us Americans and British from trying Federal Union now—on ourselves, to start with?

United, Sparta and Athens put to rout the Persian horde. Divided, they fell beneath the yoke of Rome, and for centuries supplied bolder men with Greek-speaking slaves. United again in freedom, after two thousand years, they have now driven a new invader from their land.

We English-speaking, free-speaking peoples face today a foe more ruthless than the Romans. Shall we go the way of the Sparta that was petty and the Athens that was proud? Or shall we outdo in our Union the glory that was Greece?

---

whole Manchurian conflict, I can testify to the crucial character of those first few months—when Japan could have been stopped with least danger and difficulty—and to the fact that we then practically prevented action.

The unpleasant truth is that when the Manchurian conflict first came before the League, the British and the French—with the support of the Germans and Italians—mounted the white horse. We alone discouraged them by refusing to go along, and by following for three months a policy bound to make them doubt that we could be counted on should "the guns begin to shoot." When the British were ready to act, we weren't; and when we were, they weren't. That sums up the Manchurian failure, and many another failure I witnessed at Geneva. I would blame these failures on the League system rather than on any nation.

Chapter 8

How Federal Union Works:
The American Example

Example is of the first importance in politics, because political calculations are so complex that we cannot trust theory, if we cannot support it by experience.—*Lord Acton,* Historical Essays.

WHEN THE U. S. WAS A LEAGUE

"Now the experience of the Americans is necessarily an impressive lesson to England," Lord Acton wrote in 1866. His words apply with peculiar force today, and to us Americans most of all. If only we had studied our own history with more insight, taught it more truly and followed more carefully its teachings, we could have spared ourselves this war.

It is not too late to gain from early American history precious guidance on our present problems. There or nowhere we can learn what Federal Union really means, the great difference between it and all other methods of inter-state organization, and the incalculable advantages it can bring us now. So let us turn briefly to our history.

If going to war for democracy is a mistake, then America has been a mistake from the start. Our forefathers began by fighting eight years to make just a strip of Atlantic coast line safe for democracy.

They began by making also the real mistake our own generation made, though not so badly. They assumed that the only way to have their own individual freedom was to have their states free not only from George III but from each other. Just as we sought to make the world safe for democracy by organizing it as a League of Nations to guarantee each member state the attributes of sovereignty, they sought to secure to each of the Thirteen States its own army, tariff and money. And so they organized the United States at first as a "League of Friendship," to quote their Articles of Confederation.

The League of Friendship resembled roughly the League of Nations. Each state was entitled to one vote, regardless of the size of the population. Pennsylvania and Delaware were weighted the same. The state governments named the delegates who cast their vote in Congress, paid them, and could recall them any time. Unanimity was required for any change in the Articles of Confederation. The laws of Congress could operate only on the states as units.

The League of Friendship, unlike the League of Nations, was empowered to raise an army and issue money, and did not need unanimity to act in certain new fields. But in reality action depended on the consent of each state, for this League had no power to coerce the member states, being much weaker than Geneva in this sense.

Since Virginia did not reject the Washingtonian League as the United States of America rejected the Wilsonian one, the former can be rated the stronger. Moreover, all its members spoke the same language, had the same republican form of government, and enjoyed many other common bonds.

If any league or collective alliance could make things safe for democracy the League of Friendship should have succeeded. And it failed even worse than the League of Nations.

The League Congress was feeble even while the war was on. For example, tiny "Delaware," as Madison later reminded the Federal Convention, "during the late war opposed and defeated an embargo to which twelve States had agreed, and continued to supply the enemy with provisions in time of war." Once the war was won, Congress became a debating society, and then a laughing stock, increasingly unable to secure even a quorum, let alone united action. It was afraid of its own unpaid army, and everyone was afraid of its worthless money. Thirteen other currencies and thirteen tariffs soon proved too much for even the relatively simple business and agriculture of those days. Inflation and depression ravaged the members of the League, and led to the centralizing of more and more power in the state governments.

The government of Rhode Island, for instance, gained the

power to coerce its citizens into taking its worthless money. The head of the state of New York then officially styled himself "His Excellency George Clinton, Esquire, Governor of the State of New York, General and Commander in Chief of all the Militia and Admiral of the Navy of the same."

Boston then was boycotting not Japanese but Rhode Island goods. New York was protecting its lumbermen from the woodsmen of Connecticut. Philadelphia was refusing to accept New Jersey money, and Massachusetts fathers lamented that their sons had to "reside abroad" when they went to Yale. It wasn't long before there were eleven territorial disputes among the thirteen sovereign democracies, frequent threats of withdrawal from the League and threats from Europe to invade it.

When New Yorkers sought freedom by having a commander in chief all their own, he sent them under arms to the state's eastern frontier in the conflict with Massachusetts and New Hampshire over the territory of Vermont. When Pennsylvania had an army of its own, it was committing incredible atrocities against the Wyoming Valley people who claimed that territory for Connecticut and had sent a representative to the Connecticut legislature.

Small wonder that John Jay wrote to Washington in 1786,* "I am uneasy and apprehensive, more so than during the war." Many others feared the war for democracy had been a great mistake.

But that generation of Americans did not quit the struggle as soon as they met peacetime difficulties. Instead, they went back to the basic principles of the Declaration of Independence and sought—and found—a better way to apply them.

In our misguided day many celebrate the Declaration of Independence as if the great thing it did was to separate us from the British. But to the men who signed it that separation was a mere means to the establishment of certain basic free principles that they applied equally to all men. They did not even mention Americans or British in the great passage that declares that "all men are created equal, that they are endowed by their Creator with certain unalienable Rights, that among

* In *Union Now* I erroneously attributed this statement to Washington.

these are Life, Liberty and the pursuit of Happiness; that, to secure these rights Governments are instituted among Men."

Nor did the Declaration limit its conclusion, that "whenever any Form of Government becomes destructive of these ends it is the Right of the People to alter or to abolish it, and to institute new Government, laying its foundations on such principles and organizing its powers in such form, as to them shall seem most likely to effect their Safety and Happiness."

The men who wrote and fought for those principles applied them first by abolishing the British colonial form of government and organizing themselves as a League of Thirteen "Free and Independent States." But when they found that this League form of government was also "destructive" of "life, liberty and happiness," they abolished it, too, and invented a new form of government—Federal Union, our present Constitution.

THE CHANGE FROM LEAGUE TO UNION

Essentially, just what did they do in changing from League to Federal Union? They made their inter-state government a democracy like each democracy in it. They changed from a government of, by and for states to a "government of the people, by the people, for the people," thus establishing the basic difference between all Federal Unions and all leagues or alliances. We have become so used to Lincoln's famous phrase that we now slide over its deep meaning. That meaning had to be written in his time in blood before many men could see it. We cannot ponder Lincoln's words too thoughtfully now.

Government of the people: All government must govern something, operate on something, maintain itself and enforce its laws against some sort of lawbreaker. Inter-state government has only two choices: It must either be a government of states as units, or a government of the people individually as units. Whereas the League sought to govern sovereign armed states, the new Federal Union was organized to govern the individual citizen in each state. None of the laws of the United States of America now operate on the states; all of them were supposed to do so under the League system.

The framers of the Constitution had learned from personal experience that a government could not, however, effectively operate on states—that a government of governments was, as Hamilton said, a political monstrosity. In their state governments they had not followed the absurd principle of trying to coerce and govern towns or counties as units; they governed instead the citizens in them individually. Thanks largely to George Mason, they decided to follow this same common-sense way in their inter-state government. It seems simple enough, but, as de Tocqueville pointed out, this had never been done before in all the world's various attempts to organize inter-state government. He ranked it "as a great discovery in modern political science." This device, wherever tried, has solved the sanctions problem that ruined the League of Nations as it ruined the League of Friendship.

Government by the people: Some unit must govern in any government—and inter-state government must be a government either by the states or by the people in them individually. We have noted that the state governments governed the League of Friendship through their appointees, with each state accorded equal weight regardless of the number of people in it. The new Federal Union was organized to be governed on the principle of majority rule by the citizens in each state weighted roughly as equals.

Here again the framers of the Constitution did the common-sense thing. They had tried to run none of their state governments on the grotesque league system, with one vote for each county, and unanimity necessary for action. They merely transferred to their inter-state government the system they used in their state governments, after adding safeguards against the small states being dominated by the larger ones, and against centralization.

It was this change that has allowed Federal Union government to escape the inaction and remoteness from public control that have been the curse of all leagues, and to respond to public opinion as quickly and effectively as any state democracy. This innovation, too, seems simple enough. Yet nothing in the Constitution threatened more to disrupt the Federal Convention than this shift in the basis of power from equal states to equal citizens. And nothing in American history was more completely forgotten by the drafters of the Geneva Covenant.

Government for the people: Government is always made for some primary purpose, and inter-state government must either be made for the states in it or for the people. The Articles of Confederation began, "We, the undersigned delegates of the states affixed to our names," and set out to safeguard each state's "sovereignty, freedom and independence," just as did "the high contracting parties" with whom the Covenant of the League of Nations begins. The framers of the Constitution made Federal Union—as George Mason put it—"a government for the men and not for societies of men or States." They began the Constitution with this Preamble:

We the People of the United States, in Order to form a more perfect Union, establish Justice, insure domestic Tranquility, provide for the common defence, promote the general Welfare, and secure the Blessings of Liberty to ourselves and our Posterity, do ordain and establish this Constitution for the United States of America.

Here, once more, they did the common-sense thing. They made their inter-state government clearly for themselves, like their state governments. None of these was organized for the preposterous purpose of keeping the town or county governments absolutely independent. Yet here, once more, the framers of the Constitution were doing something new in inter-state government, correcting a fatal error and making another fertile contribution to political science.

They made Federal Union a government for the people not only in clear-cut words, but in a most substantial way. Their American forefathers had learned this way to greater freedom one hundred and fifty years before—in the Fundamental Orders of Connecticut* of 1639.

* The Preamble of the U.S. Constitution stems from the preamble of this Union of 1639 which reads: "We, the Inhabitants and Residents of Windsor, Harteford and Wethersfield . . . well knowing where a people are gathered together the word of God requires that to mayntayne the peace and union of such a people there should be an orderly and decent Government established according to God, to order and dispose of the affayres of the people at all seasons as occasion shall require; doe therefore assotiate and conjoyne ourselves to be as one Publike State or Commonwelth; and doe, for ourselves and our Successors and such as shall be adjoyned to us att any tyme hereafter, enter into Combination and Confederation together, to mayntayne and presearve the libertv and

They had proved by experience that men can secure more freedom by (a) uniting instead of dividing themselves and (b) dividing instead of uniting their governors. They had learned to divide the powers of government according to whether the majority of citizens would gain more by having them local or by making them general, and to keep all who exercised these powers equally dependent on the people. Just as they employed one set of men to run their house for them, another set to run their farm, and another to run their looms, they employed one set of men to govern their town, another set to govern their country, and a third to govern their state. They kept each set as directly dependent on them as the spokes on the hub of a wheel.

But, until 1787, they had not only stopped this system at the state line, but reversed it there. They had let the men elected to govern their relations inside the state govern their relations with the peoples of outside states, too. They had let their state employees pick the men to handle this, their greatest field.

In setting up our present Constitution they arranged to choose the fourth set of men themselves—returned again to the way of common sense. They centered this spoke, too, on themselves as the hub, instead of on the rim of their wheel. They thus removed a manifest cause of friction where it was causing them the most trouble and could be removed most easily—as regards the thirteen English-speaking democracies.

Then they divided the powers of government between the new Union government and the thirteen state governments according to which would serve the people better. Wherever they agreed that they would all gain freedom by transferring a power from each state government to the Union government they transferred it—and forbade their state representatives to meddle in these inter-state affairs. Wherever they agreed that the people would be freer if the powers of government were left where they were, they kept them there, and forbade their Union representatives to meddle in such affairs. They required the Union to guarantee that all rights not specifically given it

purity of the gospell of our Lord Jesus . . . As also in our Civell Affaires to be guided and governed according to such Lawes, Rules, Orders and decrees as shall be made, ordered and decreed, as followeth."

would remain in the hands of the state governments, respectively, or in the hands of the people—whose most precious individual rights the Union Constitution requires all government in America to maintain.*

The makers of the Constitution ended by shifting only five major powers from the state governments to the Union government. But by this shift they gained for the people these five tremendous advantages:

First, they abolished those thirteen independent armies that were threatening to embroil them in war, and they secured a far more effective power for peace and for defense.

Second, they abolished those thirteen fluttering currencies and gained a common, stable means of doing business.

Third, they removed thirteen tariff walls at one blow, and gained the rich free-trade market that has been the envy of the world.†

Fourth, they brushed aside thirteen barriers to communications; they gained not only the freedom that a common postal service brings, but a cheaper, freer highway, river and coastal service—while clearing the way for steamship, railway, telegraph, telephone, automobile, airplane, wireless, and television.

Fifth, they avoided the many restrictions and dangers of being divided into Pennsylvanians, New Yorkers, Rhode Islanders, and so on, and secured the vast freedom of American citizenship, without losing the state citizenship they already had.

They gained all these advantages for all the 3,000,000 freemen of the thirteen states equally—and far more for us, their posterity, 130,000,000 strong, who now enjoy Federal Union among forty-eight instead of thirteen states. I call this making "government for the people" in a great way, both in principle

* For clarity and brevity I am including in the Constitution the first ten amendments. I consider them, moreover, as being practically part of the original Constitution since it could not have been ratified had there not been a tacit understanding to add them.

† Adam Smith brought out his *Wealth of Nations* in 1776, the year that America adopted the Declaration of Independence. The Thirteen States were the first nations to try out on themselves the free-trade principles of this Scotsman who did for economic freedom what Jefferson did for political freedom. Not only American prosperity but America itself is founded on free trade; this, rather than protection which was practiced in Europe before we succumbed to it, deserves to be called the American way.

and in practice. And this was another of the great innovations that distinguish Federal Union from leagues, alliances and all other systems of inter-state organization. It helps make the Constitution, as one of its critics, Luther Martin, told the Federal Convention, "a perfect medley of confederated and national government, without example and without precedent."

THE RESULTS OF UNION

Such, in short, was the revolutionary experiment our forefathers made when they abolished their league and established the first Federal Union. And the result?

The result, as Lord Acton has said, was an "astonishing and unexampled success." The inventors of Federal Union had thus "solved," he said, "two problems which had hitherto baffled the capacity of the most enlightened nations: they had contrived a system of federal government which prodigiously increased the national power and yet respected local liberties and authorities; and they had founded it on the principle of equality, without surrendering the securities for property and freedom."*

Can you name three of those eleven territorial disputes that were dividing the thirteen states in 1787? Speaking on the lecture platform in 1939-40, I crossed the United States six times and put that question to thousands and thousands of Americans. I never found a single one who could name even three of those disputes. That shows how thoroughly Federal Union makes for peace. It has not only settled these disputes but made them quite forgotten.

Of course, there was one Civil War—but all forms of government (centralized republics, monarchies, aristocracies, what not) have also suffered civil war. Federal Union has never once been threatened with war between two member states—the kind of war that threatened the League of Friendship and ruined the League of Nations.

So much for peace. Consider human equality and freedom. When the first Federal Union was established no country on earth could be rated a democracy by present standards—certainly not by the soured idealists who sniff so skeptically when

* Acton, *Historical Essays and Studies,* London: Macmillan, p. 124.

one talks of democracies today. The thirteen states were the most advanced democracies then. But though they declared "all men are created equal," they restricted the vote to men of property and they permitted slavery. No one in them then even suggested giving women any rights. The history of our Federal Union has been the history of the elimination of the exceptions to the great principle of equality which, as Lincoln said, "it lives by and keeps alive."

First, our Union was extended to include all white men. Next we extended it to the slaves. And then we admitted even our sweethearts, mothers, wives and daughters to the Union. All the while schools were growing by leaps and bounds, as were other opportunities equally open to all. We are still far from the ideal, but no form of government has ever brought nearly so much liberty and equality to so many millions as our Federal Union has already to its credit.

Turn to the economic side. In the first ten years of Federal Union those thirteen poverty-stricken states quadrupled their foreign trade. The Union began with a debt load of $75,000,000 inherited from the League of Friendship. Then it purchased Louisiana for $15,000,000, bought Florida for $5,000,000 and borrowed $98,000,000 during the War of 1812. But instead of accumulating debt, Federal Union was able to pay off the debt so rapidly that, by 1835, it was distributing a surplus of $28,000,000.

How are you going to account for this tremendous change from war alarms to peace, from depression to prosperity, from failure to success?

Some say it was all due to economic factors, to the frontier, free land, rich natural resources. But the old League of Friendship had all that wilderness to the Mississippi River, and it could hardly borrow a penny inside or outside the country.

Others say the success was due to the fact that we had great leaders then—Washington, Hamilton, Jefferson, Madison, Franklin. But every one of them was alive under the League of Friendship; they made as miserable a failure with it as our generation has made with the League.

Nor did success result from any change in human nature. The same Americans were alive in 1786 and in 1790. But in

1786 they were getting into more and more threatening disputes, and in 1790 they were getting out of them.

How are you going to account for that tremendous change from failure to success, *except by attributing it to the one great change that had occurred*—to the change in the *form of government* from the state-to-state basis of a league or alliance to the man-to-man basis of Federal Union, to this reapplication of the principles of the Declaration of Independence?

And so we Americans, who call ourselves today Federal Unionists, we say to you now: How much longer are we going to waste precious time, and treasure, and lives, fiddling along with the diplomatic system, the alliance system, the conference system, the collective system, the league system, the national sovereignty system, which have already failed us thrice in our time—brought us two world wars and a tremendous depression in between, all in the space of twenty-five years?

Why on earth is it, I ask you, that this great American invention is the one answer to the problem of world government and peace that we Americans have neglected most? Why is it that even now we Americans, our government, our leaders and experts, are doing so little to explore the possibilities of applying beyond our shores these 100 per cent American principles which our fathers carried steadily on, from shore to shore?

Why not at least make one more attempt to do it before saying that we can't? Why not call another Constitutional Convention in Independence Hall, invite at least the other English-speaking democracies, try to work out with them another definitive Federal Union Constitution? Why not transfer from our national democracies to this new Union democracy those same five powers which the thirteen states transferred to the Union—defense, free trade, money, communications and citizenship—since we have proved for a hundred and fifty years that this transfer makes for peace and prosperity and freedom for everyone?

Why not make The Union guarantee that all other powers of government shall remain where they are, in the hands of each nation? Why not organize The Union government broadly on the same basis as our own, with Congress, Court and Executive? Why not put it on the same population basis as our own

Union and give the smaller states the same safeguards that it does?

We run no risk in convoking this Federal Convention, we sign no check in blank. No one can tell in advance what the details of such a Constitution would provide. They have to be worked out at the Convention. We are committed to nothing the Convention does until we have not only seen and studied the text of the Constitution it produces but ratified it. If we think anything in it is too risky, we can reject it then. We run no risk whatever in starting the process, in calling the Convention. We cannot possibly tell whether or not we can work out an acceptable Federal Union until we do get round the table. And consider for yourself all we risk by refusing even to get round the table now and try our hands at Federal Union. . . .

We free-speaking peoples have got the power now to make one-third of the world safe for democracy simply by changing our own minds, simply by having the courage, and the common sense, and the vision, to do for our children what the Virginians and the Pennsylvanians and the New Yorkers had the courage, and the common sense, and the vision, to do for us a hundred and fifty years ago—to unite behind our common Bill of Rights in a Federal Union. So why not do it . . . Now?

Chapter 9

To an American Legion Official

This government has for its object public strength and individual security. It is said with us to be unattainable. If it was once formed it would maintain itself.—*Alexander Hamilton in the U. S. Constitutional Convention.*

Dear Mr. ———— :

The position you take is understandable; I trust it is therefore subject to change on a better understanding of our policy. We go a long way together, as it is. You don't want us to unite with the British government; neither do we. You think we cannot really co-operate with the British government; we agree. You think the two governments are bound to remain natural rivals; so do we. You say with such eloquence, "I believe the destiny of America lies with America and that by building our defensive strength we will have perpetuated the only type of humane, progressive and democratic government"—and we say *Amen*.

Then we go on and say that one of the grand things about our American government is that it begins by declaring that "all men are created equal." Do you say No? Of course not. And we say that another grand thing about our government is that is does try to practice this principle, to treat all men as equals whether they are of English, Irish, German, Jewish, Italian or other origin, whether they are Catholics or Protestants or Moslems. Do you say No?

You do say that in your talks with people in London you found some deep-seated prejudices about us, but you are too thoughtful a man to deny that Englishmen who come here find in their talks with us some deep-seated prejudices about them. Do you conclude that Englishmen do not and cannot make as good American citizens as Irishmen, Germans, Jews? Do you believe that it has been the ruination of America to have drawn so many citizens from England, that they and the Irish, Canadians, South Africans, Australians and New Zealanders should be kept out, or discriminated against in our immigration laws? Of course you don't say this.

Well, we go on and say that another grand thing about our American government is that it doesn't deal with people as nations or states, but as people, human beings, individuals—that that's the way it has solved the problem Europe has never solved, and has got so many people from so many nations to live together peacefully despite the fact that it divides them among forty-eight state governments. Don't you agree?

We say it isn't common sense to expect to secure prosperity, peace or freedom anywhere without good government there. Do you say that your home city can get along without effective government? That your state can? That the United States can? That the world can? That we don't need as good a government in the world to regulate, govern, the relations between nations and keep them peaceful, as we have in our Federal Union government which does this task so well among our forty-eight states? Surely you don't say that.

We continue therefore and say, well then, let's organize that government in the world, and organize it like our good old American Federal Union government, and do it as fast as we can. Let's begin the easiest way, with the other peoples that are most congenial and nearest to us in democratic principles. Let's begin with enough of them to have sufficient power to defend us all from invasion. Let's begin with the Canadians, Irish, British, South Africans, Australians, New Zealanders— organize with them a nucleus United States of the World and let it grow gradually into a world government of, by and for the people, just as our Union of thirteen states grew into one of forty-eight.

Since governments are bound to be rivals and cannot be counted on to co-operate if they are absolutely sovereign, let's arrange so that we no longer have to deal with the governments of Great Britain, Eire, Canada, and the others, that we no longer are on a government-to-government basis with them, but on the man-to-man basis of our American Federal Union.

You say that we and the British are natural commercial

rivals. Think of what natural rivals in the commercial markets of the globe—and of the United States—New York, Pennsylvania, Ohio and Illinois would be if we tried to govern their relations on the same basis that we now try to govern those between the United States and Britain. Think of the mess, the hard times, the danger that New Yorkers, Pennsylvanians, Ohioans and Illinoisans would all equally be in if they tried to secure freedom, peace and plenty by each insisting on having an army, an air force, a tariff and a money of their own, and sending ambassadors from governor to governor, instead of electing men to Congress to govern their common relations just as the men they elect to the state legislatures govern their local relations.

Don't you go along with us still? We believe so deeply that the destiny of America lies with America that, just as our fathers carried these American principles from the Atlantic to the Pacific, we want to carry them in our time beyond the Lakes and across the seas to those who are ripest for them.

And we believe this is the only way to build our defensive strength in time. We are told by authorities in Washington that the United States cannot possibly build the equal of the British fleet before 1947, that there is grave danger of Hitler forcing the British to surrender their fleet within a year, and that we would then be fearfully underprepared—at best—in every arm to prevent the invasion of America which they believe he plans. My own experience as a former *New York Times* correspondent in Europe makes me agree with them to the hilt.

Isn't our problem this: How to keep control of the seas till 1947? How do you propose to solve it? What guarantee do you offer America against the danger of a separate British peace giving Germany and Japan control of the seas by 1941? An alliance with the British? No matter what its paper pledges are, an alliance leaves each state the power to surrender its fleet separately. A Federal Union leaves no such power to any member state.

By uniting with the British in this American Federal Union way, we no longer have to build the British fleet out of our own pockets and man it with our sons. We secure it for our defense overnight, with the surest possible guarantee against losing it in a separate peace.

What about Canada? You wouldn't willingly let Hitler be New York's neighbor on the north, would you? How would you defend Canada? Along the lines that Washington is now following? Those lines leave the Canadian government free to go to war overseas when it pleases, and force us to come to its rescue in self-defense if the war goes against it. If that is good Americanism, then why should we not give the government of New York the same right? In the present meetings in Ottawa one Canadian is rated as equal to thirteen Americans, for Canada with 11,000,000 has one vote and the United States with 130,000,000 has one vote. If that is good Americanism, then why not give New York State with its 12,000,000 people at least the same voting power on this continent that Canada has in these grave problems of defense?

What is your answer? Our answer is: Let's end this diplomatic system of governing our relations which gives the British Commonwealth six votes (one for each state) to our one, and organize them henceforth on our American Federal Union basis where representation is proportioned to the population. That would give us the majority in the Union government. Are you against that?

Just where do you and I part company? It seems to me that we don't part company at all, that you wrote under a misapprehension regarding our policy. I know that a good many of our fellow Legionnaires share that misapprehension, but I don't know many who find that our policy is not their own policy, once they really understand it.

After all, we each took the same oath in the army to "support and defend the Constitution of the United States"—and its principles of Federal Union. How better can we support and defend that Constitution than by carrying on those principles in our time, organizing the world on that Federal Union basis instead of letting Hitler bring all the world under his rule?

It seems to me we ought to be a little humbler. We had the world in our hands in 1918—I was there in Paris when Wilson first arrived and I've never before or since seen such a demonstration of popular approval as the European masses gave him and America. And what did we do with our great opportunity? Why didn't we organize the world then on our own successful Federal Union basis? No one in Europe kept us from doing so. How can we blame others when none of us Americans—pro- or anti-Wilson—even proposed to begin organizing, in this American Federal Union way, the new world order for which we fought?

And, you remember, we each enlisted for "duration" in that struggle to make the world safe for democracy. Maybe it was expecting too much to expect us to hit upon the right solution at first trial. But what have we each been doing since then to achieve our great goal? I wonder what history will say of those who quit because they failed to make the whole world safe for democracy in a couple of years. Has it ever occurred to you that you and I belong to the first generation of Americans who have let their dead die for nothing?

With your position and authority and eloquence you can do a grand job in the Legion to save us all from that stigma. I hope you will clear away the confusion we've been in and line up the Legion for Federal Union before it is too late.

Sincerely,
Clarence K. Streit
(Hell Gate Post—Missoula, Montana)

August 27, 1940

Chapter 10

The Constitution Is Our Foreign Policy

We are met here as the deputies of 13 independent, sovereign
states.—*Wm. Paterson, in the U. S. Constitutional Convention.*

The United States Constitution was originally a foreign
policy, and it is still the best of foreign policies. It was, and is,
a policy for governing the relations between sovereign states by
the principles of Federal Union for the freedom and welfare of
their citizens, not of their governments.

Each of the thirteen states adopted the Constitution as the
solution of their most urgent problem in foreign affairs. By
this policy they settled peacefully eleven territorial disputes
then threateningly dividing them, and quickly turned depression
into unprecedented prosperity.

Federal Union is the foreign policy that the United States
of America has practiced most continuously since then. Its
history is the history of the extension of this policy to more
states and more people, both in number and variety. No more
successful foreign policy has ever been evolved.

In one hundred and fifty years it has been extended from
thirteen to forty-eight states, and from 3,000,000 free men and
500,000 slaves to 130,000,000 free men and women of all nationalities, races and religions. Yet it has resulted only once in
war, and that war reaffirmed it and ended slavery.

It has brought unexampled freedom, peace and plenty equally
to the people of every state that has adopted this policy. These
130,000,000 men and women have only one common oath
of loyalty. It is to carry on this policy of Federal Union—"to
support and defend the Constitution of the United States
against all enemies, foreign and domestic." And yet . . .

For a quarter-century now the Constitution has been America's forgotten foreign policy. Worse, it has been mistaken

for its exact opposite—for a purely domestic or national policy
—and been both kicked about and worshiped by pundits, politicians and patriots as doing badly what it was never meant to
do or as being what it was never meant to be. Americans have
condemned and prized it as an antique example of nationalistic policy and government—but completely forgotten it in the
field of foreign policy and inter-state government at a time
when that field was never in more lively need of it.

President Wilson forgot Federal Union at the Peace Conference and organized the world as a League. The Senate in
rejecting his League forgot Federal Union. The Republicans
forgot it when their 1920 platform proposed an "international
association." Harding, Coolidge, and Hoover all forgot Federal
Union in their foreign policy. So did the Democrats when they
returned to power with President Roosevelt.

Colleges, churches and clubs, great peace foundations and
institutions specializing in foreign affairs have been studying
and popularizing for twenty-five years all kinds of solutions to the
foreign problem . . . except the Constitution itself. And the
foreign problem has gone from bad to worse, and become
now so much our domestic problem as to determine elections
to an unprecedented degree.

Only now is our generation beginning to remember that the
Constitution is our basic foreign policy, beginning to consider
how to apply it to the world to bring back freedom, peace and
plenty. Only now are many Americans turning for salvation to
the principles of Federal Union, and urging their immediate
extension to the remaining democracies that speak English—
as the first step toward their extension round the world.

It is not too soon. Disaster is at the door. But America is at
last awakening, and there has never been a foreign policy so
swift and powerful as Federal Union. It can justify again
Benjamin Franklin's prediction the day the Constitution was
signed: "I think it will astonish our enemies."

Chapter 11

What We Are Bound to Defend

> If the spirit of America were killed, even though the nation's body and mind, constructed in an alien world, lived on, the America we know would have perished. . . . The preservation of the spirit and faith of the nation does, and will, furnish the highest justification of every sacrifice that we may make in the cause of national defense.—*President Franklin D. Roosevelt, Third Inaugural, Jan. 20, 1941.*

Our Oath to Federal Union

We Americans are now arming as never before to defend . . . just what? Something that Americans gave the world, something uniquely American. It is not land, strange as that may seem to some. The idea that we should fight for the territory of these states was deliberately omitted from the Constitution. It came up early in the Federal Convention only to be knocked out by George Read of Delaware with this brief argument:

> Mr. Read [Madison noted June 11, 1787,] disliked the idea of guaranteeing territory. It abetted the idea of distinct States which would be a perpetual source of discord. There can be no cure for this evil but in doing away with States altogether and uniting them all into one great Society.

Nor is the unique thing that we defend a ruler, race, religion, nation or class. Elsewhere men are dying to defend these things, as they have been dying for them since history began. There is not a word about them in the American oath of loyalty.

Our oath is to something else. Men had never sworn loyalty to it before this oath was enacted, as the very first statute that Congress passed. Law No. 1 of the United States of America, approved June 1, 1789 by President Washington, ordained as the American oath of loyalty:

> I, A.B., do solemnly swear or affirm (as the case may be) that I will support the Constitution of the United States.

That oath has grown only more clear-cut with time. It binds us now to "support and defend the Constitution of the United States against all enemies, foreign and domestic."

Our oath is to defend, not a continent but a Constitution, not some vague "free way of life," but definite principles of inter-state government, called Federal Union, on which our free way depends. Our forefathers discovered these principles of Federal Union in 1787 and embodied them in the Constitution. Federal Union made America out of many squabbling states and quarreling races, nationalities, religions and classes. Our oath enjoins upon us loyalty to Federal Union.

Many patriotic oaths put prejudice above common sense, make reason bow to the accident of birth, subordinate principle to place. Our oath does the opposite. That will surprise those Americans among whom old European, Asiatic, African and tribal ideas of loyalty to blood or soil or class have been growing now for twenty years. The fact remains that the American oath is to support and defend Federal Union; our patriotism centers in its principles.

Americans once fought four years on American soil against Americans for the principles of Federal Union. The men on each side believed they alone were loyal to the American oath. They all agreed that freedom lay in the balance which the Constitution struck between the rights of the Union and the rights of the states, between the freedom and equality of men and the freedom and equality of states. But the Southern Americans held that the Constitution struck this balance in favor of the states; the Northerners held the opposite. Both died to maintain Federal Union, as they saw it, against Americans whom they believed to be the enemies of these basic principles.

They all died loyal to Federal Union in the deepest sense, to determine more clearly what these principles of freedom

really were. And Lincoln did not distinguish between them
when he spoke of the "brave men, living and dead, who fought
here." He saw their common sacrifice for these principles
allowed the true meaning of Federal Union to be made clear—
and he made it clear in the Gettysburg Address.

The free way of life that Federal Union gives can be destroyed in many ways, from within as well as from without.
Giving too much power to the state governments is one way to
destroy it, and a second way is to give too much power to the
central government. The first method destroys freedom by replacing Federal Union with a futile league, alliance, or the still
worse anarchy of absolute sovereignty which Europe has suffered for so long. The second method destroys freedom by
replacing Federal Union with a highly centralized government—
and dictatorship is but the acme of centralization.

The fact that Americans once proved ready to give the last
full measure of devotion to prevent disunion still serves powerfully to preserve our freedom and Federal Union from the first
danger. But the fact that other Americans proved just as ready
then to die to prevent the opposite extreme is still a powerful
protection against overcentralization.

That is how our Federal Union was preserved for us from
both extremes, and why the loyalty of all Americans, in the
North and South alike, remains what it was from the very
first, loyalty to the free principles of Federal Union. The western hemisphere, American territory, property, and people, enter
into the picture, of course, but they are all secondary. We are
bound to defend them only insofar as defending them is the
surest means at any given time to defend the principles of
Federal Union.

The test of present American defense policy, then, can thus be
stated: Is this the surest way of defending Federal Union? It
is high time we began applying that test.

The basic question boils down to this: Can we reasonably
hope to preserve our Federal Union principles from invasion
if we wait to defend them until the western hemisphere is also
invaded? If we will fight only on our own soil to preserve these
principles? If for any reason whatever we now allow autocracy to overwhelm the British?

I find the answer is *No*. I find that the defense of our Federal Union principles requires us to prevent the triumph of dictatorship beyond the Atlantic and Pacific.

Losing Federal Union from Within

In the event of such a triumph, invasion is not the only thing I fear, although I believe that invasion can come much sooner and more dangerously than the majority now seems to think. But suppose the optimists are right. Suppose we not only successfully defend our present territory, but even extend it North and South after the triumph of autocracy overseas. Suppose we successfully defend our flag, our national sovereignty, and our nationality. Suppose we intensify our nationalism in the European sense, as so many seek to do. Even so I find that we would then no longer have our freedom and Federal Union principles to defend. We would have betrayed and lost them, and made our oath empty, before the foreign invasion began.

Suppose we successfully resisted that invasion. We still could not regain our freedom and Federal Union over here, so long as autocracy ruled overseas and remained in position to invade again. So long as we refuse to remove the danger at its source over there, we must live in a state of constant preparedness against invasion. I deeply fear that living in that state thus interminably will destroy our freedom and Federal Union more effectively than would even foreign conquest.

If we let autocracy triumph over there, we thereby set a number of factors working to destroy our Federal Union from within. They continue working powerfully, subtly and unceasingly as long as autocracy rules Europe and Asia. Conceivably these forces might work to destroy our Federal Union through divisions, anarchy, civil strife. Hitler, according to Rauschning, foresees events developing here along these lines, at least as the preliminary step to the conquest of America by himself. A number of signs point in this direction—the degree of blind, bitter and petty partisanship that still remains among us, the trend toward barriers to trade between the states, and so on. For my part, however, I do not fear the forces of disintegration in America so much as the opposite danger. I fear the triumph of dictatorship over there would destroy Federal Union over here by leading us to centralize it all away.

Consider some of the many ways in which the triumph of dictatorship in Europe and Asia would tend to do this, assuming we are willing to send our boys to fight for Federal Union in Greenland, Bermuda, Canada, Latin America, and Hawaii, but no farther away.

By this policy we allow Japan to take the Dutch East Indies, and thus assure her war machine the oil, rubber and tin it requires, while losing our present chief supplies of the latter two necessities. We might as well admit, too, that by this policy of fighting halfway across the ocean but not a drop farther, we abandon the Philippines. Japan, with nothing to fear from us in seizing them, could hardly let them threaten her communications with the Dutch East Indies.

In the Atlantic this "hemisphere defense" policy allows us no right to count on having the British navy between us and Germany, Italy and Russia. So we had better assume the worst, that the British, failing to get in time military aid from us, surrender their fleet.

We then face on either ocean a hostile navy at least the equal of ours in tonnage. The mere prospect has already caused us to start feverishly to build another fleet—one which in 1946 will have 70 per cent of the power that the British fleet now has. We must pay for it out of our own pocketbooks and man it out of our own families. But this is only a beginning. We must build much more of a fleet than that. We must keep up with the building in Japan and in Germany—and this triumphant Germany would enjoy, in addition to her own big shipbuilding facilities, those of Norway, France and Britain. Moreover, we shall have the whole western hemisphere to protect—which means still more fleet.

All this means more taxes, more spending, more deficits, more government control over heavy industries, more "Santa Claus" elections, and more armed power in the hands of one man . . . year in, year out, as long as the danger lasts.

Consider the effect on the army. We are adopting a policy which amounts to replacing the French, British, Belgian, Dutch, Norwegian, Swedish, Finnish, Polish, Czech, Swiss and Chinese armies out of our own families and pocketbooks, while taking on the defense of all Latin America and Canada. And doing it at feverish speed, which means more expense than efficiency, and leaves us at best facing the veteran armies of Germany and Japan with troops that have never been under fire. It means no temporary wartime conscription, but permanent compulsory military service. It means heavy permanent garrisons stationed at the strategic points in the ice of Greenland and the jungles of Latin America. It means heavy fortifications in many places. When we have given Japan control of our present rubber and tin supplies, we shall need to guard heavily our communications with Brazil's rubber and Bolivia's tin.

All this means more taxes, more spending, more government control over industry, more deficits, more "Santa Claus" elections and more armed power in the hands of one man. It means regimentation of all our young, drilling into them, year in and year out, increasingly blind obedience to those in authority . . . as long as the danger remains overseas.

Take the air force. It is the same story, only here we deal with expensive weapons that rapidly become obsolete, and so the pace is faster.

BUSINESS IN AN AUTOCRATIC WORLD

Turn to business, trade, money. Take just one item, rubber. We are told on high authority that we can make all the rubber we need synthetically in a year or so, at about twenty-two cents a pound, the price of natural rubber now. It doesn't look so bad at first glance, but there are several catches. Only one need now concern us. It is artificial restriction of production that now keeps the price of natural rubber up to twenty-two cents a pound. Natural rubber has been and can be produced to sell for only three cents a pound. And so the private capital needed to build synthetic rubber plants wants to be guaranteed a high tariff's production against the competition of three-cent natural rubber.

Such protection would not protect us from paying for our military and civilian rubber supplies seven times as much as would Japan, once she held the Dutch East Indies. Perhaps Germany would prefer to arm then with three-cent rubber bought from her Eastern ally. And, assuming there is still a world market open to us, how are we to compete in it with tires and other goods made of synthetic twenty-two-cent rubber against Japanese and other manufacturers who use three-cent natural rubber? Of course we can reduce the cost of synthetic rubber, but can we beat Nature, and the Japanese colonial standard?

And how is our rubber industry to avoid government control, while circumstances make its production not only expensive and uneconomic, but more than ever essential for defense?

Take another item, tobacco. Our policy has already veered the British toward Turkish tobacco. If they lose the war they, and all of democratic Europe, may well feel so bitter that they will lose their taste for our tobacco, and prefer the Turkish leaf—even if Hitler does not insist on this. Either way it means our central government will have to aid the tobacco growers as it has the cotton and wheat growers.

Always more taxes, more deficits, more government control over basic industries, more "Santa Claus" elections, more power in the hands of one man.

And it means still more of this through the disruption of our existing internal economy. For when the tobacco and cotton growers cannot sell their crops abroad they cannot buy the pork and beef from the Central and Western states. The South will have to raise its own meat then, and so the central government will have to support the hog raisers of Iowa and the Western cattlemen.

If such forces are not enough to bring all industry under the government, there remain others. Foreign trade, for one. How do we compete in what is left of the free market when we face as competitors dictatorial governments that control all industry themselves—not as a temporary war measure, but because they believe that everything must always be subordinated to the state? How are we to compete against states that trade by barter and that seek profits in power, not in prices?

"Two camps are now established," as the leading German magazine in the field of currency law has put it,* "the one under the leadership of the United States, the other under the

* *Devisenarchiv,* IV, p. 906, August 1, 1939.

leadership of Germany. In the United States the old principles of economic liberalism are in the forefront—at least theoretically—holding that the world is one unique large market in which each people shall offer what it is able to produce cheaper than others. This system is expressed by a free and unlimited system of payments. In the German group several national economies try to draw the consequences from bad experiences of the past and establish something new."

We are getting more and more evidence of what this "something new" really is. By this new German policy the government has all power at home and seeks all power abroad. Being ready to sacrifice the lives of Germans to this end, it is of course prepared to sacrifice their profits and its own in order to gain a foreign market by offering German exports below cost price. It may cut prices still lower to gain political benefits.

Under this new German Nazi system private property, in our common meaning of the term, exists now hardly more than in Russia. Everything, in theory, belongs to the state (which, as Hitler has said, is Hitler alone). Those who seem to "own" property really hold it only on good behavior or at Hitler's pleasure. Official decrees narrowly restrict the "owner's" right to dispose of his property, and give the government a positive right to take it over any time at its own artificial valuation. This applies with special force to property held by Germans abroad. The result is that German-owned firms in the United States or Latin America are really camouflaged agencies of the Nazi state.

What is the effect on us? Either this competition forces us to put the United States Government in control of our foreign selling and buying. Or the United States Government has to come to the relief of the American producers who lose their markets, or who see their profit wiped out by falling prices. Both courses lead to a much more centralized American government and a much more dependent American citizen.

Always more centralization in America, more governmental control over each man's job, farm, business, life. Consider how this trend has grown in our country since Hitler came to power in 1933 and set up his system, and how rapidly it has been growing since he conquered France. Once we let concentrated

power gain complete control in Europe, Africa and Asia, will
not our own trend toward it leap forward—to the point where
it not only ends free enterprise in America but replaces our
Federal Union with a totalitarian central government? Will our
state's rights survive longer than our property rights? In Germany they went first. One of Hitler's first acts was to abolish
the German federal system. Once he had removed the powerful
brake which state rights provide, totalitarianism sped on.

Secret Budget vs. Public Budget

We have considered by no means all the forces that the triumph of autocracy overseas would set loose inside our country.
Take another thing—the budget. Our taxes are already soar-
ing, and the higher they go, the more we democrats are inter-
ested in the budget, in seeing how our money is spent. But
under the policy of defending only the western hemisphere,
we face a world controlled by Hitler, Mussolini, Stalin, and
Japan. The budgets of the last three are notoriously misleading
and unreliable. As for Hitler, he has not even published a single
budget since 1933.

The amount Hitler was spending on armaments was guesswork until the day he launched war against Poland. Then he
said that since 1933 he had spent 90 billion marks arming for
this war. That figure represents, former Chancellor Bruening
has said, three-fourths of the cost to Germany of the war from
1914 through 1918. This is the only figure we have had.* Nothing to indicate how much of it went for navy, air force, and
army—let alone such details as tanks, cannon, bombers. No
wonder the democracies have suffered surprises—while Hitler
enjoyed the advantage of knowing on what arms the democracies were spending their money.

Where does this leave us? If we let Britain fall, it leaves
us—until we uproot autocracy overseas—in a permanent poker

* Testifying before the Senate Appropriations Committee, General
George C. Marshall, U. S. Army Chief of Staff, was asked to give some
idea of what Germany had spent on war preparations. According to
Raymond Clapper in the N. Y. *World Telegram*, he replied that the
War Department had only rough estimates but indicated it would cost
$100 billions—or twice our national debt—to reproduce the material
accomplishments of the German war machine under our laws and
procedures.

game with four heavily armed players—Germany, Italy, Russia, Japan. Each has all his cards face down, with only one man, one autocrat, playing the hand. What do we Americans do? Do we continue keeping our cards face up, as the British and French did, as a democracy must do? For democracy requires that each of us retain the right to know how our taxes are being spent, to look constantly over the shoulders of the President and Congress.

It was to control our taxes that we fought the War of Independence and established the United States of America.

How can we ourselves know where our money goes in an autocratic world without giving the game away to Hitler, Mussolini, Stalin, Japan? But if we, too, turn our cards face down, if we give up our control over the purse strings and accept taxation without representation, if, year after year in time of "peace," we let only one man know and play our cards, what is there left of our freedom and Federal Union? What are we going to do about this basic budget question if we let autocracy rule the world overseas?

FREEDOM FOR SPIES OR FOR THE PRESS?

And how are we going to learn of the surprises which dictatorship will be preparing over there against us? Even before World War II began, it was not so easy for us American foreign correspondents to learn and report what was going on in the countries that already then purged men with firing squads and beheaded women for talking indiscreetly. All the overseas world will be like that, only worse, if we let the British fall.

We shall no longer be able to depend upon newspaper correspondents to guard us against surprises. We shall have to build up a spy system of our own, a more secret and effective spy system than any democracy yet has had. But then, how shall we protect our democratic rights from the dangers inherent in equipping the head of the government with spying powers . . . interminably?

Will he not need to use these powers also here at home, to spy out enemy agents and fifth columnists? It is a great mistake to assume that these are necessarily aliens. Von Steuben, the German, was loyal to America while Benedict Arnold, an American general, turned traitor. How are we to protect ourselves from the Arnolds now—without saddling ourselves with a Gestapo? Not much freedom of speech or freedom of the press can remain when—year after year—"Fifth Columnist!" is the easy answer to every dissenter. We can no longer govern ourselves when no one can say or write what is really going on in our country without valuably informing enemies who give us no information.

Faith and trust in one another lie at the bottom of the democratic system—but gone will be the easygoing mutual confidence of our present way of life when we face nothing but autocracy overseas. It will be replaced then by a pervasive atmosphere of mistrust and suspicion. How long can democracy survive in such germ-laden air?

The Prestige of Success

And then there is the prestige of success. All through our history democracy has enjoyed this prestige. Since the Declaration of thirteen remote colonies burst upon an absolutist world in 1776, democracy has gone from one phenomenal success to another. By 1918—in less than one hundred and fifty years—it had definitely gained control of the whole world and destroyed every autocratic dynasty save the Japanese. We are used to winning, used to seeing the British muddle through. We are so used to this that even when we talk of the possibility of Britain losing, most of us cannot really imagine it.

Yet the chilling fact is that the principle of autocracy, which democracy seemed to have knocked out in 1918, has shown an amazing vitality and power. Hardly twenty years after that defeat it again rules the continent of Europe, having overcome democracy there in less than a year of war. And the policy of hemisphere defense is intended to meet a still greater triumph of autocracy—the invasion and conquest of Britain, and of all Asia and Africa.

In that event the majesty of success will no longer hedge in democracy—it will then be working for the other side. It will be working inside America for the fanatics and power-hungry demagogues in our midst who fancy themselves as dictators. It will be serving the most unscrupulous of these rabble rousers. It will be serving him while democrats are apologizing or recriminating, while many Americans are crying for "strong government," and while many forces are working, as stealthily and continuously as malignant microbes, to centralize total power in the United States in one man's hands. This invasion of our Federal Union will be going on increasingly, no matter who is President or how much he promises and sincerely desires to decentralize—if we abandon the Old World to autocracy.

Woodrow Wilson was right, dead right, when he warned us that the world must be made safe for democracy. Our Federal Union principles cannot survive in an autocratic world. And our oath of loyalty binds each of us to defend the principles of Federal Union "against all enemies, foreign and domestic."

What shall it profit us if, to defend no land outside America, we betray our oath and let our basic principles be invaded and destroyed?

Chapter 12

The United States Must Keep on Uniting States

From a small spark kindled in America, a flame has arisen
not to be extinguished.—*Thomas Paine,* Rights of Man.

Puny "Patriots" Who Would Halt America

We have seen that, even though by a miracle we keep out
of this war, and even while we keep our territory from being
invaded, we are making a mockery of our oath of loyalty if
we allow autocracy to gain control of the Old World. By this
policy we are not supporting and defending the Constitution;
we are destroying from within its principles of Federal Union,
destroying the balance between central and local government
on which our rights as men depend, speeding a process of concentrating in one man's hands all our rights—our union rights,
state rights and individual rights.

We are perverting the whole spirit of America by this course.
For, in refusing to carry on our Federal Union principles by
uniting with other democracies, we are placing the independence of the state above the independence of the citizen. We are
unnecessarily sacrificing our own freedom to the freedom of
the state. When we do that, we replace our old motto, *the state
is made for man,* with the exact opposite, *man is made for the
state.* No policy, whether of peace or war, that destroys the
heart and soul of our Federal Constitution, as does the old
European policy of nationalism that now masquerades as
"Americanism," can be considered loyal to the American oath.

If we are to save our Constitution we must support and defend most of all its principles of individual freedom through
Federal Union. If we are to be loyal to our oath as Americans
we must practice Federal Union. Our principles are dynamic
and expansionist; we must go on with them, not stop in our
tracks or turn around.

We have already stopped dangerously long. Before our time Americans were always extending Federal Union to new states and new foreigners, extending its individual rights in an always greater degree to more territory and more people. We are the first of our line to adopt the opposite policy—to adopt a narrow, restrictive, thus-far-and-no-farther policy, half-defeatist, half-chauvinist, entirely un-American.

Before our generation took control, Americans had never let more than thirteen years pass without adding another star to Old Glory. It is now twenty-nine years since the admission of a new state to the Union. It is twenty-one years since the adoption of the Woman Suffrage Amendment—the last among the great extensions of the rights of man made by the American Union. And meanwhile, with great areas of the country thinly settled and Alaska almost empty, we have practically stopped one of the most deeply American of our policies, one that was included in the Declaration of Independence,* one by which our fathers extended the Union to tens of millions of foreigners —immigration.

Of course, American history has always known these puny "patriots," these false Americans, who, having profited themselves from America's free principles, have sought to keep these for themselves alone, have opposed extending their own rights to others, and have attempted to hold down the American Union. There were plenty of them in 1776 who fought against the Declaration of Independence and its revolutionary doctrines that "all men are created equal" and that governments are made by them for their own liberty, safety and happiness.

They were present, too, at the Federal Convention. There they sought to prevent the establishment of the first Federal Union, tried to keep this country tangled up with thirteen armies, tariffs and currencies, demanded superior rights for the founder states over states admitted later, urged discrimination against those not born American, attempted to restrict high office in the Union to men of property.

---

* The indictments of George III in the Declaration of Independence included this one: "He has endeavored to prevent the population of these states; for that purpose obstructing the laws for naturalization of foreigners, refusing to pass others to encourage their migration hither."

These puny "patriots" were aghast at the Louisiana Purchase. They nearly prevented the admission of Texas to the Union. They croaked misfortune when the Union went on to California, and they denounced Seward's folly in purchasing Alaska. They did their best to prevent white male suffrage, and then black suffrage, and then woman suffrage.

And always they railed against immigration. They were using the present arguments against it when the country had only 60,000,000, only 30,000,000, only 3,000,000 inhabitants. They even formed a party against the foreign-born in 1856 when they numbered less than 4,000,000 and were mostly Irish and German. Then as now they paraded their spurious patriotism in such mottoes as "Americans must rule America." But, in those days, the great majority of Americans dismissed them as the "Know-Nothing Party." As Jefferson and Franklin had routed them before, Lincoln routed them then:

As a nation we began by declaring that all men are created equal. We now practically read it, all men are created equal except negroes. When the Know-nothings get control, it will read, all men are created equal except negroes and foreigners and Catholics. When it comes to this, I shall prefer emigrating to some country where they make no pretense of loving liberty—to Russia, for instance, where despotism can be taken pure, and without the base alloy of hypocrisy.

These anemic Americans have stayed with us as the poor always do. But they never got the upper hand until our generation, after starting out with Woodrow Wilson to carry overseas the grand American tradition, abandoned it in 1920.

How Union Decentralizes Power

It may seem a paradox, but the best way to keep our own freedom is to give it more and more to other men. The best way to extend our rights and save them from centralization is to extend our Federal Union principles to rule an always greater area till they rule the whole world.

At first glance it would appear that extending Federal Union means centralizing more than ever, since it does create a new central government where none existed. Many shy at any inter-state organization as a "super-state" because it necessarily must be greater in size than any member. They jump to the conclusion that this means greater governmental power over them.

If centralization, in the sense of tyranny, is in ratio to territory, then we should break up the United States into forty-eight sovereign states to get more freedom. Yet if we did this you and I would enjoy much less freedom, and so would our cities and counties. Each of the forty-eight state governments would then be much more centralized than any of them is now.

Imagine that the American people sought to end centralization by thus "decentralizing" into forty-eight completely independent states. You would no longer be free to seek employment anywhere in the forty-eight states, or to hire the best men you could find among 130,000,000. You would be confined to your own little state. It would have an immigration act to protect you against forty-seven new varieties of aliens—and make you just as alien to each of them. You could no longer send a letter 3,000 miles for three cents; you would have to pay foreign postage beyond your state frontier.

You could then no longer freely buy in the cheapest market in the United States of America what you need to buy, and sell in its dearest market what you have to sell. You would be free to do this only inside your own state. For then forty-eight tariff walls would be protecting forty-eight standards of living—and forty-eight national labor organizations, forty-eight national associations of manufacturers, and forty-eight national farm federations.

Could you have an automobile then for less than $1,200 (the peacetime price of the cheapest American car in "protected" Switzerland)? Mass production could never lower car prices in a home market confined to Michigan, any more than the movies could flourish on California alone. Of course, each of the forty-eight states then could boast its own highly protected automobile factory and its own Hollywood. The former would be working most of the time to defend the state against its neighbors; the latter would be devoting itself to propaganda.

The steelmakers of Pennsylvania and Illinois would then be protected against each other (at your expense), just as wheatgrowers of Dakota are now protected against the wheatgrowers of Canada. How could you then afford such conveniences as the George Washington Bridge and the Golden Gate Bridge—especially with war always hovering near?

And it would not be so easy for you to own your home when your state's shingles were protected against Washington shingles just as Washingtonians now insist on protecting their shingles against those of British Columbia. The telephone, the radio, the railways and the highways—what a mess you would be in with them if you had forty-eight states here instead of one great Union!

Your taxes then would include a bill for putting a magic Maginot line around your state, as well as perpetual, universal military service. Airplanes would then be a curse to the inhabitants of each of the forty-eight states. No matter what your state, you would be in constant danger of war from the other states, and from overseas. Forty-eight national school systems would then be poisoning the minds of the children, having them swear allegiance to only one of the stars in our present flag, drilling into them as patriotism that they should risk their lives, not to bring their state into Federal Union with the others, but to keep it independent, to "preserve its national sovereignty."

Under such "decentralization" the towns and counties, and the individual citizens in each of the forty-eight states would have lost, even in "peacetime," most of the rights they now enjoy. The degree of power centralized in the man now called the state governor would then far exceed that which President Roosevelt has.

NATIONALISM BROUGHT DICTATORSHIP

By imagining where we would be if our forty-eight states no longer practiced Federal Union, we can each understand better how much we owe to Federal Union our present decentralization—as well as our peace, prosperity and freedom. We can then understand better how much we gained when our forefathers, by taking from thirteen quarreling state governments five of their rights and transferring these to the Union, gave us all a common citizenship, a common defense and foreign policy, a common free-trade market, a common currency and a common postal and communications system.

We can then also appreciate better how much our local and

individual rights have since been preserved by extending the area of this Federal Union more and more. Imagine that Spain had remained in Florida and France had kept control of the Mississippi. Or imagine a free United States of America north of the Ohio with a slave empire south of it. Or Russia still encamped in Alaska with its long finger reaching toward Seattle. Or France owning now not simply Martinique but the Panama Canal.

Just as lack of loyalty to our Federal Union oath at any of these steps would have injured our local and individual rights, so our generation's failure to keep on extending Federal Union is the root of the centralization that we suffer now. Our misguided efforts to keep the United States of America in a sovereign watertight compartment are bringing on us bureaucracy and concentrated power as fatally as similar wrongheadedness in any of the forty-eight states would bring them on within it.

Had we Americans served our Constitution with half the zeal that we have served these twenty years the nationalistic gods of Europe, how much happier the picture now would be. To an appalling degree our taxes and governmental agencies have resulted from, and are devoted to, our attempt to maintain absolutely separate from other democracies our sovereignty as regards the five fields of Federal Union: defense and foreign policy, trade, currency, communications and citizenship. To an even more appalling degree they thwart instead of serve the purposes for which we established our government and empowered it to tax us, namely, the maintenance of our own freedom and sovereignty as individual men and women.

If, instead of nationalism, we had extended Federal Union to the advanced European democracies there would have been no depression and unemployment such as we have suffered, no Japanese adventure in China, no rise of Hitler, and this war could not have started. Now we are exposed to even greater dangers by our hesitation to govern by Federal Union our relations even with democracies that speak our language.

To defend America we must be true to American principles and apply them where they most need applying now. To save our Federal Union and its freedom we must now carry them across the seas to the British as boldly as our fathers carried them across this continent.

Chapter 13

Democracy and War

> It seems imperative that we meet physical force with physical force. . . . Can we have physical force and not use it for oppression? . . . If we can keep a guard upon ourselves which will prevent a lust for power, or a debauch of greed, then we will have done something even greater than what we envisioned on the Armistice Day of 1918.—*Eleanor Roosevelt,* My Day, *Nov. 11, 1940.*

There is a widespread and natural fear that we may lose our democracy at home if we go to war. This fear is based on fact. War is the opposite of the democratic process. War *is* dangerous to democracy. It is so dangerous that even the threat of it must be removed—as President Wilson understood so well— before the world can be safe for democracy.

The more peace preserves the possibility of war, the more dangerous it is to democracy because democracy is inherently incapable of preparing in peacetime for war as effectively as autocracy can. Therefore, as we have seen in France, democracy is much more exposed than autocracy to catastrophe in the first onslaught of war.

If it survives this onslaught, war still exposes it—while it lasts—to the evils of autocracy from within. War makes for centralization of power in the hands of one man, and for dictatorship which, even in the original Roman sense, is distasteful to democrats. It involves loss of individual rights and it tends to make for the worst emotionalism, for intolerance, blind hatred and hysteria. Consider its effects on us when we entered World War I. To show how deeply I appreciate these dangers of war, let me quote from two letters I wrote while in the A. E. F. in France in March, 1918:

I can not understand the wave of intolerance, with its determination to suppress the least expression of non-conformity, which seems to have spread over the country which has always acclaimed its freedom of speech and press. I suppose the country is only going through the same psychological stage as that experienced by England and France at the beginning of the war. May they pass through it quickly. When they have, they will realize that in a country fighting to make the world safe for democracy, intolerance, hate and forced conformity are among the enemies of the cause. . . .

A good many of our newspapers understand the President's policy about as well as the German Junker class. . . . They have not caught that spirit of democracy which is abroad in the world. . . . The American who wants to know what our aims and those of our Allies are is denounced as a pacifist. The newspapers are keen to know more of our military operations over here—they don't give a continental damn, apparently, as to where we are going but they want to know how fast we're getting there.

The subsequent American reaction to this wartime spirit was a very healthy one, and it is a very healthy sign that we are today so much on guard against recurrence. But many have now gone to the other extreme, and that is unhealthy. They forget that the existence of this widespread fear that war will destroy democracy is in itself unanswerable proof (a) that the last war ended by strengthening instead of destroying our democracy, and (b) that our democracy is much more prepared for these dangers of war now than it was then. They find "war to end war" is nonsense, but forget that the more dangerous a fire is, the more we need to fight it with fire—with the controlled fire of the fire engine or the counterfire in the forest—if we are to end it.

Then there are those who distinguish between war for democracy overseas and at home. They hold that we are bound to save our democracy if we wait till we have to fight for it over here, but fear we are bound to lose our democracy if we fight for it over there. This is a most unhealthy fear. For the nearer a war is to a democracy's own soil, the graver the danger to it. The nearer war comes, the more we must centralize power, the more we lose our individual rights, the more we are subject to hatred, intolerance, hysteria. Those who are opposed to war for these reasons should oppose most of all war on our own soil, and oppose war overseas the least. If our democracy can survive invasion, it can surely survive war for democracy anywhere on earth or on the high seas.

It survived war overseas in 1917-18 much more easily than the Civil War. Consider how the latter harms our democracy to this day, how (to mention but one evil) the South is still saddled with a one-party system. Consider how quickly and completely our democracy threw off wartime restrictions and returned to "normalcy" after the victory in 1918. That was the first great war in our history which did not put a general in the White House. Instead, it added woman suffrage to the achievements of democracy here and in Britain—where it gave the Labor party power for the first time, while in France it brought to the fore Aristide Briand and his plan for a European Federation.

It would seem reasonable to suppose that our democracy could survive the dangers of war overseas now more easily than before. There would seem to be much less danger of hatred, intolerance and hysteria. The British, French and Germans all went to war this time much more soberly than before, and so would we. If any generation in a democracy can be trusted to keep their heads and save their rights, in wartime and afterward, it is surely the one that has already been through the fire and has gained twenty years in maturity.

Renouncing some rights temporarily in wartime for the deliberate purpose of safeguarding them the better is vastly different from letting them be sapped away interminably, through unwillingness to fight for them, or lack of vision, courage and common sense. The former, not the latter, method won those rights. What people has ever lost its democracy by successfully fighting for the rights of man?

To pretend that we shall lose freedom and Federal Union

here if we form a Federal Union with Britain and have to fight for freedom there, is to talk perilous nonsense or sinister foreign propaganda. It amounts to arguing that the readier we are to risk our lives to save an ideal, the surer we are to lose it even though we succeed in removing the danger to it. If this makes sense, then we can save our lives from disease by forbidding men to risk their lives trying to cure disease.

True, when men risk their lives—to do no matter what, no matter where—some lose their lives while so engaged instead of losing them while, say, crossing traffic. For these and their loved ones, the sacrifice is not temporary; it is permanent. But the nobler the thing they risked their all to do, the more certain it is that their death will help achieve their goal.

Man has always been distinguished from other animals by a magnificent readiness to risk his life freely for intangibles, for his friends, even for the good of strangers. The progress of our species can be traced mainly to the fact that it has never lacked men who would risk their lives for what they believed in, whether in religion, politics, science or what not. That is the price some men have paid for all our great discoveries, inventions, and liberties. It will be an evil day for mankind if it should ever lack this kind of man.

I am no more afraid that America will lose its individual freedom and Federal Union by fighting to preserve them and end this war disease of the body politic, than I fear for the public health because men are risking their health to preserve other lives from influenza. If we fight clearly for freedom through Federal Union, we can be sure that when we win we shall remove all temporary restrictions on our rights and return to normal freedom—just as an influenza nurse removes the restrictions on her nose and mouth as soon as she leaves the danger zone.

Even should we lose, in fighting an invader here at home, I believe it would be relatively easy to rouse Americans to revolt against alien rule and restore our freedom and Federal Union. But how shall we restore them once we ourselves have destroyed them, stupidly or cravenly surrendering them bit by bit to some home-grown autocrat until we have lost them all—simply because we would not help save the liberties of others by uniting with them to root out the danger?

Peace cannot preserve a democracy ruled by cowardly, selfish, shortsighted fools and weaklings. War cannot destroy a democracy ruled by men and women strong in courage, generosity, vision, common sense and character; they can destroy war.

Chapter 14

The Constitutionality of Union Now

> It is said that power is wanting to institute such a govern-
> ment. . . . When the salvation of the Republic was at stake, it
> would be treason to our trust, not to propose what we found
> necessary . . . There are certainly seasons of a peculiar nature
> where the ordinary cautions must be dispensed with; and this is
> certainly one of them.—*Edmund Randolph in the U. S. Consti-
> tutional Convention.*

THE FORGOTTEN POWERS OF THE PEOPLE

How can the Union be formed quickly under the U. S. Constitution? Would not even a provisional Union take too long,
require a new constitutional amendment? Not necessarily. The
amendment we need has already been passed—it was the Tenth
Amendment. It reads:

The powers not delegated to the United States by the Constitution or prohibited by it to the States, are reserved to the States
respectively, or to the people.

In establishing the Constitution the people took from the
states certain rights and powers they had delegated to their
legislatures and governors. They re-delegated these powers to
other representatives whom they elected to Congress and the
Presidency. They prohibited the states individually from forming any "Confederation" or Union with foreign countries. But
they did not forbid the United States as a whole to do as its
component members had already done—unite with other democracies in a larger Federal Union. Instead they encouraged
this by making "a more perfect Union" their first aim.

It may be argued that they gave the power to make this
Union to the President and the Senate when they gave them

the right to make treaties and stipulated that such treaties should rank with the Constitution as the "supreme law." It can also be argued that the provisional Union could be formed under the vast executive and war powers the Constitution gives. But suppose these powers are held insufficient, and decisive importance is attached to the fact that the Constitution does not explicitly delegate to the United States Government the power to form a Federal Union with other peoples. Then the power to form such a Union falls among those unspecified powers which were forbidden to the states and not granted to the United States Government, and were carefully reserved to the people in the Tenth Amendment.

The importance that the people attached to this reservation of unspecified powers is indicated by the fact that they also safeguarded such rights in the Ninth Amendment. It reads:

The enumeration in the Constitution of certain rights, shall not be construed to deny or disparage others retained by the people.

Both the Ninth and Tenth Amendments put into the Constitution basic principles already embodied in the Declaration of Independence.

No machinery, it is true, is provided for the people to exercise these unspecified powers. So far as I know, we the people have never exercised these powers since the adoption of the Constitution. To conclude, however, that we have thereby lost our powers under the Tenth Amendment would be worse than nonsense. It would go against the spirit of both the Constitution and the Declaration.

The Tenth Amendment can be likened to a great waterfall in the public domain which has not yet been harnessed, but which can be harnessed whenever its owners, the people, see fit. Measured by the development of relatively minor grants of power in the Constitution, such as the inter-state commerce clause, the sweeping powers reserved to the people in the Tenth Amendment have gigantic possibilities. Our representatives in Washington, D. C., and in the state capitals have developed enormously the powers delegated to them. The powers which we the people reserved to ourselves remain untapped.

How can we tap these powers? Only by another amendment to the Constitution? If so, there was little point in adopting the Tenth Amendment, for it added nothing to the sweeping power the Constitution already gave the people to amend it.

It is reasonable to believe that something different was intended in the Tenth Amendment. It was meant, for one example, to allow the people, when as gravely endangered as we are now, to save themselves and the whole spirit and substance of the Constitution by swift radical action—by swifter radical action than the machinery of the Constitution allows in more normal times. The American people came into being through revolutionary action. This was very fresh in their minds when they adopted the Tenth Amendment.

There is no doubt that they wanted both to keep their right of revolutionary action, and yet to act always constitutionally. The problem was how to reconcile the two, how to make revolution safer by domesticating it, keeping even revolution within the Constitution, and preventing the Constitution itself from inducing revolution by proving too rigid in time of exceptional emergency. This is one of the most serious problems facing any written Constitution, and the Tenth Amendment solves it.

CAN THE CONSTITUTION BE UNCONSTITUTIONAL?

This problem was much in the minds of men when this amendment was proposed. The adoption of the Constitution itself was then under attack as being itself unconstitutional, in flagrant violation of the existing Articles of Confederation. Washington was denounced as "twice a traitor" for having "betrayed" the Articles as well as George III. The Thirteenth of these Articles explicitly provided that they could not even be altered except by consent of "the legislature of every state." Yet the Constitution was not even submitted to any of them. Why? In his introduction to the Sesquicentennial edition of *The Federalist*, Professor Edward Mead Earle explains:

It would have been a counsel of perfection to consign the new Constitution to the tender mercies of the legislatures of each and all the thirteen States. Experience clearly indicated that ratification then would have had the same chance as the Scriptural camel passing through the eye of a needle. It was therefore determined to recommend to Congress that the new Constitution be submitted to conventions in the several States especially elected to pass upon it and that, furthermore, the new government should go into effect when it should be ratified by nine of the thirteen States (to be binding, however, only upon the States actually ratifying).

This was an act of revolution, a *coup d'etat*. But assuming that the nation under the Confederation was in a state of virtual paralysis, it was also an act of great political courage and perspicacity. Hamilton vigorously defended it [in *The Federalist* No. 22] on the ground that ratification by the people would give the new Constitution greater moral power and prestige. And Madison, in a long and ingenious argument [in *The Federalist* Nos. 40 and 42], both denied that the Convention had exceeded its powers and asserted that, even if it had, it would have been justified in the welfare of the nation.

This issue had already caused much debate in the Federal Convention. On July 23, Madison noted this significant argument of George Mason:

Col. Mason considered a reference of the plan to the authority of the people as one of the most important and essential of the Resolutions. The Legislatures have no power to ratify it. They are the mere creatures of the State Constitutions, and can not be greater than their creators. And he knew of no power in any of the Constitutions, he knew *there was no power in some of them, that could be competent to this object*. Whither then must we resort? *To the people with whom all power remains that has not been given up in the Constitutions derived from them.* It was of great moment he observed that *this doctrine should be cherished as the basis of free Government.* (My italics.)

Madison then supported this view, saying that he

. . . considered the difference between a system founded on the Legislatures only, and one founded on the people, to be the true difference between a *league* or *treaty*, and a *Constitution*. The former in point of *moral obligation* might be as inviolable as the latter. In point of *political operation*, there were two important distinctions in favor of the latter. 1. A law violating a treaty ratified by a pre-existing law, might be respected by the Judges as a law, though an unwise or perfidious one. A law violating a constitution established by the people themselves, would be considered by the Judges as null & void. 2. The doctrine laid down by the law of Nations in the case of treaties is that a breach of any one article by any of the parties, frees the other parties from their engagements. In the case of a union of people under one Constitution, the nature of the pact has always been understood to exclude such an interpretation. (His italics.)

The Federalist, as Prof. Earle says, "has been cited as a source of constitutional law by the Supreme Court of the United States." And on this same problem, Madison wrote in *The Federalist* (No. 40):

They [the framers of the Constitution] must have reflected, that in all great changes of established governments, forms ought to give way to substance; that a rigid adherence in such cases to the former, would render nominal and nugatory the transcendent and precious right of the people to "abolish or alter their governments as to them shall seem most likely to effect their safety and happiness,"* since it is impossible for the people spontaneously and universally to move in concert towards their object; and it is therefore essential that such changes be instituted by some *informal and unauthorized* propositions, made by some patriotic and respectable citizen or number of citizens.

They must have recollected that it was by this irregular and assumed privilege of proposing to the people plans for their safety and happiness, that the States were first united against the danger with which they were threatened by their ancient government; that committees and congresses were formed for concentrating their efforts and defending their rights; and that *conventions were elected* in *the several States* for establishing the constitutions under which they are now governed; nor could it have been forgotten that no little ill-timed scruples, no zeal for adhering to ordinary forms, were anywhere seen, except in those who wished to indulge, under these masks, their secret enmity to the substance contended for.

They must have borne in mind, that as the plan to be framed and proposed was to be submitted *to the people themselves*, the disap-

---

* Madison would have made his point still stronger had he not garbled his citation from the Declaration of Independence. It reads: "it is the Right of the People to alter or abolish it, and to institute new Government, laying its foundations on such principles and organizing its powers in such form as to them shall seem most likely to effect their safety and happiness."

probation of this supreme authority would destroy it forever; its approbation blot out antecedent errors and irregularities. (His italics.)

Is it any wonder that it was Madison himself who, a little later, piloted the Tenth Amendment through Congress? Thanks to him and it, the American revolutionary right to establish a Federal Union more swiftly in time of grave danger than ordinary procedure permits is now also a constitutional right reserved to the people.

No Amendment Needed for Union Now

How can this power be exercised except by constitutional amendment, or special convention, or direct vote? By a method even less informal than those by which, as Madison pointed out, the United States began, and to which we can always return. By the President and Congress initiating the procedure. When war faces them with the choice of combining with the British either in an alliance or in a Federal Union, and they decide in favor of Federal Union, they are simply returning some of their powers to the people for the people to re-delegate. True, they must first arrange with the representatives of other democracies for all of them to shift these same powers to a common Union government. It would be impossible for the peoples to negotiate this directly, but they can agree on this question through their existing representatives.

So long as the agreement requires these powers to be exercised in the new government by representatives chosen expressly for this purpose by the people, and in accordance with the principle of a free and equal vote for every citizen, then there is no real re-delegation of power by anyone except the people themselves. Nor is there any loss of power by the people; the relation of each citizen to the representative he chooses to exercise these powers for him in the new government remains precisely the same as in the old government.

Because of the exigencies of war it would seem wisest to have the representatives of the people in the new government named by the President and Congress temporarily till they could be elected directly by the people. This might be a period of three months or so. No doubt those who had been appointed would have the best chance of being elected later by the people. But the fact that they were confirmed in their position by the people, who had full power to throw any or all of them out, would greatly strengthen their position and would be in accord with the spirit of the Tenth Amendment.

Moreover, because of the exigencies of war, the new Union would be only a provisional Union; a Constitution Assembly would work out more leisurely a permanent Constitution. Its ratification by the people would remove the last doubt as to the constitutionality of the whole procedure.

The dangers facing the thirteen states justified them, Madison held, in violating by revolutionary right the Articles of Confederation in order to establish the present United States Constitution. Today we face worse dangers, the allied might of the three most powerful aggressor governments on earth—the gravest dangers our people have faced since Jamestown, President Roosevelt has said. Surely such dangers justify the American people in using now the constitutional powers they reserved in the Tenth Amendment to establish provisionally another Federal Union.

Chapter 15

Some Questions and Answers

The Government we mean to erect is intended to last for ages.
—James Madison in the U. S. Constitutional Convention.

Can it be supposed that this vast country including the western
territory will 150 years hence remain one nation?—*Nathaniel
Gorham in the U. S. Constitutional Convention.*

I foresee the difficulty . . . of drawing a representation from
so extensive a continent to one place. What can be the induce-
ments for gentlemen to come 600 miles to a national legislature?
The expense would at least amount to £100,000.—*Alexander
Hamilton in the U. S. Constitutional Convention.*

WOULD THE BRITISH ACCEPT?

Q. *Would forming this Union mean our joining the British
Empire?*

A. Of course not, no more than Virginia joined New England when they combined to form the United States. Our thirteen states didn't join each other then; they joined the American Union. Similarly we and the British would be joining The
Union of the Free. We wouldn't be ruled by their King any
more than we are now, and they would have no more voice in
electing our President than they have now. Nor would they be
subject to our laws.

We and they, of course, would all be equally subject to the
laws of the Union, in the few fields where it governed, but each
of us would have the same vote in making those laws—or electing representatives to make them—that each of them would
have. Since there are many more of us than there are of them,
we would have more voice—in that sense—than they in The
Union.

For this reason, and because they would be endorsing the
basic principles of the Declaration of Independence the same

as we do, and accepting our Federal Union system instead of
our accepting their British Commonwealth of Nations system
as the basis of our world government, you could argue with
more reason that they were joining us than that we were joining the British Empire. But, as I said, they would not be joining
the United States of America. The fact is we would all be joining together to form something new, The Union, which would
resemble the United States without being the United States.

Q. *But would the British, Canadians and others agree to a
Union that was so American as this?*

A. The Canadians have already adopted our Federal system,
and so have the Australians and South Africans. The British
didn't object to that; they encouraged it. Why should they object to using this same system themselves, then? They have
already offered to form a Federal Union with the French, which
shows they are ready to adopt our system.

And, after all, we use a system of representative government,
jury trial and common law that we got from them, don't we?
So why should they balk at a good thing simply because it was
invented here? They didn't refuse to use airplanes because
they were invented in America any more than we refused to
use steam engines because the British invented them. So why
should national pride keep people from adopting the best political inventions, simply because they didn't happen to invent
them?

The best way to find out whether the British would accept
Federal Union with us is send them an invitation. If they refuse
to do with us what they offered to do with the French, then the
responsibility of destroying, without a trial, the hope that Union
gives for peace and freedom would be theirs alone. Surely they
would not refuse.

Q. *They might fear that, since our population is greater, they
would be the tail to our kite, that they would be degraded.*

A. The delegates of the smaller states raised the same objection in our Constitutional Convention, and James Wilson,
who represented one of the largest states, Pennsylvania, answered by asking: "Will the Citizen of Delaware be degraded
by becoming a Citizen of the U. S.?" Who would now say that

tiny Delaware is the tail to Pennsylvania's kite because they are both in the same Union? But if they were separate, sovereign nations, each with its own army, then Delaware would really be the tail to the Pennsylvania kite, just as Esthonia is to Russia.

Q. *But wouldn't the British and Canadians and others fear that they would be outvoted by us in the Union Congress, since there would be more American members than all theirs put together, on a population basis?*

A. No doubt some of them will object on this ground, but the objection is easy to answer. If this isn't a fair basis, then Ontario should give Alberta an equal voice with it in the Canadian Parliament, and England should give an equal voice to Scotland.

As a matter of fact, we borrowed from the English the idea of representation on a population basis when we drafted our Federal Constitution. There was a very sharp fight in the Convention on this question of putting representation in the Union government on a population basis, for the small states were afraid they would then be dominated by the larger ones. Benjamin Franklin then helped save the day by pointing to the example of the United Kingdom. He said (Madison noted):

I do not at present clearly see what advantage the greater States could propose to themselves by swallowing the smaller, and therefore do not apprehend they would attempt it. I recollect that in the beginning of this Century, when the Union was proposed of the two Kingdoms, England & Scotland, the Scotch Patriots were full of fears, that unless they had an equal number of representatives in Parliament, they should be ruined by the superiority of the English. They finally agreed however that the different proportions of importance in the Union of the two Nations should be attended to, whereby they were to have only forty members in the House of Commons, and only sixteen in the House of Lords; A very great inferiority of numbers! And yet to this day I do not recollect that any thing has been done in the Parliament of Great Britain to the prejudice of Scotland; and whoever looks over the lists of public officers, Civil & military of that nation will find I believe that the North Britons enjoy at least their full proportion of emolument.

The American contribution to this problem was to safeguard the position of the small states much more than England did with Scotland; this was done by giving each state two Senators, while putting representation in the House on a population basis. Since experience proves that no small state has suffered under the Federal Union system, there is no cause now for the British to fear we would "swallow" them.

Q. *It's true that our small states do not feel in an inferior position. Yet you would think there might be some danger to them in this inequality. Why isn't there any, in fact?*

A. Because there is no real inequality between the people of the large and small states in a Federal Union. In the division of powers between the Union and the state governments, all the state governments, large and small, get exactly the same powers. Pennsylvania has no more rights than Delaware, and the whole Union guarantees any small state from encroachment by its larger neighbor. Moreover, as regards the powers given the Union government, the citizen of the small state is at no disadvantage; he has the same voice as the voter in the large state in exercising these powers because the Union representatives are apportioned according to the number of citizens. And so in The Union a Canadian would gain no greater power by moving to the United States, and the American who moved to Canada would lose no power.

PARTY LINES IN THE UNION

Q. *Wouldn't the party system also help to remove the fear of one state dominating another?*

A. Of course, it would be a great help. Once power is based on the citizen, as in a Federal Union, the party system can operate, whereas it cannot work in a league or alliance, where each state has only one vote, which is cast by the party governing it. Once The Union was formed, the divisions in The Union government would be along party lines, and no longer between British and Americans. British and American conservatives would be voting together against British and American liberals. The lines of capital and labor would divide British and Americans as they now divide New Yorkers and Pennsylvanians. The

Americans, Canadians and Australians who came to the Union Congress from the wheat belt in their countries would vote together where wheat was concerned, just as the representatives from the Dakotas, Nebraska, Kansas and other wheat states now make common cause in Washington.

No doubt one of the first party divisions in The Union would be between those now working in each democracy for the establishment of The Union and those opposing it—between the Federal Unionists and the isolationists or nationalists. Curiously enough, establishment of The Union would serve to bring together in one party the extreme British and the extreme American nationalists who now criticize each other so—just as the creation of the American Union brought the isolationists of that time together to defend state's rights.

Q. *You frequently refer to our early history, but, after all, it was much simpler to unite then than now.*

A. Of course, the parallel is faulty; all historical parallels are. But it is the best we have, and no one yet has gone wrong who followed it to the extent of trying out the Federal system. And what is the alternative to seeking guidance from our own experience? It is to rely on pure guesswork, logic, speculation. Is that safer, less open to error? As for its being harder now to form a Union, was it really simpler, easier, to invent Federal Union, as they did then, and get people to try it out for the first time on themselves, than to apply these same principles after one hundred and fifty years of successful experience with them?

Q. *But this Union would be so much larger.*

A. The vast size of the proposed American Union was one of the chief arguments against the Constitution when it was established, though the United States then extended only to the Mississippi. Oliver Ellsworth of Connecticut argued in the Federal Convention that "each of these states (Massachusetts and Virginia) is too large for a republican system." Even Hamilton, bold as he was, kept recurring to this difficulty, and went so far as to tell the Convention, "I have grave doubts whether a more energetic government can pervade this wide and extensive country."

The fact is that democracy was never tried, before or since, on so vast a scale as when the Constitution was established. Before then democracy had worked only in small areas. Thereafter, the advent of steam and of still faster means of communication lessened the difficulties of big-scale democracy. If we measure size in minutes rather than miles—and the former is the measure that counts in this problem—The Union of the Free would be much easier to form and govern than the American Union in 1789. Eight years after its formation Washington still felt the need of pleading, in his Farewell Address, that Union on so great a scale be given at least a fair trial. (See the citation in the Introduction to this book.)

Yet only a few years later, in 1803, Jefferson got the American people to go still further and double the size of the country by purchasing Louisiana. They were bold men then, able to see and secure our future needs when most of America hadn't yet reached the horse-and-buggy stage, when men nowhere dreamed of railroads—let alone airplanes and wireless—when the argument against a big Federal Union was a really stout argument. If we are afraid of size and cannot look ahead in our electrical age as boldly and as far as they did then, we are not fit to govern even what we have inherited, we are already too big for ourselves.

Q. *Where do you get all these quotations from the U. S. Constitutional Convention that salt this book?*

A. Straight from Uncle Sam. From the autobiography he published under the title: *United States—Formation of the Union.* You can get it from the U. S. Government Printing Office for $2.85, though it's 1,115 pages long. It is a mine of wisdom on the biggest problem of our day, inter-state constitution making. Had it only been among the best-sellers, and required reading for Presidents, Senators, Representatives and diplomats, we would be basking in The Union now, and would have avoided both the depression and this war.

Formation of the Union should be in every school and college and editorial and really big business office; in every organization dealing with foreign policy and in every minister's study —not only here but in every democracy. A well-thumbed copy of this document is the sure identification mark of a trust-worthy Member of Congress or Parliament.

You can be fairly certain that no American "patriot" who opposes Union now has had the patriotism to study this book. It gives all the official information available on the debates in the Federal Convention in which the United States was con-stituted. *Formation of the Union* contains not only all of Madi-son's voluminous notes, but also those of Yates, Hamilton, Pat-erson and others.

Isn't the Economic Problem More Pressing?

Q. *Don't you think other questions, economics, for example, are more pressing?*

A. Not just now. This problem of constituting Federal Union in the world is *the* problem of today, just as geography was *the* problem in 1492. Economics has been having its inning lately, science almost monopolized the scene in Darwin's day, but now it is again the turn of political science as in 1787. We have been neglecting political science shamefully, and we need to dig into it quickly and deeply if we are to do soundly the big task of the day.

Once it is done, then we can give first place again to the other fields clamoring for attention—economic and social questions, better distribution of wealth and work and play, science, engi-neering, good living, the arts, and the things of the mind, heart and spirit. Of course, they are all affected by The Union; it will help in many ways to ease their problems, but each of these fields needs mankind's special attention when we can get round to it.

The first essential, however, is to get agreement on the ma-chinery for peacefully getting and keeping agreement among the peoples of the world; this is a political problem, a constitutional problem. Until we provide the political machinery we need, our other problems can neither gain solution or even gain sufficient attention—they are bound to be crowded out by wars, revolu-tions and counter-revolutions.

Q. *Would you recommend a few other foundation books for one who desires to get a thorough grasp of Federal Union?*

A. Gladly. And, as I say, the man or woman who really goes into the subject now, soaks himself in it, will be wise—as wise as those who soaked themselves in maps in 1492. There are any number of books in this field; I would like to mention them all but that might help defeat their purpose, for the longer the list, the more forbidding it is bound to seem. And so I shall simply give a few books which I have found most valuable. Though they are substantial, they are not hard to read or dip into:

The Federalist. The Sesquicentennial and also the Everyman's editions are excellent, cheap, and equipped with very helpful introductions, the former by Prof. Edward M. Earle, the latter by W. J. Ashley.

Lincoln's Speeches. (The Everyman's edition covers the ground fairly well.)

Paine's *Rights of Man.* (Also obtainable in the Everyman's edition.)

De Tocqueville's *Democracy in America.* Perhaps the most penetrating study of America yet written, and sadly neglected, even in France.

Lord Acton's *History of Freedom* and his other books, especially the all too few chapters on America that are scattered through them, every one of which is highly stimulating. So, too, is his prophetic chapter on nationalism in his *History of Freedom.* (Macmillan.)

Fiske's *Critical Period of American History, 1783-1789.* (Houghton Mifflin and Co., Boston.) To be read with *Formation of the Union* and *The Federalist.* Had this fascinating volume appeared in 1918 instead of 1888, it might have saved us the mistake we made in organizing the world then as a league instead of a union.

Commager's *Documents of American History.* (F. S. Crofts and Co., New York.) Handy, yet comprehensive. Includes the early colonial charters which have been so neglected, here and abroad, but are of high importance in the development of democracy and federal union everywhere.

Lionel Curtis' *World Order.* (Oxford University Press.) A monumental recent work by the statesman who for a generation has been the outstanding British champion of federal union.

A world history of the development of the idea of world federal union from prehistoric times down to today. It brings out— among its details—how England's union with Scotland made possible the British Empire—and how England's failure to form a similar union with Ireland directly helped bring on the American War of Independence.

Whitman's *Leaves of Grass*. Whitman is not only America's greatest poet, but *the* poet of democracy. He gives an insight into democracy, federal union and America that is essential to an understanding of them, and can be had nowhere else. This is especially true of his poem, *By Blue Ontario's Shore*.

Q. *How would you define "democracy"?*

A. Many of the critics of democracy still talk as if people today meant by democracy either something perfect, or simply a government by the people—majority rule without the checks on it which we Americans associate with "republic." I think most of us mean by democracy what I mean by it—"the way to individual freedom formed by men organizing themselves on the principle of the equality of man," government not merely by the people but, as Lincoln stressed, of the people and *for* the people, (the people being composed of individuals all given equal weight in principle).

"By democracy I mean government of the totality by the majority for the sake equally of each minority of one, particularly as regards securing him such rights as freedom of speech, press and association. (If merely these three rights are really secured to all individuals they have the key, I believe, to all the other rights in all the other fields, political, juridicial, economic, etc., that form part of individual freedom.)" *Union Now*, p. 5.

Q. *Would you call the British a democracy? What about —?*

A. You don't realize how your type of mind, when born in Britain, will be asking, "Would you call the United States a democracy? What about —?" Perhaps you haven't read the address of the English workingmen to President Lincoln urging emancipation? You will find extracts from it at the beginning of Part II of this book. Perhaps your British twin hasn't read Lincoln's Message to Congress on emancipation? There are extracts from it in the Introduction of this book. And these are only two from many proofs of British and American democracy.

The fact is that both we and they are far from perfection in democracy, but we have both been moving toward it steadily for generations. If you can't call us both democracies, then there are none. If we are more democratic in some ways, they are more democratic in others. Personally, I love the deep, friendly, equalitarian quality in the American democrat and the quick, staunch fairness in the British democrat. And I hate the smugness, hypocrisy and race prejudice too often found in both. I feel sure that we and they will greatly gain in democracy by uniting together, and with other peoples.

Is Union Just Another Imperialism?

Q. *But is this Union not just another kind of imperialism?*

A. No, despite all that the Nazis, the Stalinists and their stooges say, the Union policy is the opposite of imperialism. Imperialism means extending the power of a nation or ruler over others against their will. Unionism means:

(a) reducing considerably the power of every national government in The Union and restricting the operations of each strictly to its own territory;

(b) giving each citizen of every nation admitted to statehood an equal voice in the Union government—just as much voice in it as he has in his national or town government—and thus extending considerably the individual power of all the citizens;

(c) aiming at no conquest of additional territory, but seeking deliberately to prepare for full nationhood in it as soon as practicable every part of the nonself-governing territory it inherits from its member nations; and

(d) leaving the door wide open for all outside peoples to become full member nations but—far from imposing membership on them—granting it only to those that voluntarily ask it and that offer the guarantees of freedom that all the member democracies do, each application being judged on its merits.

Q. *Wouldn't The Union's great and growing preponderance of power cause outside powers to fear it, and combine against it?*

A. The outside combination already exists. But this is the result of *disunion*, not Union of the democracies. The Union can hope to break up the Triangular Alliance by promising to admit to membership either the Italian or the German people —whichever first restores its democratic rights. Once the Axis loses one wheel it is broken.

Consider how strong The Union will be (1) through the hope all outsiders will have of being admitted to it, too, (2) through Italy or Germany shifting its power from the Axis to The Union and (3) through victory. Just *who* is going to combine with *whom* against so strong a Union? If there should be two powers who seek to combine against it, there will be twenty who will seek to join The Union. The historical fact is that democracies need not fear alliances against them when they are preponderantly powerful, but they do need to fear that a serious decline in this preponderance will lead to combinations against them.

Q. *Historical fact? For example?*

A. One. There were no alliances or combinations made against the British when they were at the peak of their power in the nineteenth century. The alliance of Germany, Austria and Italy before World War I was made against Russia, not Britain.

Two. No alliances were made against the British and French in the period of their greatest power after World War I. Germany and Italy formed the Axis only after the democracies had weakened themselves by their chronic differences. Even then Mussolini stayed neutral till France was practically knocked out and the whole British expeditionary force had been driven from the Continent, after losing all its equipment.

Three. The United States has always had the preponderance of power in the western hemisphere, but the other nations of the New World have never formed an alliance against it, though many of them had not only language to unite them but fear of the "colossus of the North."

Q. *But now an Old World alliance has been made against the U. S.*

A. Yes, and it proves the point. For this, the only alliance ever made against us, was made . . . when? After our legendary prosperity had crashed. After we had adopted for motto, "The Yanks Are Not Coming, No Matter What Happens Overseas." After we had merely sighed while heroic Finland fought. After we had shuddered and turned away when our historic friend, France, fell, appealing piteously to us. After we had lethargically watched our British bodyguard gallantly suffer wracking bombardment. After we had done our worst as a people to convince the enemies of freedom that we had fallen into second childhood—weak in our arms, slow in building them up, shrill and insistent in criticizing others, blurred in vision, set in our ways, soft and flabby in our moral muscles, petty in our purposes, paltry in our patriotism, mean in spirit, wobbly in will.

Q. *Still, if we had such preponderance of power as The Union brings, might we not become arrogant and domineering toward outsiders, forget our principles, misuse our power?*

A. History teaches us to fear this more when democracies are weak than when they are strong. As Britain grew in power she grew less grasping and more humane and tolerant, both at home and abroad. Will even the most embittered Irishman argue that the last hundred years of British policy toward Ireland have been far worse than her policy in previous centuries? How does it happen that the ideas of Gandhi could make such headway in India after Britain had won World War I, and not in the time of Napoleon? Contrast the way the British used to lead in the slave traffic with the way they have led the fight against it during the last hundred years.

As for us Americans, our imperialistic war with Mexico happened a century ago, when we had one-fourth our present population and much less power. In 1812, we invaded Canada; in 1940 we volunteered to defend Canada. Do you suppose our Indians would have preferred the treatment they got from us when we were weaker, to the treatment the Filipinos have had? When were Americans willing to die to abolish slavery—when there were 3,000,000 free Americans, or when there were ten times more?

The United States was never more powerful than it was after

it won World War I—and it was in this period that it began the policy of the "good neighbor" toward Latin America. But let Britain fail and the United States be thrown in imminent danger of invasion from East, West and South, let us be weakened to that point—and will our Latin-American policy, particularly as regards the Caribbean, be more good neighborly in character, or more imperialistic? It is a weak United States, not an all-powerful Union of the Free, that the Latin Americans need fear.

WHAT ABOUT LATIN AMERICA?

Q. *What about Latin America, the Monroe Doctrine, hemisphere defense?*

A. The formation of The Union would enormously strengthen the Monroe Doctrine, for it would put behind it the combined power of the United States and the British Commonwealth. It would do the same for hemisphere defense. That policy was born to meet the contingency of the British fleet being lost to democracy. But were that fleet lost before our two-ocean navy is ready in 1946, full hemisphere defense would hardly be possible, for we would not have the ships it would require.

And if we form The Union, we remove the chief danger of losing the British fleet, and have a better hemisphere defense than we could possibly build in ten years. Once we put the British and American fleets under the Union government, The Union controls the seas, and there is no longer any danger to the Latin-American states of Nazi penetration, whether military, economic, or otherwise.

Under the present policy we have to do all the defending of the western hemisphere, supply practically all the soldiers, sailors, fliers, and dollars, for the Latin-American republics are debtor nations, almost unarmed for modern war. Only by Union do we get any real help all along the line in this big job, for the British are the only ones in position to help effectively and immediately.

Q. *What would be the status of the Latin-American republics?*

A. The same as now as regards the United States and the rest of the world. If they desired to enter The Union they would apply for admission. Personally, I would hope that at least some of them would apply and be admitted as soon as The Union was established.

It would be for the Union Congress to decide whether those with a very high rate of illiteracy and instability of government should wait till they gave better guarantees of democracy, or whether their standards could be raised more rapidly by admission into The Union. And it would be for each Latin-American republic to decide for itself if it wanted to join The Union. We should lean backwards not to appear to be trying to force any of them in.

A good many Americans seem to think that the Latin Americans would be so eager to enter The Union that they would be offended if they weren't included among the founders. But the fact is that it has always been possible for them to ask admission as states in the United States—a similar Union. Yet they have shown no inclination to do so, and no offense at not being urged by us to enter our Union.*

Nor was there anything to prevent the Spanish-speaking American colonies from joining together in a federal union as the English-speaking American colonies did. But they have never done so, or seriously tried to unite this way. Even the little republics of Central America cling each to their own absolute national sovereignty. And they have not worked together too well even on that basis in existing international organizations.

Latin-American genius so far, in short, has shown little natural inclination toward federal union, least of all on a big

---

* On the contrary, Latin Americans have taken offense at proposals to include them in the U. S. Thus, *The New York Times* reported Jan. 26, 1941, in a special dispatch from Havana:

"The Cuban Secretary of State, José Manuel Cortina, today issued a statement observing that a resolution to admit Cuba as a State of the Union introduced in the United States Congress by Senator William H. Smathers [Democrat, New Jersey] was contrary to President Roosevelt's foreign policy, to pan-Americanism and to the opinion and decision of all Cubans. He said he believed it would be forgotten within a few days since it had no basis, no foundation and no reason. . . .

"A group of youths late last night threw several bottles through the plate glass windows of the Woolworth store here. Police said the bottles contained notes that said 'Down with the American Senate. This reply to the American Senator.'"

scale and with English-speaking people. Until the Latin Americans have shown strong evidence that they have changed their minds in this respect, it should not be assumed that simply because we and the British want to unite they will want to unite with us at once—even before we definitely unite ourselves.

Moreover, we need to remember that we would be forming this Union in circumstances of grave danger. Is it right or wise that we, the most powerful American republic, should try in any way to get these weaker neighbors to involve themselves to this degree in our policy? If any of them volunteer spontaneously to go the limit with us—that is quite different. But meanwhile is it not for us, the stronger, to take the lead alone in so dangerous a time?

Q. *Shouldn't the European democracies that have governments in exile, such as Holland, Norway, Free France, be invited to join in founding the Union?*

A. That is a very delicate question. Personally, as *Union Now* should prove, I am very favorably inclined; and their inclusion would have the great advantage of helping prove that no English-speaking hegemony was sought in founding the Union. But would their inclusion, under the present circumstances, help get The Union formed faster? Or would the dangers and difficulties involved tend to make the American people hesitate longer before offering Union? If it will speed our action, let us do it by all means; but let us first make sure that their inclusion in this present preliminary stage will not cause dangerous delay.

In any event The Union should maintain the closest relations with all the exiled governments. And I would be strongly in favor of working out some arrangement whereby not only their leaders, but representative Swiss, Swedes, Finns, and others, including competent German and Italian exiles, could help the Convention that would be drafting the definitive Constitution of the Union.

WHAT OF CHINA? JAPAN?

Q. *What of China?*

A. I have the greatest respect for Chinese civilization, and for the courageous, persevering struggle of the builders of the modern Chinese Republic. It seems to me that we do not appreciate nearly enough the political achievements of ancient and modern China—to mention only the one thing with which we are now concerned.

We are inclined to compare China to this or that nation of the West, and think of it as the chaotic, happy hunting ground of a troop of war lords. But China is comparable in area and population to *all* western Europe, rather than to any one fragment of it. If we keep that in mind, we must concede that Europe rates still lower than China in chaos and war lords. And we shall then understand better the really remarkable political achievement of the Chinese in attaining so early and maintaining for so many centuries a much higher degree of political unity than Europe has known since the fall of Rome. It is no small achievement the Chinese accomplished in establishing a common language so soon over so huge an area of slow communications, and keeping it long after Latin had ceased to serve this purpose in the West.

By our western provincialism, we have failed to enrich political science with the study of how the Turks, the Persians, and above all the Chinese succeeded in holding huge empires together through centuries of the chariot age. Yet to do this they had to solve problems in political structure and functioning much too knotty for their contemporaries.

The Chinese have my admiration and sympathy, but I think their leaders will recognize that, for Federal Union to work successfully, a different type of political experience is needed. Federal Union requires in the masses of its citizens a much higher individual average in self-governing experience and tradition, and in economic and literacy standards than does any other political system. Once a sound core is strongly established, the Federal Union system, as the history of the United States has shown, is capable of being successfully extended to large masses of inexperienced citizens of all races and nationalities.

But I believe Chinese leaders would agree that there is such a thing as overloading the cart to the point where it cannot be started at all or breaks down, and that an attempt to include

China's masses in this Union at the start on the normal basis of membership would serve only to prevent any Union nucleus from being created. The first essential is to get that nucleus created before it is too late—and it is hard enough to overcome the prejudices and economic difficulties that are still preventing Union even in the English-speaking world.

Once we and the British have attained the wisdom and courage to unite ourselves, but not before, there will be hope, increasing hope, of successful solution—from the standpoint of all concerned—of such difficult problems as China presents. Meanwhile China would lose nothing by our Union and would gain enormously by it.

Q. *And Japan?*

A. What I said of China applies also to Japan, with changes in details that do not change the basic sense or spirit. To me the "awakening" of Japan, the amazing development of this people in the last ninety years, is another of the glories of our species.

This westernization of Japan, like the establishment of a republic in China and the feat of the Turks who turned defeat into the emancipation of women, the adoption of a western alphabet and the establishment of one of the few republics in the Old World that have proved sturdy—all this is, to me, proof of the magnificent, infinite possibilities scattered through all mankind . . . and of the stupidity of our prejudices. It is proof positive of the soundness, of the universal appeal and of the astonishing stimulating power of our basic American principle, "All men are created equal."

The pity of Japan is that it swallowed so much of the bad of the West along with the good. Japan's insular geographical position in Asia is strikingly similar to England's in Europe, and it is hardly surprising that it should adopt toward China the policy that England followed so long as regards Europe. But it is still a great pity to see a people begin fighting the Hundred Years' War hundreds of years too late—in the twentieth century when the development of machines and communications makes such a policy suicidal, while the improvement in political methods permits a much better solution.

INDIA? SOVIET RUSSIA?

Q. *What about India? And colonies?*

A. My attitude toward India is no less friendly, appreciative, equalitarian and practical than toward all the others. One of The Union's most urgent problems will be that presented by such dependencies as India which it will inherit from the member democracies along with their nonself-governing territory.

One can hardly conceive of a federal union in which a member state, instead of The Union itself, governs colonies. The Union's Constitution should make clear that its policy is to prepare all nonself-governing territory for full membership as rapidly as prudent experiment justifies. Such a policy should transform existing colonial psychology and greatly soften the problem.

As for India itself, however liberal one may be he must concede, if he is at all practical, that India's politically inexperienced masses cannot be included in this Union from the start on the same population basis as the member democracies. To try to start that way would not advance the interests of the Indians; it would merely prevent the formation of The Union, and hand the world over to autocracy and war.

On the other hand, the conservative must concede, if he is practical, that India must be given much more help toward raising the standards of its population than it has been getting, and more voice than it has had in its own affairs. It should also have some voice in the Union government, certainly as regards questions directly affecting India. Between the present status of India and the status of full membership in The Union there is wide room for compromise—for the kind of wise compromise that will allow steady progress from the former to the latter.

This problem is also discussed in Chapter X of *Union Now*. It may be added here that the framers of the first Federal Union had to wrestle with a problem even harder than India is for Union now. For they had to reckon with the existence of slavery in some of their member democracies.

This question threatened to prevent the formation of the American Union. Had it done so no one would have been better off, slaves, masters, or freemen. Compromise allowed the Constitution to be established, and that led to the freeing of the slaves . . . and to the opportunity we now have to take another great step forward by forming the nucleus of the United States of Man. All concerned in the present problem will profit if they allow this opportunity to be taken, even at the cost of compromise.

Q. *There remains Soviet Russia?*
A. It has nothing to gain from the triumph of the Triangular Alliance, and everything to lose—first of all, every one of its three maritime windows on the world: The Baltic, the Black Sea and Vladivostok. The Union could have no aggressive intentions toward Russia; it would have to play its cards very badly indeed to drive Moscow into joining the Triangular Alliance. And such a combination would have the profound weakness of any misalliance.

As for membership in The Union, there is no likelihood of that question being seriously raised so long as the present Russian government is in power, since the guarantee of free speech and a free press, which we would make The Union to secure, seems to be no inducement to it to seek admission. On the contrary, Stalin leaves no doubt that he fears his position would be destroyed if his opposition were as free as the opposition to President Roosevelt is.

Democrats cannot, however, quarrel with Soviet Russia or any other nation because of its economic collectivism, for democracy itself introduced the idea of collective machinery into politics. It is a profound mistake to identify democracy and Union necessarily or entirely with either capitalist or socialist society, with either the method of individual or collective enterprise. There is room for both these methods in democracy, room for different states in The Union to experiment as they please in this regard, so long as they make their experiments peacefully and keep them under the continuous control of free speech and a free press.

Democracy not only allows mankind to choose freely between capitalism and collectivism, but it includes marxist governments, parties and press as well as *laissez-faire* governments, parties and press, and plenty of gradations in between. Soviet Russia allows no such choice and no such freedom in its territory. But this difference has not prevented normal, peaceful diplomatic relations between Russia and the American Union; it should not prevent them between Russia and The Union of the Free.

This whole problem is discussed more fully in Chapter V of *Union Now*.

WHERE WOULD THE CAPITAL BE?

Q. *Where would the capital of the provisional Union be?*

A. On this side of the Atlantic, at a place to be determined by Congress. Some have suggested Ottawa, others have suggested some point in our Central States—Chicago, Detroit, Milwaukee, or some other Lake city, or in Indiana, Ohio or Kentucky near the population center, or in the Ozarks or Black Hills for climate and central geographical position. There are lots of cities, small and large, in the Central States and Canada that might compete for this great prize.

Q. *You mean that the center of isolationism might become the center of the world through this Union?*

A. Why not? The world may seem remote to some in the Mississippi Valley, but if you will look on the map you will see that this region would be fairly near the center of this Union that stretches from the British Isles to Australia.

Q. *In this superstate* ——

A. Do you call the United States a "superstate"? This Union would be no more of a superstate than is our American Union. If you are worried that this will be a superstate, you can find in *Union Now*—especially in Chapters VI, VII and X—the detailed reasons why a Federal Union does not form a superstate, while leagues, alliances and nationalism do.

Q. *How would the Union avoid the dangers of sanctions and yet provide collective security?*

A. Just as the United States of America does. If this book, particularly Chapter VII, hasn't made clear enough to you how and why a union solves this problem of sanctions, and why a league cannot solve it, you will find this subject discussed at length, and in the light of Geneva experience, in *Union Now*, Chapters IV, VI, VII, and Annexes 3 and 4.

What of the Economic Problems?

Q. What about the problems of tariffs, unemployment, debts, immigration?

A. I must repeat that the object here is not to cover again the ground covered in *Union Now* where this can be avoided. You will find these and other economic questions discussed in *Union Now*, notably in Chapters VIII and IX and Annex 2. They show how groundless are the fears of Union entertained on these grounds and how the transitional difficulties can be worked out in a Union of fifteen democracies.

These fears are even more groundless, and the difficulties much less, in the present proposal whereby only the seven English-speaking democracies—the peoples with the highest standards of living—form the nucleus. Moreover, these problems were even harder to solve without Union before the war—and the war has made them much worse. It is piling up a fearful postwar reckoning for us all in the economic, financial and social fields—piling up problems that are bound then to bring depression, revolution, chaos and more war if we fail to begin solving them by Union now.

Q. But wouldn't Union harm our industries and farmers, and lower our standard of living?

A. It would do just the opposite for every member people, just as every Union has always done for every people that had the sense to unite this way with others. This was strongly brought out by *Fortune* in a long editorial on *Union Now* in the April, 1939, number. *Fortune* then called this plan

. . . the greatest political and economic opportunity in history, by comparison with which the opening of the North American continent was a modest beginning. . . .

Gigantic opportunities would be opened up. A rise in the standard of living of millions of consumers would result from the expansion of markets and the consequent lowering of prices for mass-produced goods. Even a relatively slight expansion in their known market would enable U. S. automobile manufacturers (to take only one example) to cut prices, and cars would thus become available to more persons, not only in other states of the union but also at what we call "home." The economic history of the U. S. demonstrates that this process is cumulative and that it would almost certainly result in lower automobile prices than even Mr. Ford has dreamed of. There would be an inevitable revival in shipping and in railroads, and hence in the capital-goods industries behind them. Industrial unemployment might, therefore, almost disappear. And at the same time the union's agricultural products would obtain preference in union markets, as against the products of nonmember states.

A genuine union of the democracies, then, opens up a vista of industrial growth to which the only enlightening parallel is the growth of the United States itself. At the time the American Union was formed the eighteenth-century libertarian economists were preaching free trade. And the abolition of tariffs within the borders of the U. S. provided for this doctrine the most spectacular practical demonstration that any economic theory has ever had. It may be true that free trade in the U. S. would not have caused such rapid expansion if there had not been protection from the outside world, on the one hand, and plenty of unexploited land and resources on the other. But the proposed union of the democracies could also protect itself from cheaper labor in the rest of the world. And the proposed union of the democracies would also have plenty of undeveloped land and resources, together with vast substandard "domestic" markets to be financed and built up. In short, while the abolition of tariffs would cripple certain highly protected enterprises, it can scarcely be doubted that it would produce a *net* economic expansion of unprecedented proportions.*

Think out for yourself all the ways you and your town gain from being part of the American Union and you can begin to imagine how much you and it would gain by being part of this larger Union.

WHAT WOULD I GAIN OR LOSE?

Q. *What are some of the things that I, as an average citizen, stand to gain by getting my country to join this Union?*

A. Much greater security from war. Safety from dictatorship and revolution, too. Far greater protection than any tariff, subsidy, pump priming or dole can give against the depression and unemployment that will follow the present war—and be

* Reprints of the entire editorial in *Fortune* are available at Federal Union, 10 East 40th St., New York City.

worse than anything we have yet known—if we come out of it with no better means of peacefully governing the relations between nations than we had in 1938.

New frontiers of all kinds. Wider opportunities for business and jobs and markets. Less armaments, less bureaucracy, less government, less taxation. Security against your life insurance and savings being wiped out by inflation.

More freedom of all kinds. Freedom to travel, work or seek work, to buy, sell and trade, to study, play and live anywhere in all that third of the world that would be Union territory from the start. More security and freedom than you dream of now. And always more and more of them for you as the Union grew.

Q. *But surely some citizens would lose something by the formation of The Union?*

A. Of course. But they would form a small minority. Most of them would be hurt only temporarily, and all of them would gain in many ways. Most of those who would be hurt are the very ones we have to help already. They are, for instance, the producers who produce so inefficiently that they can't sell their goods even to their neighbors and countrymen in competition with distant foreigners unless they get the government to put up a tariff to "protect" them. (Not to protect their neighbors, mind you; the tariff forces them to pay for this inefficiency by making prices higher than they need to be.)

These inefficient industries are efficient, however, in lobbying, and undoubtedly they will set up a howl against Union. But financial aid to tide them through the transition period should calm them, and it would cost less than they now cost us, and be temporary, not permanent as it is now.

There would be another group of losers—the politicians who couldn't meet the competition in The Union. Take a U. S. Senator or a British Member of Parliament. The power he now has over treaties, war, trade, currency and a few other fields of government would be transferred to the members of the Union Congress. He would lose importance—unless he was big enough to be elected to the greater Congress. Then he, too, would gain; he would be helping govern one-third of the world.

The really big men in the U. S. Senate and British Parliaments will champion the Union, once they understand it. Only the most petty politicians, those who know they are so small that they have no chance of being elected to the Union Congress, will oppose its creation to the bitter end. None of us can measure the Union idea, but it can give the measure of each of us.

How Can I Help Get the Union Made?

Q. *How can I help get the Union made?*

A. Spread the word to your neighbors, to your friends wherever they are, to strangers. By word of mouth, and by letters—to acquaintances, to newspapers and magazines, to prominent people of all kinds, and, of course, to Members of Congress or Parliament, especially your own representatives. The very thing that makes you hesitate to do this—the fact that you can express only one person's will for Union—is the thing that gives it weight. One sincere, thoughtful message outweighs 100 stereotyped "pressure" messages. The more individually, sincerely, you express your will, the more weight it will have.

You have some special gift—everyone has—and you can find the way to use that gift most effectively to advance The Union. Perhaps you have a gift for organizing people, or for public speaking, or for writing; or perhaps you are a specialist in trade, or production, finance, defense, communications, research, advertising, or something else. Whatever it is, you can make it help The Union.

Time was when men with a gift for writing, speaking, organizing went to prison or the stake so that others with such gifts might freely use them. To preserve and extend such rights today, you need only give The Union some of your gift. You need but give a bit of the thing you are richest in, and can best afford to give—and can get most happiness from giving.

And the more you yourself *practice* Union, by joining with other Unionists to obtain it, the sooner you will succeed. You will find at the end of this book a list of existing Federal Union organizations. If there isn't already such an organization in your community, you can help form one.

Don't wait for your neighbor. Start now, individually and

collectively. And don't stop till The Union is made, not only provisionally but definitely. It is ours together, or no one's. And it shall be ours—if we each remember what Winston Churchill told the Pilgrims, Jan. 9, 1941 :

"There we stand, all of us, upon the watch towers of history and have offered to us the glorious opportunity of making the supreme sacrifices and exertions needed by a cause which it may not be irreverent to call sublime."

Chapter 16

End, or Beginning?

I have fought a good fight, I have finished my course, I have kept the faith.—St. Paul, II Timothy, 4:7.

The present moment is favorable, and is probably the last that will offer.—Edmund Randolph in the U. S. Constitutional Convention.

The issue now depends largely on what you decide to do. Nobody can share that responsibility with you. . . . And before the Judgment Seat of God each must answer for his own actions. —Lord Lothian's last public words.

Through the world today sweep what seem to be revolutionary movements—Nazi, Fascist, Japanese and Communist. But these are only different names for the same old dogma of autocracy— that the people are made for the nation, state, king, collectivity. All four form really a tremendous counter-revolution against the democratic revolution—against the English Revolution, against the French Revolution, and above all against our own American Revolution and its great Declaration that the state is made for the people equally.

The times in which we live are so revolutionary that our American Revolution must quickly come to life. How do we measure up to the measure of 1776 and 1787?

While Hitler plans to decide now the future of mankind for a thousand years to come, what are we planning to do? What are you, yourself, planning, doing? Are you one of those who think the American Revolution can continue without men of revolutionary vision, courage, energy and spirit? Who count on the oceans to protect American freedom?

They have protected it as the shell protects the egg. But the shell can*not* protect the egg from rotting inside it. Only life can. And if there is life in the egg, it is evolving. In a gently moving miracle it is growing from a little germ into muscles, legs, beak, brain. Outwardly for days and weeks that living egg looks the same as a lifeless egg, so imperceptibly gentle is the change from germ to chick.

But then comes an hour—a very definite hour—when either the chick breaks quickly through the shell and steps out into the world, or suddenly that protecting shell turns into a deadly danger—smothers the chick inside it.

You know as well as I do that this is the way of life: First, a long period of invisible evolution, then, abruptly, in a fraction of that period, the convulsive drama of birth where life and death wage the war that never ends halfway. You know that there has been going on for generations behind our oceans an evolution comparable to the one within the egg. You know the time is bound to come when the American Union must break through its protecting oceans and step out into the world, or it must die.

Behind our oceans there has been evolving not simply another state, but a new form of government—Federal Union.

In one hundred and fifty years our Federal Union has evolved from a government of 3,000,000 free men of one nationality divided among thirteen squabbling, poverty-stricken "sovereign" states into a government of 130,000,000 free men of every nationality united in forty-eight states whose wealth has become legendary. It has grown from ocean to ocean, changed a wilderness into a civilization, brought the world inventions that have transformed it—made the problem of world government our urgent problem now.

Sooner or later our American Federal Union must break through its oceans and begin the era of the Federal Union of the World. When the appointed time comes for that, we must summon all our power and break through those oceans at once, to a newer, freer, more marvelous life than was dreamed of in the shell. If we fail to do so, then all that Americans have done before us for liberty and union is bound to perish.

You know that this is true. But is *now* the appointed hour?

No more awe-inspiring question could possibly face each of us. The equal freedom that Federal Union has given each American is balanced by an equal responsibility to know truly when the hour of birth has come for Federal Union of the World, and to throw then all our power against the shell.

How shall we know when the hour has come to carry Federal Union across the oceans as our fathers carried it across this continent?

Shall we say it is here when our stratoliners cross the Atlantic within a day, within half a day, or when? Shall we doubt the hour has come for the United States of the World to be born when the pains of birth reach the intensity of world war twice in twenty-five years?

We Federal Unionists answer: *Now* is the time, that hour men always long for till it strikes with all its peril and its pain. Now comes that awesome hour of birth when life contends with death for a better, freer life.

This ordeal from which we shrink—this is the hour for which the Pilgrims dreamed, for which Washington, Jefferson, Lincoln dreamed, for which myriads of men and women like you and me have dreamed and lived and died—the hour when the United States of the World is to be born. Now is that great hour of Union . . . *Now*.

We urge you to avoid the blunder of assuming that The Union of the Free is still remote because it has been remote so long already. And to avoid the blunder of believing that so great a thing as this Great Republic will ever be born easily, without intense human suffering, without grave danger, without the best men and women giving the best they have to carry it through the supreme moment—being ready to risk for it all that is dearest to them. And above all to avoid the blunder of supposing that we have plenty of time left to bring The Union safely through these convulsions of birth.

Whether it takes life twenty-one days as with the egg to reach the hour of birth, or hundreds of years as with World Federal Union, it takes death but one moment, one instant more than the fearfully brief time that God allows for birth, to end that whole evolution. When death wins at birth, then life, to renew the attempt, must begin, not where it left off, but far back, at the very beginning. It must conceive again the microscopic germ and bring it safely through all the weary brooding time that God requires before the test of birth can come again.

In all earnestness I would say that if we Americans do not, within a year or so, bring into the world this nucleus Commonwealth of Man, then you and I will not have another chance to do it. Nor will our children, nor their children. Today's opportunity will not come back again to men for who knows how many hundred years of painful struggling up through darkness.

These are again times that try men's souls, and we must each answer for our own. We must each satisfy our conscience either that there is something more worthy of us—and of our time, money and devotion—than is the cause of Union now, or that we are really doing all we can to create The Union now, that we are helping till it hurts. You have helped many things that no one will remember. Are you helping to create The Union now? You and I must risk our life knowingly or unknowingly every day. Is there something more worth living and dying for than Union now? It is for you to answer, and may your answer satisfy your conscience.

Is it Walt Whitman or conscience that calls us now on to Union?

> Come my tan-faced children . . .
> For we cannot tarry here,
> We must march, my darlings, we must bear the brunt of danger,
> We the youthful sinewy races, all the rest on us depend,
> Pioneers! O Pioneers!
>
> See my children, resolute children,
> By those swarms upon our rear we must never yield or falter,
> Ages back in ghostly millions frowning there behind us urging,
> Pioneers! O Pioneers!
>
> Has the night descended?
> Was the road of late so toilsome? Did we stop discouraged nodding on our way? . . .
> Swift! to the head of the army!—swift! spring to your places,
> Pioneers! O Pioneers!

Annexes

ACTS OF UNION

Having in all the preceding parts of this work endeavored to establish a system of principles as a basis on which Governments ought to be erected, I shall proceed in this to the ways and means of rendering them into practice. — Thomas Paine, Rights of Man.

Annex 1

Illustrative Declaration of Inter-Dependence and Union

> The opportunity confronting this country is infinitely grand
> if we view the crisis as opportunity and draw from it the
> courage, boldness and competence inherent in our people.
>
> For unless we allow all those to fall who together with us
> may carve out the structure of the coming era, and, giving up,
> resign to organized force or the threat of it, we shall emerge
> from the struggle with our feet on the pathway to a great
> destiny.—Dorothy Thompson, *On The Record*, New York
> *Herald Tribune*, Dec. 22, 1940.

The Declaration of Inter-Dependence and Union that follows
is meant to illustrate chiefly two points. One is to suggest the
kind of Declaration that the provisional Union's Inter-Continental Congress could sign and issue to the world soon after it
assembled, as the announcement of the creation of The Union.
The other aim is to show how well the principles and form and
phrases of the original Declaration of 1776 fit the present purpose, how the heart of that Declaration lives today as it did
then, how soundly and enduringly we shall be building if we
build closely on this great model.

To see how closely the text here follows Jefferson one need
but compare it with the original. The basic paragraphs—the
second and third—are copied textually from the original; the
first and forth are only slightly changed to make them apply to
union instead of separation. Where the original Declaration
then indicted and threw off the absolutism of George III, this
one indicts and abolishes the absolutism of the sovereign ruling
every people now—the dogma of *absolute* national sovereignty.
For, as the rise of democracy has replaced the principle of royal
sovereignty with that of national sovereignty, the old wolf our

205

fathers fought—*the divine right of kings*—has come sneaking back into our midst, clothed as *the divine right of nations.*

It should be stressed that the present Declaration, in denouncing this usurper and restoring the democratic principle of the equal sovereignty of Man through Federal Union, attacks only the *absolute, unlimited* claims of modern nationalism and maintains that essential of Federal Union—the principle of a *limited* national or state sovereignty.

This Declaration deliberately refrains from naming any person or people; it centers its fire on principle in the belief that bad principles rather than bad men are the true enemy of mankind.

To our British friends who may think the Declaration of 1776 too American a model for them to follow now with dignity, I would say this: Since you do believe in these universal democratic principles what quicker, better, more enduring way can there be to end the separation that began in 1776 than for us all to underwrite them now together?

It was not the British people's but a British ruler's rejection of these principles that caused the great separation. And while the American people were rebelling against his absolutism, the British were attacking it, too. No sooner had the Americans succeeded in rejecting his pretensions over here than the British practically ended his personal rule over there by restoring to Parliament its powers, and adding considerably to them. As Lionel Curtis, the British historian and statesman, has pointed out:

The successful revolt of the American colonists had started the great revolution which was destined to end the rule of dynasties and call into being the national states of the modern world.

In England public opinion was quick to recognize and deal with the cause which had brought the commonwealth to the verge of destruction. In 1782 Lord North resigned, and measures were passed which deprived the king of his power to control votes in the House of Commons. . . . On December 23, 1784, Chatham's son, William Pitt, became Prime Minister at the age of 24 . . .

He remained in office till the year 1801 . . . in the seventeen years the principle was finally established that in the British Com-

monwealth the ruler is the minister who for the time being can
command a majority in parliament or the electorate. . . .

As Professor Seeley has said, the prime minister is the real suc-
cessor of Plantagenet kings. Their descendants on the throne are
hereditary presidents of a commonwealth who hold for the sovereign
electorate their final power of attorney.*

I would also recall that the first voice boldly raised for independence in America was that of an Englishman, Thomas
Paine, who had arrived in America only a *few weeks* before his
pamphlet, *Common Sense,* changed a demand for redress of
grievances into a war for independence. On January 10, 1776,
that pamphlet, to quote a contemporary, "burst like Jove upon
a startled world." Six months later the Declaration of Independence was signed. And of it Paine himself wrote, in his
Rights of Man:

"The Independence of America, considered merely as a separation from England, would have been a matter of but little importance, had it not been accompanied by a Revolution in the
principles and practice of Governments. She made a stand, not
for herself only, but for the world."

Proposed Declaration of Inter-Dependence and Union

When in the course of human events it becomes necessary for one
free people to unite with other free peoples, and form a common
government embodying the fact that they do depend on each other
for their freedom, a decent respect to the opinions of mankind
requires that they should declare the causes which impel them to
the Union.

We hold these truths to be self-evident: That all men are created
equal; that they are endowed by their Creator with certain unalienable rights; that among these are life, liberty and the pursuit
of happiness; that to secure these rights, governments are instituted
among men, deriving their just powers from the consent of the
governed: that, whenever any form of government becomes destructive of these ends, it is the right of the people to alter or abolish
it, and to institute new government, laying its foundation on such
principles and organizing its powers in such form as to them shall
seem most likely to effect their safety and happiness.

Prudence, indeed, will dictate that governments long established

* Curtis, *World Order (Civitas Dei)*, Oxford University Press, 404-5.

should not be changed for light and transient causes and, accordingly, all experience hath shown that mankind are more disposed to suffer, while evils are sufferable, than to right themselves by abolishing the forms to which they are accustomed. But when a long train of abuses and usurpations, pursuing invariably the same object, evinces a design to reduce them under absolute despotism, it is their right, it is their duty, to throw off such government, and to provide new guards for their future security.

Such has been the patient sufferance of these free peoples, and such is now the necessity which constrains them to alter their system of governing their mutual relations and common interests, and consign the dogma of *absolute unlimited* national sovereignty on which it is based to the limbo where they long ago consigned the dogma of absolute royal sovereignty. The history of the dogma of absolute national sovereignty has become a history of repeated injuries, divisions, excesses and usurpations, all having in direct object the establishment of an absolute tyranny over the free peoples. To prove this, let facts be submitted to a candid world:

Absolute unlimited national sovereignty has prevented the adoption of agreements the most wholesome and necessary for the public good.

It has made the free blind to the truth that they do depend on each other for their freedom.

It has sown dissension among them, and thereby deprived them of the peace and freedom they won in 1918 at the cost of tremendous sacrifices made in common.

It has kept some people from joining and others from operating the League of Nations for which so many gave their lives, and so it has destroyed the first world government our species ever succeeded in establishing.

It has turned to ashes the hopes and promises of disarmament, and piled on us all in peacetime an increasingly heavy armaments burden while giving us each less and less security.

It has with equal falsity promised each people prosperity and given them instead inflation, depression, and unemployment, making money unstable, business bad, farming worse, jobs rare, and misery always mounting.

It has erected in every free people a multitude of new offices, with swarms of officers to harass the people and eat out their substance.

It has made government in every free people cost more and more while giving the citizen less and less security for his job, his freedom and his life.

It has in every people centralized more and more power, and made the citizen increasingly dependent on the national government for life, liberty and happiness.

It has delivered great peoples totally into the hands of bloodthirsty dictators who have carried the dogma of absolute national sovereignty to the most grotesque extremes, making everything depend on the accident of birth, deifying one nationality and race, pretending they are above all, wantonly vilifying and torturing persons whose only fault lay in their blood, and raging with the utmost frenzy against our principle that all men are created with an equal right to life, liberty and happiness and that government is made by them equally to secure these ends.

It has allowed these dictators to exceed all previous armaments, to excite insurrections among other peoples, to attack them without warning and in brazen violation of the most solemn and recent pledges, to wage the most treacherous, ruthless and destructive of wars against them, to plunder the seas, ravage the land, burn and raze cities, befoul the heavens and maim and slaughter myriads.

Its dictators are even now preparing to transport large armies to complete the work of death, desolation and tyranny already begun, with circumstances of cruelty and perfidy scarcely paralleled in the most barbarous ages, and totally unworthy the heads of civilized nations.

It has already delivered other free peoples one after another to dictatorship from without or from within, and will deliver to it each of us in turn if we continue to let it divide us and fail to abolish at once this misery-making dogma of *absolute unlimited* national sovereignty.

We, therefore, the representatives of The Union of the Free, in Inter-Continental Congress assembled, with malice toward none, with charity for all, with firmness in the right, as God gives us to see the right, do, in the name and by authority of the good people of our democracies, solemnly publish and declare:

that these united democracies are, and of right ought to be, a free and independent Federal Union;

that they have abolished the principle of absolute, unlimited national sovereignty in their relations with one another;

that they maintain equally in each member nation the principle of a *limited* national sovereignty—limited, as is the sovereignty of the Union government itself, to such fields as the people of

The Union shall, from their own full sovereignty, delegate to them by constitutional law;

that they intend to hold a Constitutional Convention at the earliest practicable time to establish definitely among them, as the first step toward a world government of, by and for the people, a Federal Union on the broad lines of the American, Canadian, Australian, South African and Swiss Federal Constitutions;

that the Constitution shall guarantee all persons living in The Union a Bill of Rights that shall include at least freedom of speech, press, religion and peaceful association; and shall provide that all rights not granted specifically to The Union or forbidden to the member democracies shall be reserved to the latter respectively, or to the people;

that the Constitution shall provide that non-members shall be admitted to full membership as states are admitted to the U. S. A.—on a basis of equality with the founders, and without being required to give more effective guarantees of democracy and disarmament than the founders themselves give—until The Union shall gradually become the government of all mankind and armament be reduced to a world police force;

that meanwhile the people for whom we speak have organized themselves as a Provisional Federal Union in which the citizens of each member democracy are equal citizens, with a voice in its government roughly proportionate to their numbers, and have established this Inter-Continental Congress as its government on this basis;

that it has full power to levy war, contract alliances, conclude peace, establish commerce and do all other acts and things which independent states may of right do;*

that The Union deeply desires to establish at once normal peaceful relations with all outside nations;

that it takes the opportunity which its creation provides to propose to those at war with any of its members that peace be restored on a basis of no annexations or occupation of foreign territory, no indemnities or reparations except the return of returnable property, and the settlement by arbitration, conciliation or judicial action of all disputes that led to this war, as well as all subsequent questions that cannot be settled by direct negotiation; and

* This passage is taken textually from the original Declaration.

that, to hasten the establishment of real peace, The Union pledges itself to admit to The Union, once normal conditions are restored, those European peoples who have long governed themselves democratically, or who prove their readiness and and desire for membership by the way in which they restore at home their own free rights as men.

And for the support of this declaration, with a firm reliance on the protection of Divine Providence, we mutually pledge to each other our lives, our fortunes and our sacred honor.*

* This passage is taken textually from the original Declaration.

Annex 2

Illustrative Constitution

In the end all depends upon whether men see themselves greatly or meanly. These are times which try men's souls, exposing most terribly what is low and false, revealing whatever is great and, therefore high-hearted. There is no peace of mind for the frightened and no happiness left except among the brave. For in such times as these men rise to the occasion—making their duty their opportunity—or they hesitate and quiver and quake and stumble into the ditch.—*Walter Lippmann,* Today and Tomorrow, *New York* Herald Tribune, *Jan. 9, 1941.*

THE DEFINITIVE UNION

The draft constitution that follows is taken from *Union Now,* with a few revisions to adapt it to seven founders in place of the fifteen in the original. It is meant, like the draft Declaration, to make the proposed Union clearer by illustrating how the democracies might unite.

For a commentary on this illustrative constitution and a discussion of the Union's constitutional problem, the reader is referred to Chapter X of *Union Now.*

Although it was stressed there that this draft was submitted, not as a hard and fast plan but by way of illustration, a minority has insisted on giving it the character it disclaimed and then criticizing it as being a final "blueprint." The final blueprint can be made, of course, only by the Union's Constitutional Convention and, as was pointed out in *Union Now,* it is bound to be far superior to any existing constitution, let alone the draft that any one person can produce. For the convention will have the advantage of including authorities from every successful democratic union, each of which has its own valuable contribution to make. It can thus draw in the best way on the rich store of experience in federal union that the world has accumulated in the one hundred and fifty years since the first such constitution was drafted in Philadelphia.

Before the final blueprint can be adopted, many preliminary ones must be made. I know of no better way to bring this subject down from the clouds of generalities, in which it has too long reposed, and begin to eliminate the loose, fuzzy, easy thinking —or rather, dreaming and fearing—that now prevents progress, than to try to reduce one's principles to concrete constitutional law.

Some British critics have complained that my illustrative draft follows the American Constitution in all important respects. Yet it incorporates what many foreigners consider the most distinctive and best feature in the British Constitution—the parliamentary system of responsive government.* It proposes for Chief of State a Board that, without following exactly the Swiss example, resembles it rather than the White House. My draft also adopts the Canadian idea of giving the very populous members a somewhat larger representation than the less populous ones in the Senate, without, however, giving them control in it or so large a voice as in the House, whereas in the U. S. every state is entitled to have the same number of Senators, two.†

With these important exceptions, it is true that my draft is taken almost entirely from the United States Constitution. A fraction is drawn from the practice that has developed under it (notably Art. II, sections 1, 2, 4, 5). The rest is drawn from its text, though sometimes the provisions of the United States Constitution have been rearranged with a view to greater clarity and condensation. Once or twice they have been made more explicit and somewhat expanded. The Preamble is the only serious example of this last. In the American Constitution the Preamble reads:

* *Union Now,* Chap. X, gives the reasons for this and the other departures from the American system.
† *Federation and World Order,* by Duncan & Elizabeth Wilson (Nelson and Sons), 1939, provides a handy digest of the Canadian and Australian constitutions focused, like its digest of the U. S. Constitution, on the problem of world federal union.

We the People of the United States, in order to form a more perfect Union, establish Justice, insure domestic Tranquility, provide for the common defence, promote the general Welfare, and secure the Blessings of Liberty to ourselves and our Posterity, do ordain and establish this Constitution for the United States of America.

No important element in the United States Constitution has been omitted, and *all important changes have been put in italics.* It can thus be seen at a glance how much of this draft is taken from the time-tested provisions of the United States Constitution. The remainder—with the exception of the Executive Board —has been equally time-tested in Britain and Canada.

I have relied so greatly on the American Constitution because it has behind it twice as long a record in successful achievement as any other in the field of Federal Union. Moreover, the Union it governs resembles more nearly than any other, by its vast territory, its large number of states and its great and mixed population, the problem we seek to solve. In such circumstances it seems to me that our safest, surest course, in taking the first step from the nation to the world state, is to stick closely at the start even to the details of the United States Constitution, while making it reasonably easy—as this draft does—to amend them should they prove unsatisfactory in this larger field. Certainly this would seem to be the best way to get the American people to make the Union offer in good time—and that is no small consideration.

The draft that follows was made to meet the problem of constituting a permanent rather than a provisional, emergency Federal Union. It might, of course, be adapted to the needs of the latter along the lines discussed in Part I.

Illustrative Constitution

We the people of The Union of the Free, in order to secure freedom equally to every man and woman now and to come, to lessen ignorance, poverty, and disease, to insure our defense, to promote justice and the general welfare, to provide government of ourselves, by ourselves, and for ourselves on the principle of the equality of men, and to bring peace on earth and union to mankind, do establish this as our Constitution.

PART I

THE RIGHTS OF MAN*

ARTICLE 1.—In the individual freedom this Constitution is made to secure we include:

1. Freedom of speech and of the press and of conscience.

2. Freedom to organize ourselves for any purpose except to change by violence this Constitution and the laws made under it; freedom to assemble peaceably and to ask redress of grievances and make proposals.

3. Freedom of our persons, dwellings, communications, papers and effects from unreasonable searches and seizures, and from warrants unless issued upon probable cause, supported by oath or affirmation, and particularly describing the place to be searched and the persons or things to be seized.

4. Freedom from ex post facto law and from bills of attainder.

5. Freedom from suspension of the writ of habeas corpus except when public safety may temporarily require it in case of rebellion or invasion.

6. Freedom from being held to answer for a capital or infamous crime except on indictment of a grand jury—save in the armed forces in time of war or public danger—and from being twice put in jeopardy of life or limb or liberty for the same offense, and from being deprived of life, liberty, or property without due process of law and from having property taken for public use without just compensation.

7. The right when accused of any crime to have a speedy public trial by an impartial jury of the country and district wherein the crime shall have been committed, as previously ascertained by law, and to be informed in good time of the nature and cause of the accusation, to be confronted with the witnesses against one, to have compulsory process for obtaining witnesses in one's favor, to be under no compulsion to be a witness against oneself, and to have the assistance of counsel for one's defense.

8. Freedom from excessive bail or excessive fines or cruel and unusual punishments.

* Some have criticized this Bill of Rights as omitting "economic rights." I have not gone beyond the U. S. Bill of Rights because I believe that if these rights are really secured we have then the key to all other rights. Moreover, I wish to avoid arousing controversy on points which, important though they are, are not essential to present purposes. Personally, I would favor adding to this bill the following sweeping "economic right":—"Freedom from both overwork and unemployment, as defined by law."

9. Freedom from slavery, and from involuntary servitude and forced labor except in legal punishment for crime.

10. The right to equality before the law and to the equal protection of the laws.

11. The preceding enumeration is not exhaustive nor shall it be construed to deny or disparage other rights which we retain.

PART II

THE GOVERNMENT OF THE UNION

ARTICLE II.—THE PEOPLE OF THE UNION.

1. All persons born or naturalized in the self-governing states of The Union are citizens of The Union and of the state wherein they reside. All citizens above the age of 21, except those in institutions for the feeble-minded or mentally deranged or in prison, are entitled to vote in all Union elections, and to hold any Union office for which their age qualifies them.

2. All other persons in the territory of The Union shall enjoy all rights of citizens except the right to vote in Union elections. The Union shall seek to extend this right to them at the earliest time practicable by helping prepare their country to enter The Union as a self-governing state.

3. *The self-governing states of The Union at its foundation are Australia, Canada, Eire, New Zealand, the Union of South Africa, the United Kingdom, and the United States of America.*

4. The nonself-governing territory of these states and of all states admitted later to The Union is transferred to The Union to govern while preparing it for self-government and admission to The Union.

5. *Before casting his or her first vote, and before taking civil or military office in The Union, each citizen of The Union shall take this oath in conditions to be prescribed by law:* "I do solemnly swear (or affirm) that I will preserve, protect and defend the Constitution of The Union of the Free against all enemies, foreign and domestic."*

6. Treason can be committed only by citizens against The Union and can consist only in levying war against it or in adhering to its enemies, aiding and comforting them. No one shall be convicted of treason unless on the testimony of two witnesses to the same overt act or on confession in open court.

* The American Union requires this oath only of naturalized citizens or of citizens entering the Union service or applying for a passport.

ARTICLE III.—RIGHTS OF THE UNION AND OF THE STATES.

1. The Union shall have the right to make and execute all laws
necessary and proper for the securing of the rights of man and of
The Union and of the states as set forth in this Constitution, and to
lay and collect income and other taxes, duties, imposts, and excises,
provided these be uniform throughout The Union, and to incur and
pay debt, provided that no money shall be drawn from the treasury
except by lawful appropriation and that an account of all receipts
and expenditures be published regularly.

2. The Union shall have the sole right to

a. grant citizenship in The Union and admit new states into The
Union;

b. treat with foreign governments, provide for The Union's defense, raise, maintain and control standing land, sea and air forces,
make war and peace, regulate captures, define and punish piracies
and felonies committed on the high seas, call forth the militia to execute the laws of The Union, suppress insurrections and repel inva-
sions, organize, arm, discipline, and govern such part of the militia
as The Union may employ, and punish treason;

c. regulate commerce among the member states and in The Union
territory and with foreign states;

d. coin and issue money, regulate the value thereof and of foreign
money, provide for the punishment of counterfeiting, fix the standard of weights and measures;

e. own and operate the postal service and own, operate or control
all other inter-state communication services;

f. grant authors and inventors exclusive right to their work for
limited periods;

g. provide uniform bankruptcy laws throughout The Union;

h. govern any district The Union may acquire for its seat of government or for forts, magazines, arsenals, dockyards, and other
needful Union plant.

3. The Union shall have no right to establish a Union religion,
grant hereditary or noble titles, levy any tax or duty on inter-state
commerce, subject vessels bound to or from one state to enter, clear,
or pay duties in another, grant preference by any regulation of
commerce or revenue to one state over another.

4. The rights not expressly given to The Union by the Constitution
nor forbidden by it to the states or the people are reserved by it to
the states respectively, or to the people.

5. The Union shall guarantee to every state in it a democratic
form of government and shall protect each of them and all the terri-

tory of The Union against invasion; and on application of the state legislature or executive The Union shall protect each state against domestic violence.

6. Each state has the right to maintain a militia and a police force, but may engage in war only if actually invaded or in such imminent danger as will admit of no delay.

7. Each state has the right to guarantee to the people in it greater rights than those enumerated in this Constitution.

8. No state has the right to

a. abridge the rights, privileges and immunities of citizens of The Union;

b. exercise, except temporarily by consent of The Union, any of the rights given by this Constitution to The Union alone;

c. raise any barriers to inter-state commerce or communications without the consent of The Union;

d. adopt any law impairing the obligation of contracts;

e. enter without the consent of The Union into any pact or agreement with another state or foreign power.

9. Full faith and credit shall be given in each state to the public acts, records and judicial proceedings of every other state in The Union.

10. The citizens of each state shall be entitled to all privileges and immunities of citizens in the several states.

11. A person charged in any state with crime who shall flee and be found in another state shall on demand of the executive authority of the state from which he fled be delivered up to it.

ARTICLE IV.—THE LEGISLATIVE POWER.

1. The legislative power of The Union is vested in the Congress, which shall consist of a House of Deputies and a Senate. Each shall choose its own officers, judge the elections, returns, and qualifications of its own members, determine its rules of procedure, have the power to punish its members for disorderly behavior, to compel their attendance, and to expel them by two-thirds majority; keep and publish a record of its proceedings, meet and vote in public except when two-thirds shall ask for a private meeting on a particular question, vote by roll call when one-fifth of the members ask this, form with a majority a quorum to do business though fewer may adjourn from day to day, act by majority except where otherwise stipulated in this Constitution.

2. The Congress shall meet at least once a year at a regular date it shall fix. During a session neither branch shall adjourn more than three days or to any other place without the other's consent.

3. Members of Congress shall not be questioned outside their branch of it for anything they said in it, nor shall they be arrested on any charge except treason, felony, or breach of the peace, during attendance at a session of Congress or while going to and from it.

4. No member of Congress shall hold other public office in The Union or in a state during his term, *except in The Union Cabinet.*

5. The Deputies shall be at least 25 years old, and shall be elected directly by the citizens every *third* year.

The number of Deputies from each state shall be determined according to population, a census being taken at least every ten years, and shall not exceed one for every district of *1,000,000* inhabitants or major fraction thereof, though each state shall have at least one.

6. Senators shall be at least 30 years old, shall have resided since at least 10 years in the State by which elected, and shall be elected at large from each state directly by the citizens every *eight* years, except that in the first election half the Senators of each state shall be elected for only four years. There shall be two Senators from each state *of less than 25,000,000 population, and two more for each additional 25,000,000 population or major fraction thereof.*

7. To begin with, the apportionment of Deputies and Senators shall be :*

Australia	7	2	U. of S. Africa	2	2
Canada	11	2	United Kingdom	47	4
Eire	3	2	United States	131	10
New Zealand	2	2			
			Totals	203	24

8. To become law a bill must pass the House and the Senate and be approved and signed by *a majority of the Board.*† If *a majority of the Board* shall return the bill with its reasons for not

* To give an idea of how the representation would look as new states were added, here is the representation of the other democracies who were included as founders in the original *Union Now* proposal and would be admitted as soon as they are free to enter:

Australia	7	2	Norway	3	2
Belgium	8	2	Sweden	6	2
Canada	11	2	Switzerland	4	2
Denmark	4	2	Union of South Africa...	2	2
Finland	4	2	United Kingdom	47	4
France	42	4	United States	131	10
Eire	3	2			
Netherlands	8	2	Totals	282	42
New Zealand	2	2			

† The executive, see Art. V. The United States Constitution gives to the President the powers this paragraph gives to the Board.

signing it, the bill shall become law only if passed again by House and Senate by two-thirds roll-call majority, and if a *member of the Board* shall ask to be heard by House or Senate during its debate thereon he shall be heard. A bill not returned by the Board within fifteen days (holidays and Sundays excepted) after presentation to it shall be law, as if signed, unless adjournment of Congress shall have prevented its return. This shall also apply to every order, resolution, or vote to which the concurrence of the House or Senate may be necessary, except on a question of adjournment, and to every expression of The Union's will, unless otherwise provided herein.

9. The Congress shall have the power to declare war, make peace, and exercise all the other rights of The Union unless otherwise provided herein.

10. The Congress shall have the right to admit new states into this Union; but no new state shall be formed or erected within the jurisdiction of any other state nor any state be formed by the junction of two or more states or parts of states without the consent of the state or states concerned.

ARTICLE V.—THE EXECUTIVE POWER.

1. *The executive power of The Union is vested in the Board. It shall be composed of five citizens at least 35 years old. Three shall be elected directly by the citizens of The Union and one by the House and one by the Senate. One shall be elected each year for a five-year term, except that in the first election the citizens shall elect three, and the House shall then elect one for two years and the Senate shall then elect one for four years, and the Board shall then by lot assign terms of one, three, and five years respectively to the three Members elected by the citizens.*

2. *A majority of the Board shall form a quorum, and it shall act by majority thereof unless otherwise provided herein.*

3. *The Board shall establish a system of rotation so that each Member may be President of it one year.*

4. The *Board** shall be commander-in-chief of all the armed forces of the Union, shall commission all officers of The Union and appoint ambassadors, ministers and consuls, may grant reprieves and pardons for offenses against The Union, shall have the power to make treaties by and with the advice and consent of the *Premier and Congress,*† and to appoint with the advice and consent of the

* President, in the United States Constitution.
† Senate, in the United States Constitution.

Senate the justices of the High Court and of all lower Union Courts, and to make any other appointments required of it by law.

The *Board** shall from time to time report to the people and Congress on the state of The Union, *its progress toward its objectives, and the effects and need of change,* and shall recommend to their consideration such policies and measures as it shall judge necessary and expedient; it may require the opinion of any one in the service of The Union on any subject relating to the duties of his office.

The *Board** may convene extraordinarily Congress, adjourn it when its two houses cannot agree on adjournment, *or dissolve it or either branch of it for the purpose of having it elected anew as shall be prescribed by law.*

The *Board** shall receive ambassadors and other public ministers.

5. *The Board shall delegate all executive power not expressly retained by it herein to a Premier, who shall exercise it with the help of a Cabinet of his choice until he loses the confidence of House or Senate, whereupon the Board shall delegate this power to another Premier.*

ARTICLE VI.—THE JUDICIAL POWER.

1. The judicial power of The Union is vested in a High Court, and in such lower courts as The Union may from time to time establish by law. All Union judges shall be appointed for life. The number of High Court judges shall be fixed by law, but shall not be less than *11*.

2. The judicial power extends to all cases in law and equity arising under this Constitution, the laws of The Union, and treaties made by it; to all cases affecting ambassadors, other public ministers, and consuls; to all cases of admiralty and maritime jurisdiction; to controversies between two or more states; between a state and citizens of another state; between citizens of different states, and between a state, or citizens thereof, and foreign states, or persons.

3. The High Court shall have original jurisdiction in all cases affecting ambassadors, other public ministers, and consuls, and those in which a state or a foreign state shall be party; in all the other cases before-mentioned it shall have appellate jurisdiction, both as to law and fact, under such regulations as shall be made by law.

* President, in the United States Constitution.

ARTICLE VII.—THE AMENDING POWER.

1. The power to amend this Constitution is vested in *the citizens of The Union acting by a majority of those voting on proposals made by two-thirds majority of the House and of the Senate with the approval of three-fifths of the Board, or by two-thirds majority of either House or Senate with the unanimous approval of the Board,* or by a special constituent assembly established by law, *or by petition signed by at least one-fourth the voters in one-half the states. No state, however, shall be deprived without its consent of its right to have its own language and its own form of democratic government.*

ARTICLE VIII.—GENERAL.

1. This Constitution, and the laws of The Union which shall be made in pursuance thereof; and all treaties which shall be made under the authority of The Union, shall be the supreme law of the land; and the judges in every state shall be bound thereby, anything in the Constitution or laws of any state to the contrary notwithstanding.

2. All persons in the service of The Union, and the legislative members and executive and judicial officers of each state, shall at the beginning of each term renew their oath to support this Constitution.

3. All Union elective offices, unless otherwise stipulated herein, shall be filled on the same day throughout The Union, to be fixed by law; the exact date when their terms shall begin and end shall also be fixed by law, as well as the manner for filling vacancies.

4. All persons in the service of The Union shall be paid from the Union treasury as shall be fixed by law, but the compensation of no judge shall be decreased during his term nor shall that of any elected officer of The Union be increased during the term for which he was elected.

5. Any one in the service of The Union, on impeachment for and conviction of treason, bribery, or other high crimes, shall be removed from office and may be disqualified from holding office again, and if convicted remains liable to indictment, trial, judgment, and punishment according to law.

The House shall have the sole power of impeachment and the Senate the sole power to try an impeachment, and it shall convict only by two-thirds majority of the Senators present sitting under oath or affirmation. The Chief Justice shall preside when a President *or Member of the Board* is tried.

6. No religious test shall be required as a qualification to any

office or public trust under The Union, nor shall there be any
official Union religion.

ARTICLE IX.—RATIFICATION.

1. The ratification of this Constitution by *the people of the United
States, and the United Kingdom or Canada* shall suffice to establish
it between them.

•   •   •   •   •

THE PROVISIONAL UNION*

The preceding text can also serve, with only minor alterations, as an illustrative emergency constitution for the Provisional Union. The alterations could be limited to the following:

1. Insertion of "provisional" before "Constitution" in the
Preamble, and wherever necessary to make this clear.

2. Replacement of Article IX by a text to this effect:

ARTICLE IX.—PERMANENT CONSTITUTION.

1. The Congress of the Provisional Union shall convoke, at the
earliest practicable time, a Federal Convention to draft a definitive
Constitution for The Union, which shall be submitted to each Member Democracy for appropriate adoption by the people thereof.

2. Provision shall be made in such Constitution for the admission
of new members to The Union on a basis of equality with the
founders so that it may grow ultimately into a universal Union of
Mankind. To help hasten the establishment of real peace, it shall
promise admission to The Union, once normal conditions are restored, to those European peoples who have long governed themselves democratically, or who prove their readiness and desire for
membership by the way in which they restore at home their own
free rights as men.

3. The definitive Constitution shall provide for the assumption of
all debts, obligations and undertakings theretofore assumed by the
Provisional Union, and it shall supersede the provisions establishing
this Provisional Union.

ARTICLE X.—DURATION OF THE PROVISIONAL UNION.

1. The Provisional Union shall continue as regards each Member
Democracy for the duration of the emergency created by the present

*I am greatly indebted to John Foster Dulles, the author of *War,
Peace and Change* (Harper & Brothers), for his legal advice on a
number of provisions in this section.

state of international anarchy and violence, or until the definitive Constitution, referred to in the preceding Article, shall have earlier superseded it as regards each Member Democracy, or until such Member Democracy shall have earlier rejected such definitive Constitution, in which event such Member Democracy may thereafter within _____ months withdraw from The Union or be excluded by it.

2. In the event of a Member Democracy withdrawing or being excluded, or the Provisional Union being disbanded, the former Member or Member Democracies shall continue liable for the debts and financial obligations of the Provisional Union theretofore incurred, in proportion to its or their self-governing population. In the event of any dispute, it shall be finally determined by the High Court.

3. The Provisional Union Constitution shall be deemed established on acceptance by the United States and the United Kingdom or Canada.

Two other insertions are proposed. One would be to add to Article III this new section:

12. It shall be discretionary with the Provisional Union whether to exercise, and to what extent to exercise, the powers conferred upon it; and it shall exercise such discretion with a view to allowing to each Member Democracy the maximum of independence which, in the judgment of The Union, is compatible with the achievement of the ends for which The Union is founded. But to the extent that The Union shall act in any of its lawful fields of power, its action shall be supreme and may not be frustrated by the action of any Member Democracy.

The other insertion would be to add this clause to Article IV, section 7 (composition and election of the first Congress):

In the first Congress of the Provisional Union, the Senators and Representatives of each Member Democracy shall be chosen by its Congress or Parliament from a list nominated by its Chief Executive to serve a preliminary term, not exceeding _____ months, until The Union can hold the direct popular elections required in other sections.

In Article V, section 1 (The Executive), the fourth sentence, providing for the first election of the Board members, should be amended to read:

One shall be elected each year for a five-year term, except that in the first election the Union House shall elect two, the Union Senate shall elect two, and the House and Senate sitting jointly shall elect the fifth member; and the five shall serve a preliminary term, not exceeding _____ months, until The Union can hold the first direct popular elections. At that time the citizens shall elect three Members of the Board, and the first popularly elected House shall elect one for two years, and the first popularly elected Senate shall elect one for four years, and the Board shall then by lot assign terms of one, three, and five years respectively to the three Members elected by the citizens.

The advantages of using the illustrative Constitution for the Provisional Union, with such alterations as have been suggested, include the following:

a. It would provide all the major machinery needed, thus allowing the Provisional government to concentrate as it should on winning the war and the peace, and avoid the delays, debates, and distractions that are bound to ensue if it has to organize any of its major machinery itself.

b. It would provide machinery which (with the exception of the Board) is time-tested and familiar, and would thus promote swift emergency action by insuring that it would proceed along lines to which the statesmen involved are already accustomed.

c. It would be more acceptable to many people since it would give them a clearer picture of what they were doing than would the alternative course, which would simply establish the provisional Congress and authorize it to set up whatever executive machinery it required.

d. Its two-house Congress allows the classic federal compromise to be made between the United States and the British Commonwealth, for the former would elect a majority of members of the House, and the latter would elect a majority of the Senators.

The alternatives discussed in Chapter 1 would involve further change in the Illustrative Constitution, mainly as regards Arti-

cles IV and V—the legislative and executive departments.
Provision for a single executive, or a double executive, or a
Board of Three, or some other solution, could easily be drafted
to replace the Board of Five, and be coupled with a two-house
or a one-house Congress. Similarly provision for the latter type
of Congress could be inserted in the Illustrative Constitution
and its Board of Five left intact.

The simplest alternative would be to replace Articles IV and
V with a single brief article, to this effect:

The powers vested in the Provisional Union shall be exercised
by and through a one-house Congress, in which the people of each
Member Democracy shall be entitled to have one representative,
plus one additional representative for every 5,000,000 self-governing inhabitants, or major fraction thereof, as follows:

Australia	2	Union of S. Africa	2
Canada	3	United Kingdom	11
Eire	2	United States	27
New Zealand	2		—
		Total	49

The representatives of the people of each Member Democracy
shall be chosen by its Congress or Parliament from a list nominated by its Chief Executive, to serve a preliminary term, not exceeding _____ months. Pending this time the Provisional Congress
shall arrange for its members to be elected by direct popular vote
for a term of _____ years. The Provisional Congress may provide
for exceptions to this in certain Member Democracies should wartime conditions make a popular election impracticable there.

The members of the Provisional Congress shall receive such
emoluments as the Congress may determine to be reasonable, the
same to be paid out of the Treasury of The Union.

No Member of this Congress shall hold any office in any Member Democracy.

The Congress shall fix its own rules of procedure and its time
and place of meeting, except that its capital shall be in North
America and its initial meeting shall be held at such time and place
as may be fixed by Executive Agreement between the Member
Democracies.

The Board may establish such administrative and executive
organs as seem to it appropriate to its proper functioning and exercise of its powers and the discharge of its responsibilities.

This course, too, would have a number of advantages:

a. It would be not only the simplest but the most supple solution.

b. Its smaller one-house Congress should make for swifter emergency action than a larger two-house Congress, while still safeguarding the position of the less populous democracies.

c. It allows the members of Congress to work out gradually together the executive and other machinery that they find the circumstances require—it permits more experimenting in this new field, more adapting of machinery to actual emergency conditions.

d. It follows the precedent of the Continental United States Congress, while at the same time allowing evolution along the lines of the British House of Commons and Cabinet system.

There are, of course, other advantages and disadvantages to this solution and to the major and minor alternatives. The purpose in making all these concrete suggestions here, I repeat, is not so much to plead the case for them as to stimulate thinking in concrete terms and give the whole problem a rapid preliminary airing. The final thing to be noted is this: Any of these provisional solutions, or the variations of them that Federal Union permits will—whatever their faults—be much better than the best alliance.

Last Word

OF LIFE AND DEATH

Greater love hath no man than this, that a man lay down his life for his friends. — Jesus.

Of Life and Death

These two letters were exchanged while France was falling:

Dear Mr. Streit:

In connection with your plan for the federation of the democracies, I am writing for your advice in regard to questions which have arisen in my mind. Your answer will no doubt play a large part in any immediate, as well as long range, action that I may take.

Dating from my first reading of your most excellent book, *Union Now,* I have been convinced of your reasoning and now hold your ideal as my own.

The question that I have in mind is the course I should take to be of most benefit to, if you will permit me, our mutual cause. It has seemed to me that of primary importance at present is an Allied victory. I believe that it would be best for the U. S. to remain neutral, if possible, so that at the close of hostilities we might play a part unmutilated by hate and similar emotions. However, it has seemed that we cannot determine at what point the U. S. would thus cease to be of aid toward Allied victory, in the event, which at present we cannot know, that they are fighting a losing war. Granted, also, that I as an individual, will play a small part in any event, I have tentatively concluded that the only course for me to follow in accordance with my conscience and my ideals, is to enlist in the Canadian Army.

I believe myself ready to lay down my life, insignificant as I agree it is, for our cause. I have also thought that, to the extent that I am able, I would further our ideas within the Allied Army itself. The men in the army, it has seemed, would play no little part in the thought trends of the countries which will, if they are victorious, make the peace settlement. The Union plan would, I think, reach its first crisis at that settlement.

You no doubt see by now my purpose in writing to you. Can

you detect any fallacies in my reasoning? Is there any other way in which I might be of more service? I have tried to keep the hysteria, now enveloping a large part of our country, from influencing my present decision, and I certainly labor under no delusions as to the "glory" of war. Up to this time I had thought it best to continue my education by going to college. At present I am eighteen and have completed my high school education.

In appreciation of any advice which you may find time to give me, I am,

Very sincerely yours,
John B———, Jr.

Shell Service Station
———, Maryland
June 5, 1940

[Note: This is the true signature. It does not stand for John Brown, Jr. . . . and yet . . . his soul goes marching on.]

·   ·   ·   ·   ·

On Speaking Tour
Newton, Kansas
June 14, 1940

Dear John:

Your letter, which just reached me here, went to my heart, and will remain there. For I see you are a boy after my own heart, the kind of son any father would be proud of. And I am happy to have you for a comrade in this great task.

You have learned, and done, early in life a great·thing. You will be the better for having reached coolly, of your own free will, the most momentous decision any mortal can reach—the decision that there is a truth one is willing to give one's life for. You say your life is insignificant—but by your willingness to lose it for what you believe in you have given it the highest significance. Not only are you the better for it, but I am the better for it, we are all ennobled by it.

When I stop at a service station now, I shall look with higher and friendlier esteem on the lad who fills the tank, wipes the windshield. I shall remember that one such lad, I know, is ready to give the last full measure of devotion for my freedom, for the freedom of mankind—and how can I know that here at this service station is not, or will not be, another such man? You can see how it goes, how much you have already done.

I pity those who have no truth for which they are willing to live and die. They have not yet really lived, and they will really die, and die fearfully many times before their death. For them death has its sting.

I shall never forget the experience I had when it suddenly dawned on me one day six years ago that federal union of the democracies was *the* solution of the world problem for which I had been groping for so long. It came as a great light, suddenly, humbling and exalting at the same time. I felt deeply happy, joyous beyond anything I have known. And out of the nowhere there flashed on me vividly this thought in these words: "Now I can die in peace." It impressed me the more since I had not been worrying or thinking of dying one way or another. With it came the vivid feeling, "Now I have done the thing I was born to do, that I came into this life to do, and so death no longer matters. The idea is here, on paper, it will remain, and it will not die."

I had not been thinking on these lines either . . .

Since that experience, I have found there was a great deal more to be done for this Union idea than just simply putting it down on paper the first time. It had to be re-written and re-written, and re-thought out. I found no end of things remaining to be done for it, and that still remain to be done. It has taken more and more of my life. But ever since that experience, John, I have felt, so to speak, comfortably at home with death, knowing it would come when it would come, and could no longer kill The Union, and could help it. And to keep always working for The Union while one lives is surely the best way of insuring that one's death—no matter how or when it comes—will also serve The Union.

You ask me if I find any fallacies in your reasoning. I find none, but I do find you too young in years to go—though you show in mind and courage a maturity I wish more older persons had. I do not know what to advise you. With all my heart I want you to live—the world so sadly needs men, and you are a man—but how to secure this? Some survive through every danger, and some die in the midst of safety.

There are questions each must settle in his own conscience, and this is one of them. I have always found it wise to obey at such times the voice within when it speaks clearly and persistently—but to make sure first that it does speak clearly and persistently, despite everything.

And do not lightly dismiss practices that embody the common, long-term judgment of men. One such practice, based on many sound reasons, is to exempt from war service those under 21 until there is a lack of men over 21. That emergency has not yet arisen.

And you have much to do here at home. The best hope for liberty and Union now, here and elsewhere in the world, lies in your spirit spreading through the American people in time to save freedom's last foothold in Europe. Already you are doing much more to awake America than you imagine. I read your letter to my audience here tonight and they listened spellbound. One mother told me later it shook her to the roots.

Yours is the spirit that led another young man—Lafayette—to cross the seas to fight for man's freedom when the outlook for it here was as dark as it is now in France. In these days when so many of our young men seem deadened with the cynicism of frustrated age, it is good to know that the true spirit of youth lives on. You are of a noble line, and I, who have a son only a little younger than you are, I say *Sir* to you. God keep you.

Sincerely,
Clarence Streit

Index

Acton, Lord, quoted, 125, 133
Adams, John Quincy, 45
Alaska, xi, 17
Alliances, system of collective, 68
Arnold, Benedict, 153
Articles of Confederation, 126
  quoted, 25
Ashley, W. J., 181
Australia, 17, 19, 122
  founder Democracy, 11, 14
  in Union, 4, 39
Austria, 64
Autocracy, 8, 15, 17, 28, 45, 63, 72,
  118, 120, 151, 154 ff., 162. *See
  also* Dictator, Dictatorships.
Ayres, Col. Leonard P., quoted,
  76 f.n.

Babcock, Major D. S., quoted, 79
Bank for International Settlement,
  84, 123
Barter business, 107
Belgium, 66 f.
  founder Democracy, 11
  non-European possessions of, 14
Bible, quoted, 53, 66, 89, 199, 229
Blockade, 29, 80
Boer War, 121
Briand, Aristide, 105, 122, 164
Briand's Committee, 106
British dominions, role of, in
  Union, 34
British power, preponderance of, 63
Bruening, Chancellor, 152
Building of the Ship, The, Longfel-
  low's, 1
Bureaucracy, 60, 161
Burke, Edmund, 45, 53
  quoted, 3

Caesar, 119

Canada, 19, 34, 36, 122
  founder Democracy, 11, 14
  French in, 6
  in Union, 4, 39
  Union between British and
    French, 12, 22
Caporetto, 77
Case of Federal Union, The, xii.
  See also Curry, W. B.
Centralization of power, 35, 159,
  162
Channel ports, 113
Château-Thierry, 77 f.
Chicago Daily News, The, quoted,
  75 n.
China, 108
Churchill Cabinet, 37
Churchill, Winston, 1, 42 ff., 44 n.,
  52
  quoted, 198
Civil War, American, 121, 133, 164
Clapper, Raymond, 152 n.
Clinton, George, 127
Commager, 181
Commonwealth of Man, 70
Compulsory military service, 62,
  149
Conciliation of America, On the, 3.
  See also Burke, Edmund.
Congress of Vienna, 64
Connecticut, Fundamental Orders
  of, 130
Conscription, 105, 149
Constitutional Convention, The
  U. S., 3, 27, 135, 142, 167, 199.
  See also Madison, James; Pat-
  erson, Wm.; Randolph, Ed-
  mund; Gorham, Nathaniel;
  Hamilton, Alexander.
Continental Congress, 41, 51
Coolidge, Calvin, 143

Cortina, José Manuel, 187 n.
Coudenhove-Kalergi, Count Richard N., 122
Critical Period of American History, 181. *See also* Fiske, John.
Curtis, Lionel, xii, 181
  quoted, 206
Curry, W. B., xii

Darius, 119
Darwin, Charles Robert, 180
Davis, John W., 40
Declaration of Independence, 4, 26, 31, 127 f., 132 n., 135, 157, 171 n., 174, 207
Declaration of Inter-Dependence and Union, 27
Democracy, 108, 120, 124, 162
  dangers, problems, virtues, 110 f.
  defense problem, 112
  fighting for, 125
  France's service to, 117
  machinery, 121
  philosophy, 114
Democracy in America, 181. *See also* Tocqueville, Conte de.
Denmark, 66 f.
  founder Democracy, 11
  non-European possessions of, 14
Deuel, Wallace R., quoted, 75 n.
Devisenarchiv, quoted, 150
Dictators and Dictatorship, 9, 17, 19, 21, 28 f., 35, 42 f., 46 f., 68, 72, 95, 106, 108, 120, 148, 160, 162
Documents of American History, 181. *See also* Commager.
Dunkirk evacuation, 115 f.
Dutch East Indies, 148

Earle, Prof. Edward Mead, 169, 171, 181
Economic Conference, London, 84
Eire, 60, 122
  founder Democracy, 11, 14
  in Union, 4, 39
Ellsworth, Oliver, quoted, 178
European Federation, 164

Faraday, Michael, 53
Farewell Address, Washington's, xv, 179
Federal Convention, 8
Federalist, The, xv, 169 ff., 181. *See also* Madison, James; Hamilton, Alexander; Earle, Edward M.
Fifteen Founder Democracies, 11
Finland, founder Democracy, 11
Fiske, John, quoted, 26, 122, 181
Ford, Henry, 195
Fortune, polls, 19, 194 f.
Fox, Charles James, 45
France, 64, 66 ff.
  founder Democracy, 11
  non-European possessions of, 14
Franco-British Alliance, 7, 21 f., 34, 61
Franco-German relations, 105
Franklin, Benjamin, 45, 53, 158
  quoted, 62, 91 f., 108, 134, 143
Freedom and Union, xi
Freedom, general, 215
  of press and speech, 5, 31, 154, 192, 215
  of religion and peaceful association, 5, 31, 215
French Empire, 46

Gallup, polls, 19
Gandhi, Mahatma, 185
Geneva, 105, 129. *See also* League, etc.
George III, 157 n., 169
Germany, 45, 64 ff., 68, 70 f., 108
Gettysburg Address, 146
Goebbels, Joseph, 75, 86
Goldsmith, John Francis, xii
Gompers, Samuel, 123
Gorham, Nathaniel, quoted, 174
Government of, by, for the people, 128 ff.
Grant, Ulysses, 53

Halifax, Lord, 113 n.
Hamilton, Alexander, 45, 53, 134

Hamilton, Alexander, quoted, 1, 137, 174, 178
Hapsburg, Dynasty, 95
Harding, Warren G., 143
"Harding Gang," 97
"Hemisphere Defense," 148, 154, 186
Henry IV, 122
Herald-Tribune, New York, quoted, 205, 212
Historiarum Mundi, 103. *See also* Pliny the Younger.
History of Freedom, 181. *See also* Acton, Lord.
Hitler, Adolf, 17, 19, 29, 38, 46, 51 ff., 63, 66 ff., 71 f., 79, 86, 93, 105 ff., 112 f., 119 f., 139, 147, 150 ff., 161, 199
Hobbes, Thomas, 53
Hohenzollern Dynasty, 95
Holland, 66 f.
    founder Democracy, 11
    non-European possessions of, 14
Hoover, Herbert, 40, 143
Hughes, Charles Evans, 40
Hull, Secretary Cordell, 84

Independence Hall, 23, 135
Inter-Continental Congress, 26, 31
International Labor Organization, 123
Invasion of Britain, 113 ff.
Invasion of United States, 147
Isaiah, 119
Isolationism, 93, 97, 105
Italy, 45, 64, 68, 70 f., 80, 108

Jamestown, 173
Japan, 17, 19, 45, 49, 52, 63 f., 70 ff., 108, 148, 152 f.
Jay, John, quoted, 127
Jefferson, Thomas, 45, 132 n., 134, 158, 179, 201
Joint Co-ordinating Committee, 22
Joint Defense Board, 34

Kant, Emanuel, 122
Kellogg Pact, 84

Kennedy, Sinclair, xii
"Khaki Election," 48
King, Mackenzie, 44
Kipling, Rudyard, quoted, 110

Labor Party, British, 37, 164
Landon, Alfred, 40
Layton, Sir Walter, quoted, 114, 117
"League of Friendship," 126, 133 f.
League of Nations, xi, 55, 63, 83, 96, 105, 107, 123, 124 n., 125 f., 143
    assembly, 105
    council, 84
    covenant, 84, 108, 123, 129
    failure of, 12, 133
Leaves of Grass, 182. *See also* Whitman, Walt.
Lee, Robert E., 22, 53
"Lend-Lease Bill," 36
Liberal Party, British, 37
Lincoln, Abraham, 24, 89, 119, 128, 182, 201
    quoted, xv, 23, 53, 90, 134, 146, 158
    second inauguration, 31
Lincoln's speeches, 181
Lindbergh, Col. Charles A., 104
Lippmann, Walter, quoted, 212
Lodge, Senator, quoted, 95
Longfellow, Henry W., quoted, 1
Lothian, Lord, quoted, 62, 199
Louisiana Purchase, 158, 179

Madison, James, 45, 134, 172
    quoted, xv, 3, 144, 170 f., 174, 176
Maginot Line, 111
Magna Carta, 120
Manchester workingmen, England, quoted, 89
Manchurian conflict, 84, 124 n.
Marshall, Gen. George C., 152 n.
Martin, Luther, 133
Mason, George, 45, 129 f., 170
    quoted, 91, 130
Mediterranean Sea, 80 f.

Message to Congress, Lincoln's, 1862, xv
Milton, John, 53
Monnet, Jean, 22
Monroe Doctrine, 17, 186
Montana Kaimin, quoted, 82
Mussolini, Benito, 19, 29, 46, 52, 69, 71 f., 108, 116, 152 f., 184

Napoleon Bonaparte, 113, 119, 185
quoted, 110
Nationalism, dangers of, 54, 160 f.
Naval bases, lease, 36
Nazi centralization, 107
Newfoundland, 122
New Mexico, Spanish in, 6
New Zealand, 17, 122
founder Democracy, 11, 14
in Union, 4, 39
Nine Power Pact, 108
Ninth Amendment, 168 f.
North, Lord, 206
Norway, 66 f.
founder Democracy, 11

Oath of loyalty, 145
Oberlin College, 107. *See also* Wilkins, Ernest.
Ottoman Dynasty, 95
Ownership, individual, in Germany, 151

Paine, Thomas, quoted, 3, 19, 102, 156, 203, 207
Palestine, 122
Pan-Angeles, The, xii. *See also* Kennedy, Sinclair.
Paterson, William, quoted, 142
Pax Americana, 65
Pax Britannica, 63 ff.
Peace Conference 1918-19, 83, 143
Peace Pact, 108
Philippine Islands, 148
Pitt, William, 45, 206
Platt Amendment, 83
Pliny the Younger, 104
quoted, 103

Preamble to U. S. Constitution, 130 n.
President Randolph as I Knew Him, xii. *See also* Goldsmith, John Francis.

Racial fanaticism, 106
Randolph, Edmund, quoted, 167, 199
Rauschning, Hermann, 147
Read, George, 144
Reichstag, 106
Rights of man, 52, 120
Rights of Man, 3, 102, 156, 181, 203, 207. *See also* Paine, Thomas.
Rights of nations, 5
Romanoff Dynasty, 95
Roosevelt, Eleanor, quoted, 35 n., 162
Roosevelt, Franklin D., 1, 35 n., 40, 42 ff., 44 n., 105, 143, 173, 187 n., 192
quoted, 111 n., 144
Roosevelt, Theodore, quoted, 95
Root, Elihu, 123
Rubber, natural vs. synthetic, 149
Ruhr occupation, 106
Russia, 46, 63 f.

"Safe for Democracy," 94, 96, 112, 125 f., 136, 141, 155
Scandinavian Campaign, 113
Scapa Flow, 113
Sedan, 113
Seeley, Prof., 207
Senate Appropriation Committee, 152 n.
Seward, William Henry, 158
Shakespeare, William, quoted, 54
Shelley, Percy B., 53
"Short-of-War" policy, 62, 74 ff.
Smathers, Senator William H., 187 n.
Smith, Adam, 132 n.
Smith, Alfred E., 40
Socrates, 119

South America, 17
Spanish War, the, 83
Stalin, Joseph, 49, 52, 95, 152 f., 192
Stimson, Henry Lewis, 123 n.
Stresemann, Gustav, 105
Suez Canal, 67
Sweden, founder Democracy, 11
Switzerland, 19
 founder Democracy, 11
 union among Germans, French, and Italians, 12

Tenth Amendment, 167 ff., 172 f.
Thirteen States or Colonies, 25 f., 50 f., 125 ff., 131 f., 132 n., 134, 138, 142, 169 f., 173
Thompson, Dorothy, quoted, 205
Times, The New York, 105, 111, 113 n., 123 n., 139
 quoted, 113, 187 n.
Tobacco, Turkish vs. American, 150
Tocqueville, Conte de, 181
 quoted, 19
Trade, loss of, 17
Triangular Alliance, 70, 184, 192
Turkey, 46

Unemployment in Germany, 106
Union
 admission of new members, 6
 aims of, 4
 air superiority, 80
 Bill of Rights, 5
 board of five, 44
 capital city, 43
 citizenship in, 5
 congress, 43 ff., 61
 congress, composition of, 39 ff.
 constitution, 8
 executives, 42
 means toward, 5
 peace terms, 6
 purpose of, 7
 reasons for, 6 ff.
 representation in, 5

Union—(Continued)
 rights, 5
 steps toward formation, 7
 supreme council, 34
 U. S.—formation of, 179
Union of South Africa, 19, 121 f.
 Dutch Afrikaners in, 6
 founder Democracy, 11, 14
 in Union, 4, 39
 union between Boers and British, 12
United Kingdom, the
 founder Democracy, 11, 14
 in Union, 4
United States, 19, 64, 67
 founder Democracy, 11, 14
U. S. Constitutional Convention, 91, 129
United States of Europe, 63, 105

Valera, Eamon de, 44
Versailles, Peace Treaty, 63, 68, 83, 95, 105 f.
Vichy Government, 22
Von Steuben, Baron Frederick William, 153

Wall Street, 105 f.
Washington, George, 45, 98, 134, 145, 169, 179, 201
 quoted, xv
Wealth of Nations, 132 n. See also Smith, Adam.
Webster, Daniel, 39
Wheeler, Senator, 66 f.
 quoted, 66 n.
Whitman, Walt, 53, 182
 quoted, 202
Wilhelm, Kaiser, 86, 113, 117
Wilkins, Pres. Ernest, quoted, 107
Willkie, Wendell, 1, 40
 quoted, 37
Wilson, James, quoted, 175
Wilson, Woodrow, 36, 76, 82 ff., 92, 95, 111 f., 123, 143, 155, 162
 quoted, 94, 112, 158

SEP 22 1978

Woman Suffrage Amendment, 157
World Court, 123
    Protocol, 84
World Government, Organization
    of, 10 ff.
    need for, 109

World Order, xii, 181, *See also*
    Curtis, Lionel.
World-Telegram, New York, 152 n.

Young, Owen, 123
Young Committee, 84